A practical blueprint for preparing and taking law school exams.

Mastering the
Law School
EXAM

SUZANNE DARROW-KLEINHAUS

THOMSON

WEST

MAT# 40394484

© 2007 Thomson/West
     610 Opperman Drive
     P.O. Box 64526
     St. Paul, MN 55164–0526
     1–800–328–9352

Printed in the United States of America

ISBN–13: 978–0–314–16281–6
ISBN–10: 0–314–16281–X

 TEXT IS PRINTED ON 10% POST CONSUMER RECYCLED PAPER

TO BENJAMIN, WHO TEACHES ME

ABOUT THE AUTHOR

SUZANNE DARROW-KLEINHAUS is the Director of Academic Development and an Assistant Professor of Legal Process at Touro College Jacob D. Fuchsberg Law Center in Central Islip, New York. She has published in the area of academic support and bar exam preparation.

PREFACE AND ACKNOWLEDGMENTS

STUDENTS ARE AT ONCE OVERJOYED and overwhelmed when beginning law school. In awe and frightened, the student sees the professor as all-knowing and wonders, "how will I ever know?" The universe of what there is to learn seems to be without end. Often, the student gets lost in the theoretical and philosophical aspects of class discussions and case readings. And since the law school exam typically looks nothing like what goes on during an ordinary class, the student is left at a loss in knowing how to prepare and how to respond on the exam.

I wanted to write a book that would address these concerns and provide a method the student could use to bring order to the learning process. Without reducing the enormity of the enterprise, I wanted to make it manageable so students could settle down and focus on the individual task at hand.

I also wanted to make the book practical rather than theoretical so the emphasis would be on providing the type of detailed examples necessary to show students precisely "how to do it" and "how to write it." Consequently, in some instances, *Mastering the Law School* Exam resembles a "how-to" manual. It even features a chapter modeled after a troubleshooting section in a technical guide where the user's difficulty is identified followed by a series of applicable solutions. For example, the student seeking assistance for "sketchy on the law" or a "conclusory analysis" first finds a description showing how the problem manifests followed by how the problem can be cured. When used alone or in conjunction with an academic support professional, this type of neutral classification of common performance errors guides the student in learning to consider his or her own work objectively and removes some of the sting of not performing up to expectations.

At its core, the book provides a blueprint for preparing for and taking law school exams. However, in so doing, it also links and explains the conceptual path from note-taking -to outlining-to exam writing. It identifies the thought processes involved in these activities because the problems students have in writing about the law are often "mirror images" of the problems they have in thinking about the law. Most study aids do not address this gap in conceptualization since they tend to focus on the discrete tasks and not their connections.

In the end, only you, the user, is in a position to judge whether this book accomplishes all I've intended it to do. If it serves as a useful and effective learning tool, it will be found in your growing sense of comprehension and competency and the reality of improved exam grades. Only then will it have achieved its purpose.

This project has been a major enterprise and would not have happened without the support and assistance of others. As always, my husband Murray, for his love and constancy, so essential to helping me get where I need to go, my daughter Meredith, for becoming such an amazing young woman that I am constantly surprised and delighted, and for my parents, who never fail to encourage me, especially to write.

My deepest appreciation to Dean Lawrence Raful and Vice Dean Gary Shaw for their unhesitating support of my work. I am especially grateful to Gary for his confidence in my ideas and encouragement. I would also like to thank my colleagues for permission to include their exam questions: Myra Berman, Rodger Citron, Nicola Lee, Judge Pratt, Gary Shaw, and Teddy Silver.

I would also like to offer my heartfelt gratitude to Myra Berman, once my student, and now my dearest friend and colleague. Her insights, suggestions, and just plain presence throughout it all has been a comfort and true source of support. Thank you for listening to my progress reports and commenting on the early drafts. I am forever grateful.

No writing project becomes real without the vision and support of a publisher and this one is no exception. I am grateful to Louis Higgins and Heidi M. Hellekson at Thomson-West Publishing Company. I am especially thankful for Heidi: her receptivity to new ideas and ability to match an author's enthusiasm with her own is a true gift.

Finally, I would like to thank my students. There are far too many to name individually, but a few made very real contributions. Specifically, I'd like to thank Randi Schwartz and Rachel Basher, Class of 2006. I'd also like to thank Spencer Horn, Class of 2005, for his eagerness to learn, his willingness to work hard, and his infectious enthusiasm. Spencer sought me out voluntarily before he had even taken a law school exam. He realized that law school learning was different from other kinds of education and wanted to take advantage of every opportunity to succeed. We met regularly to work on legal writing and analysis, time management, and exam preparation. You might say that much of what is in this book is a result of our work together. He encouraged me to write about it because he believed it would be valuable to others. In many ways, this book is as much his as mine. Thank you, Spencer.

— Suzanne Darrow-Kleinhaus
Bellmore, New York
June, 2006

The MBE questions have been "Reprinted by Permission" from the following NCBE publications: Sample MBE 1996 (© 1996 by the National Conference of Bar Examiners), Sample MBE III July,1998 (© 1998 by the National Conference of Bar Examiners) and the 2006 Information Booklet (© 2005 by the National Conference of Bar Examiners).

HOW TO USE THIS BOOK

IF YOU ARE A LAW TEACHER:

While this book was conceived initially for law students only, I realized it had practical value for law teachers as well, and especially those of us working in academic support. I saw how useful it might be when I found myself using sections I had written to illustrate points I was making in class or in working one-on-one with students. It was helpful to have examples and explanations for what we were discussing at the moment, whether it was choosing between outlining formats, answering multiple choice questions, or showing why a sentence was conclusory and how it could be corrected. It was easy to see that if I found myself turning to these materials, others might do so as well.

CONSIDER THIS BOOK IN WORKING WITH YOUR STUDENTS:

- To supplement individual student meetings with detailed explanations of the most common questions regarding such law school basics as note-taking, outlining, and exam preparation.
- As a source for additional hypotheticals with evaluation sheets so students can practice their exam-writing skills and get immediate feedback.
- To provide opportunities for students to direct their own learning through examples with detailed explanations of "how to write it right."

- To provide illustrations of correct and incorrect essay answers so students can learn to see for themselves the difference between the two.
- To help students cultivate the skills of active reading and self-awareness by developing their "thought-monitor."
- To explain the conceptual path from note-taking -to outlining-to exam writing.
- To provide detailed step-by-step guidelines for answering multiple choice questions.
- To help students learn to organize their writing through IRAC diagraming.

IF YOU ARE A LAW STUDENT:

Consider using this book if you want to make law school exams a lot less terrifying, infinitely more manageable, and ultimately more successful for you. It will:

- Provide a knowledgeable, reasonable, and rational voice to navigate the intricacies of law school exams and impart a practical strategy for success.
- Walk you through the entire law school learning process, showing you how to integrate case readings, class discussions, and secondary source materials to achieve a working knowledge and understanding of the required materials.
- Fill the gap between what the professor refers to as learning to "think like a lawyer" and the practical means for doing so.
- Show you how to tailor an individualized study program that works from the your strengths while accounting for weaknesses.
- Dispel the misconception that the skills needed for success in one subject are somehow different for another.
- Identify the basic skills that exams seek to test and the precise manner in which they are tested.
- Examine each type of law school exam through examples and detailed analysis of sample answers.
- Provide instruction in the precise use of language and, in particular, guidance in the use of specific "signal" language in the writing of issues, statements of the rule, and analysis of the facts.
- Explain what a "disorganized exam" really means and how to correct it.
- Provide practical applications in the context of the substantive law.

WHERE TO BEGIN:

Like everything else you'll read in law school, how you read this book will be a little different. Let's face it – it's not a novel you read for enjoyment but a guide you're turning to because you need it.

Typically, the stage of your legal education will determine where you begin. This is a practical book intended to help you with the practical side of law school. Use it that way. Turn to the section that addresses the area in which you are having difficulty at the moment. It might be outlining a subject where your earlier methods don't seem to be working. On the other hand, it might be that you've just learned your Constitutional Law exam includes multiple choice questions and you've always had difficulty with them. You will find that each chapter provide references to related topics so you will learn what you need to know wherever you choose to begin.

> > > > > **Begin here: CHAPTERS 1 THROUGH 3**

If you are reading this book before you begin your legal studies or early in your first semester of law school, then you should start with the first three chapters. It will acquaint you with what to expect in law school and guide you in the most effective approaches to the tasks of law school learning.

These chapters can be equally valuable after your first semester when you look back on your initial experiences and want to make the most of what's yet to come. For many students, the first semester passes in a blur and it's only afterward that they are able to understand it. At this point, the chapters will resonate with your new awareness and be incredibly helpful.

> > > > > **Begin here: CHAPTERS 4 AND 5**

After you've attended a few classes – and by this I mean only enough to give you a sense of what goes on – you'll want to read Chapters 4 and 5. Here you'll learn how to take notes, use commercial study aids, craft your outlines, set up a study group, and begin the process of preparing for exams. It also makes sense to return to these chapters over the course of the semester as you become more familiar with the process of law school learning.

> > > > > **Begin here: CHAPTERS 5, 6, AND 7**

Even if you have not read any of the other chapters in this book and it's the end of a semester, begin here. These chapters provide all you need to know about exam taking, from the various types of exams and how to prepare for them, to what to do the night before and exactly how to budget your time on the exam. Chapter 7 will take you through every step of reading and answering exam questions, including short answer questions, multi-issue fact patterns, and multiple choice questions.

> > > > > *Begin here: CHAPTER 8*

If you've received a disappointing grade on a quiz, mid-term, or final exam, turn to this chapter for an exam make-over. I would also recommend beginning here if your grades are anything less than an "A" because you'll learn how to make that happen.

What you want to do is jump start the process by beginning where you encountered the difficulty – with exam performance. This chapter provides examples of "what not to do," the reasons why you're not supposed to do it, and precise instructions on exactly what you should do.

> > > > > *Begin here: CHAPTER 9*

If you're looking to improve your exam-taking skills, then begin here. Chapter 9 shows you, sentence by sentence, what is required to comport with the structure and substance of solid legal analysis. The first part of the chapter applies forensic IRAC principles to essays and examines each sentence in terms of its place in the IRAC structure of legal analysis. The process unfolds like a troubleshooting section in a technical manual where faults are identified and possible solutions are provided. The second part applies forensic IRAC elements to multiple choice questions by examining the reasoning behind incorrect answer choices to identify flaws in the thought process. The third part of forensic IRAC involves sentence diagraming.

> > > > > *Begin here: Chapter 10*

Chapter 10 provides hypotheticals so you can practice what you have learned. You should begin writing out sample answers as soon as you have covered enough "law" to analyze a factual situation. This usually occurs within the first two to three weeks of class. You can use the sample answers and evaluation sheets to check your answers and then apply the principles in Chapter 9 to correct any problems you encounter.

MASTERING THE LAW SCHOOL EXAM — AN OUTLINE

PREFACE AND ACKNOWLEDGMENTS

CHAPTER 1:
A HYPOTHETICAL UNIVERSE

A. YOUR FIRST LAW SCHOOL EXAM

■ *Imagine the following:*

It's some mid-December morning at the end of your first semester of law school. You arrive for your first final exam. You've studied all your class notes and reviewed all your case briefs. You understand the reasoning in the cases and can compare and contrast the facts from one case to another. You're as ready as you're ever going to be to take this test – or at least you think so.

When told to begin, you open your exam booklet and find something like this:

On June 8, Ben and Jen, owners of Muffin Morning, received from Minster, a manufacturer of muffin tins, the following letter dated, June 6:

"We are having a special this month on muffin tins. Our super size tins are priced at $15 a dozen and our mini muffin tins are priced at $10 a dozen. This offer requires a minimum order of 10 dozen of each type of tin and will be held open until June 30."
/s/ Michael of Minster

Ben and Jen created a new line of health food muffins. On June 10, they placed an order with MilkMan for 100 gallons of soy milk for immediate shipment at $2.00 per gallon. They also placed an order with ChipMan for 500 bags of carob chips at $1.00 per bag. No sooner had they placed the order for soy milk and the soy market crashed and was selling for 25 cents per gallon on the spot market. Ben immediately called MilkMan and asked for a price reduction. He said "No way. I bought the soy milk when it was $1.75. Too bad. Who knew the market would plunge. Besides, I already shipped your order." Ben refused the shipment when it arrived and failed to arrange for refrigeration. The soy milk went sour. When the invoice arrived, Muffin Morning refused to pay it.

Meanwhile, things were not going well in the kitchen. Jen burned all of the muffin tins when she tried to shorten the baking time by baking at 600∞ F. On June 26th, Ben and Jen received a letter from Minster revoking its June 6th offer. In desperate need of muffin tins, Ben and Jen sent their acceptance to Minster on June 27th for 10 dozen super size tins and 20 dozen mini tins at the prices listed in the June 6 letter. Minster refused to deliver the muffin tins at this price claiming that the offer had been revoked. Ben and Jen bought substitute tins from PotMan and paid $25 per dozen for the super size tins and $20 per dozen for the mini tins.

Ben and Jen have come to you for legal advice. MilkMan is threatening suit and Ben and Jen want to know if they have any rights against Minster. What would you advise?

Now imagine that this is the very first time you've seen a problem like this, let alone tried to answer one. What would you do? Where would you begin?

If you've been spending the last three and a half months diligently attending class, taking notes, and reading and briefing cases, then my guess is that you'd be pretty surprised. Nothing you've been doing or experiencing in class would have led you to expect this type of exam – or so it would seem. Still, you should have known and, more important, your professor will deem you to have known. This is because if you've been thoughtfully attending class, you should have realized that class discussions, while organized around cases and the rules presented in the cases, were really about understanding how a particular rule was used to solve the problem presented by the facts of the case. Further, each time the professor varied the facts and asked "what result?" you were supposed to "think like a lawyer" and analyze the new legal problem raised by the change in the facts. This is legal reasoning and it's pretty much the way it's taught and tested in law school.

B. THE ENDPOINT IS YOUR STARTING POINT

This book proposes a unique approach to succeeding in law school. It suggests that you work backwards from the end result. By beginning at the end point of your studies – the exam – you'll remain focused from the beginning of your studies on what you need to do. By identifying the basic skills that exams seek to test and the precise manner in which they are tested, you'll learn how to tailor an individualized study program that works from your strengths while accounting for any weaknesses. As a result, you'll save countless hours that otherwise would have been spent on wrong turns and missed opportunities.

Knowing what is expected of you is essential to knowing how to prepare and preparation is the key to avoiding unwanted surprises. Unlike some activities where you're not supposed to skip ahead and check out the ending because it will spoil the surprise, a good lawyer does not want to be surprised. Not ever. Neither does a good law student. Surprise is avoided by always knowing what to expect. For law students, part of knowing what to expect means knowing what to expect on exams. The only way to know what to expect on exams is to practice them well before exam day. You practice them to get good at them, the same way you develop any other skill. The more you do something, the better you get at it, whether it's playing the piano, shooting hoops, or solving legal problems.

But there's another side to exam-taking you need to consider. If properly written to reflect the material covered during the course, exams serve an important function. They are endpoints in the task of learning, no less a part of the process than deadlines are in the attorney's everyday world of client meetings, conferences, and court appearances. But even more important, they require that you learn the material in a way that you would not do otherwise. Without the impetus of an impending exam, cases would not be reviewed, outlines would not be written, and the rigor required to synthesize, understand, and master the material simply would not be expended. This effort is required for the study of law and not just for taking the exam. Most, if not all of the information learned about a subject is necessary and relevant, if not for the exam, then for the actual practice of law. In law school, it's not possible to study too much – only incorrectly, inefficiently, and ineffectively, as this book will show you.

C. TAKING CONTROL

The only way to know what's expected of you on exams is to become familiar with them ahead of time – both with the structure, format, and content of exams and with your responses to them. You can be sure there are no classes in law school that address this topic and very few professors, if any, discuss the final before the end of the term. Even then the discussion is mostly about form – how many questions there will be, whether there will be multiple choice questions, or essays, or both. While useful, this discussion won't help you learn how to approach the questions and how to write solid exam answers. This book will.

Still, it's critical that you don't mistake the importance of using the structure of exams to inform your learning process with the more important goal of learning the law. Your primary goal is to learn the law and, if you do, good grades will naturally follow. While grades are important for a number of reasons, they're not the reason I'm recommending we begin our work with an understanding of law school exams. Rather, it's because exams simulate the same types of problems and require that you apply some of the same skills you'll use in actual law practice. Despite the funny names and almost comical situations you find on law school exam questions, they test such basic lawyering skills as reading comprehension and reasoning, identifying and formulating legal issues, organizing information, following directions, and writing ability. From day one of law school, your professor's goal is to develop these skills; your job on an exam is to show that you've mastered them.

Of course these are not the only skills you'll learn in law school. You'll learn to think critically, read carefully, communicate orally, counsel clients, conduct research, engage in negotiations, work collaboratively, and above all, you'll learn what it means to be a member of the legal profession. The cultivation of these and other vital lawyering skills, while an essential part of your development as a conscientious, ethical, and knowledgeable lawyer, will not be addressed here. We'll be dealing with the more immediate and practical side of your law school performance – spotting issues, engaging in legal analysis, and communicating that analysis in writing. These are the primary skills your professor tests on written exams and therefore the primary focus of this book.

D. WHAT'S SO DIFFERENT ABOUT LAW SCHOOL

Most of you are not expecting law school to be so very different from your prior educational experiences. Consequently, you're not prepared for the strangeness of it all: the way the material is presented and how you're supposed to learn it, the nature of class interactions and the Socratic method, how long it takes to read court cases and how much work there is to do, and especially the difference between the skills emphasized in class and the ones tested on exams.

What's also so very different is that the learning process will not be explained or taught to you – at least not directly. Here's where I can help. I'll show you how to listen and learn from your professors because they will teach you – just not the way you're accustomed to learning. Professors are role models. Much of what they have to teach you is communicated in the way that they think, speak, listen, and question. Each of your professors will teach you something and it will be more valuable than the rules. You can always look up the rules but what they teach can't be found in books. If it could, you wouldn't need three years of law school. And you do.

Most of law school learning is self-learning and requires that you become your own guide. This is one of the major differences between law school and most other educational experiences. Not only does the burden of learning the material fall on you, but much of it is dense and challenging and learning means more than memorizing and regurgitating it on the exam. You need to own it.

On an exam, you must be able to show that you can identify the legal issue, apply the relevant rule, and reach an appropriate outcome on problems you've never seen before. This requires original thinking because the problems you're asked to evaluate will be unique. Even if they seem to be like the cases you've read or ones you've discussed in class, they will never be exactly the same. That's because your professor has twisted and tweaked the facts of the problem to make it precisely unlike anything you've seen before. This is done deliberately because it's intended to simulate the nature of legal practice. Each client will present a different problem, new and special in its own way, and you will have to figure it out. This is what makes the study and practice of law at once so exasperating and exhilarating: it is dynamic and you can shape it, thus allowing for creativity and originality – the catch is that you must do so within a required structure.

You have a choice. You can let yourself be overwhelmed by the demands of this environment and spend your law school years in a perpetual state of anxiety or you can accept the ambiguities, embrace the legal dynamic, and get on with learning the law. I expect that you've chosen the latter path since you're reading this book.

E. BECOMING YOUR OWN TEACHER

I can almost hear you thinking, "okay, here's another guide to law school that tells me that law school is different from other academic experiences and, better yet, that I need to teach it to myself. Well, how am I supposed to do that? Why doesn't somebody tell me how I become my own teacher?"

That's where this book comes in. I'm not merely going to tell you that law school is different – I'm going to show you how. While the truly best part of the study of law is learning to appreciate its complexity, intricacy, and precision, sometimes when you first take up the enterprise, what you really need (and really want) is just a way to get started.

Here's what you can expect:

- A knowledgeable, reasonable, and rational voice to navigate the intricacies of law school exams and impart practical approaches for success.

- A guide through the entire law school learning process, showing how case readings, class discussions, and outlining are used to prepare for exams.

- A "deconstruction" of each type of law school exam by example and analysis of sample answers where the role of each sentence is explained in terms of the IRAC structure of legal analysis.

- A step-by-step tutorial to writing exam answers where you're led through the appropriate thought process and provided with specific guidelines, organizational approaches, and writing techniques.

- A method of "objectifying" your own thought process through the use of "forensic IRAC."

But there are some things you should not expect. I won't be providing strategies or tactics. While there are approaches to learning the law and I will be making quite a few suggestions in how you should go about it – there are no magic tricks or short-cuts to learning the law. What you learn is meant to last a lifetime; tricks are short term devices.

Accordingly, we're going to begin with the understanding that the type of learning that goes on in law school is highly interactive. How and whether you learn the material is integrally related to the way you think, read, and write about the material. In turn, these cognitive processes are reflected in the notes you take in class, the case briefs you prepare, the course outlines you compose, and the exam answers you write. Even though we will take up these activities individually in terms of the specific role each plays in the learning process, it's an artificial distinction because they are fundamentally connected. Once we start working with the material, you'll see how what you write on an exam answer is directly related to what you wrote in your outline and, going back further, to the notes you took in class when that topic was discussed by your professor. Further, you'll see that if there's a flaw in your writing, it's a reflection of a flaw in your thinking. The activities of writing and thinking are not divisible. But that's getting a bit ahead of ourselves for now.

F. ADDRESSING THE "HOWS"

In addition to the basics of taking law school exams, we'll consider the following questions which concern all law students – and are intimately related to success on exams:

- How do I sort the relevant from the irrelevant facts since everything seems to be "material" to me?

- How do I stay focused and read actively when I don't know what most of the words mean?

- How do I take notes in class when the professor just asks questions and never answers them?

- How do I find the time to start outlining and studying when it takes every waking minute just to read and prepare for class?

- How do I know what goes in my outline?

- How do I get the type of feedback that I need to succeed when I'm not getting much in the way of individualized instruction?

- How do I find the "magic words" my professor is looking for in an essay answer?

- How do I learn from the professor's comments on my papers?

- How will I ever learn all that I'm supposed to know?

As you may have noticed in reading these questions, each asks for the "how" in accomplishing a defined task. That's because if you're seeking help, you want to know exactly what to do and how to do it. I'll provide answers to these questions and many more like them. This book is performance-oriented, providing practical applications in the context of the substantive law.

Even so, I'm pretty sure you won't like some of my "answers." That's because if you're like most law students, and I have no reason to believe that you're not, you're probably in search of a magic formula for figuring out the law – and there just isn't one. But there are ways to make your learning experience more meaningful, manageable, and ultimately, more rewarding.

So let's get back to where we started – how do you go about addressing a hypothetical question like the one at the beginning of this chapter? The answer is simple: you learn from every case you read and brief, from every note you take in class, from every outline you prepare, and from every practice problem you take the time to answer and analyze. In short, you learn from active participation in every part of the law school learning process.

CHAPTER 2: UNDERSTANDING LAW SCHOOL EXAMS

A. LEARNING WHAT YOU'RE SUPPOSED TO DO

Students are told from the beginning of their law school education that their job is to learn to "think like a lawyer." What's not so clear is what this means and how to go about it. The other thing that's not so clear is how quickly you have to figure it out since law school has an incredibly steep learning curve and an incredibly short time in which to climb it.

I thought I was supposed to learn the names of the cases and their holdings and the final exam would test me on how well I memorized the information. This seemed to make sense since all my assignments were to read cases, the texts contained nothing but cases, and all we did in class was discuss cases. I began with Civil Procedure and charted the case names and rulings so I could learn them. I was so pleased with my work that I asked my sister, who had just graduated from law school and taken the bar exam, to look at it. I expected her to be impressed by my organizational skills and study strategies. Instead, she said this wasn't what I was supposed to do with the cases and left it at that. If I wasn't to recite the case holdings and explain the court's reasoning, then what was I expected to do?

Fortunately, I found out early enough in the semester when there was still time to adjust my learning strategies. The Teaching Assistant for my first year Torts class provided a short problem by the end of the second week of classes and I was introduced to the unique law school universe of hypotheticals.

If it hadn't been for this Teaching Assistant, I don't know when I would have realized what was expected of me. Of course, my professors informed the class that they kept exams on file in the library and we should take a look at them, but the value of this advice was lost to me. The last thing I wanted to think about, let alone look at, were exams. I had always done well in college and never found it necessary to think about tests before the end of the semester. This plan may have worked in college but it never would have worked in law school. That's because the very nature of what you are expected to do in law school is so very different.

B. RECOGNIZING THE GAP BETWEEN WHAT'S DISCUSSED IN CLASS AND WHAT'S ON THE EXAM

It's easy enough to get lost in the theoretical and philosophical aspects of class discussions and hard to know what to expect on the exam when you spend most of your class time being questioned on cases. Much to your dismay, you're asked to judge the cases that you read – sometimes in your very first law school class. You're asked whether you think the court was correct in reaching its decision or whether you would have found differently. Then you get to the exam and there's nothing about cases. Or at least nothing that's obvious. You have to wonder: why does the exam seem so different from what went on in class?

The gap, if indeed there is one, comes from the style of the process more than its substance. Most law professors don't lecture and present the law in neat little packages for you to digest. Instead, they rely on the Socratic Method and ask questions. They ask lots of questions and only sometimes give answers. Supplying the answers is your job. Professors assume that you'll do the reading, learn the material, and put it all together in a way that's meaningful to you. They did it when they were in law school and they expect you to do the same. Some students make the mistake of waiting all semester for the professor to tie it together and this just doesn't happen. At least not usually. It's pretty much up to you to make the connections.

Making these connections is the first step in learning to think critically. Law school asks you to think about things you've never thought about before and in ways that are new to you. The process can be frustrating but it can also be intoxicating. This is the stuff of a legal education. It's about figuring out how the rules work, what they mean, why we have them, and questioning everything about them.

So if you think about it, really think about it, what goes on in class is related to what's on the exam. In class, you talk about the cases. You dissect them. The professor hurls questions at you to test your understanding of what you've read and your ability to use what you've learned. Then she changes the facts and asks another question. And yet another. The professor's goal is for you to learn to ask the same kinds of questions for yourself. On the exam, the hypos are longer and more complex but they're pretty much like the ones you discussed in class. They're just new problems for you to solve.

C. KNOWING THE GOAL

If learning the names of cases and holdings or a set of rules was all that was required in law school, then memorization alone would suffice. But that's not the goal of law school learning and you cannot do well simply by memorizing. Instead, you must be able to use the law that you've learned from the cases you've read to solve new problems. It's a lot like math – while it's essential to know the formulas and principles, they're not all that useful by themselves. It's what you do with them that counts. That's why law school exams test the following rather than rote memorization:

- Identifying and formulating legal issues
- Applying the rule
- Analyzing the rule with respect to the facts
- Organizing information
- Separating relevant from irrelevant facts
- Communicating effectively in writing
- Managing time efficiently

Most of these are practical skills and require problem-solving. If you spend all of your time studying only the substantive law, you won't be adequately prepared for the exam. While it's absolutely essential that you learn the rules, you must also develop your understanding of how the rules work.

D. WHAT LAW SCHOOL EXAMS TEST

The good news is that problem-solving is a skill. And because it is a skill, you can acquire it much like any other, through practice and more practice. It also requires a level of self-awareness, a willingness to explore how you think and write, and knowing how to look at these processes objectively. Exam performance is pretty much tied to the time spent in learning the material, reflecting on what is learned, and applying that knowledge in the context of simulated exam questions.

In many respects, law school exam questions are written to simulate client problems. As a result, what you're expected to do on the exam is pretty similar to what you're expected to do for your client: listen to the story, sort through the facts to see what's legally significant, identify the controlling rule of law, analyze the facts with respect to that law, determine whether your client has a viable claim, and, if so, assess the likely outcome. This process – both on the exam and in practice – tests your substantive and analytical skills: you need to know the law to "spot the issues" in the facts and you must analyze those facts with respect to the law to predict the likely consequences.

Let's take a closer look at what's involved in law school exams and how each part of the process serves a particular purpose in preparing you for the practice of law.

1.   YOUR SUBSTANTIVE KNOWLEDGE

Exams test your substantive knowledge. Let's face it: you're in law school to learn the law and until a better system is devised for accomplishing this task, testing is the only way to ensure that you'll do the necessary work.

While it's a common argument that lawyers can use books to look up answers, the truth is that a lawyer must know the law. It has to be there when it's needed and for an attorney, it's needed at a moment's notice. Quite apart from the picture created by television dramas, lawyers really do need to be able and articulate. The ability to think on one's feet and respond quickly is an essential skill for every practicing attorney, and not just the trial attorney. Any attorney who meets with clients, negotiates with adversaries, and appears before the court must have this skill. It's a skill that's based on a solid mastery of core substance; when exams test a student's knowledge of black letter law, it does so in the best interests of the profession.

2.   YOUR ANALYTICAL SKILLS

Law school exams test your ability to "think like a lawyer." This means mastery of the fundamentals of IRAC, the "Issue, Rule, Application, Conclusion" structure of legal analysis. All professors share the same expectation from a student essay: a well-reasoned argument based on an analysis of the relevant issues and an application of the law to the facts. The ability to reason in a logical, lawyer-like manner is critical. Generally the value of an answer depends not as much upon the conclusion as upon the demonstrated understanding of the facts, a recognition of the issues, an explanation of the applicable rules, and the reasoning by which the conclusion is reached.

3.   YOUR COMMUNICATION SKILLS

Finally, exams test such basic skills as reading comprehension and writing ability. Each of these skills is fundamental to the competent practice of law. The ability to read carefully, thoughtfully, and actively is essential to your success in law school.

You must be able to read and brief cases, interpret statutes, and decipher critical documents. Further, you must understand what you read to learn the material.

Exams test reading comprehension skills indirectly so it's easy to overlook the role that critical reading skills play in the process. For example, the consequences of faulty reading show up on exams when you fail to follow directions, confuse or ignore the facts, and address a question that is not asked of you. These problems show up most dramatically on short answer and multiple choice questions where every word is critical to the meaning of the passage.

The essence of lawyering is written communication and essay exams afford an objective measurement of your ability to communicate knowledge of the substantive law in an organized and articulate manner. Writing a well-constructed essay is a learned skill that requires mastery of the law and the nature of logical argument. Essay exams also demonstrate your ability to manage time effectively, organize the material, and use the proper legal terminology. "Sounding like a lawyer" in writing your exams is essential to marking your transition from novice to law student to practicing attorney.

E. THE PROCESS OF INTERNALIZATION AND "OWNING THE MATERIAL"

Students often come to see me after an exam, telling me that they "knew the material" but nonetheless failed to do well. What they are really saying is that they recognized the material when they saw it on the exam because it was familiar to them from their reading and class discussions. However, when it came to having to respond with the detailed specificity required to provide a thorough legal analysis, their "knowledge" fell short.

Since the first requirement for successful exam taking is knowing the law, we need to discuss exactly what this means. In short, "knowing the law" means that you internalize the material in such a way that you truly "own" it. It must become such a part of your understanding that you're able to see connections between and among concepts. Clearly, this is not the same as thinking you know something because a term or concept seems familiar. There's a big difference between recognizing something because you've seen it before and really knowing it.

Gaps in knowledge become readily apparent when students are required to distinguish between answer choices on a multiple choice exam or work their way through complicated fact patterns on essays. Preparing for exams simply by reading class notes, even if read several times, would not allow for the type of internalization of the material necessary to respond to these questions. First, since a law school professor typically does not lecture on the law but instead engages in a Socratic exchange, your notes are not likely to yield the type of complete, clear, and organized statements of the law necessary for complete understanding; and, second, even if your notes contain reference to rules, they are neither synthesized nor connected in the way necessary to allow you to use them in a subsequent application. This type of critical assessment, so vital to the learning process, is something you must do for yourself.

One of the primary goals of this book is to show you how to do this. You'll learn how to work with practice questions to prepare for exams and use model answers and checklists to evaluate your answers. More important, you'll be shown how to critique your own work to see what you've done right and where you've gone wrong. By learning to apply "forensic IRAC" to your own essays and multiple choice answers, you'll be able to identify the flaws in your work and correct them. In this manner, you'll move beyond a mere familiarity with legal terms and concepts and gain the true understanding necessary to excel on law school exams .

Understanding law school exams gives you the perspective necessary to bring order to the learning process. By identifying the basic skills that exams seek to test and the way in which they do so, you can target your study efforts and design an effective study plan that incorporates skills practice as well as substantive review.

Here's what you'll find in this book to help in this effort:

- Clear guidelines, useful explanations, and practical approaches for each step of the learning process.

- A blueprint for preparing for and taking law school exams, including instruction in the precise use of language and illustration of correct and incorrect essay answers so you can learn to see the difference.

- Practical applications in the context of the substantive law with the type of detailed examples necessary to show you precisely "how to do it" and "how to write it."

CHAPTER 3: ACCOUNTING FOR SUBJECT DIFFERENCES

A. THE FIRST YEAR

A great deal has been written about the experiences of first year law students. The truth is that as much as you may read about it and try to prepare yourself for what's to come, nothing quite compares to the real thing. You just have to live it to fully appreciate it. Having said that, however, there is still much to be gained from having some idea of what to expect.

1. IT'S A STEEP LEARNING CURVE

The first semester of law school is by far the most exacting in terms of its demand on you physically, emotionally, and intellectually. As I've said, everything about law school learning is different from what you've experienced previously. Even a library is suddenly unfamiliar territory when it requires figuring out a system of legal citation before you can do so much as locate a court case.

Of course it's not only the manner in which you learn that's new and different but the substantive material itself. It's the combination of these two factors that makes the learning curve so precipitous. The good news, however, is that while it's steep, it's also relatively short. By the end of your first semester, which is only a matter of 14 weeks or so, you'll go from knowing no more about the law than would any avid viewer of *Law and Order* to one who has researched and written a legal memorandum, read and briefed somewhere between 300 to 500 cases in three or four areas of doctrinal law while developing a working knowledge of the vocabulary and structure of the American legal system. Even though you'll still have a long way to go, the most intense, exhausting, and challenging period in law school will be behind you – that is until you study for the bar exam. But that's a whole other story and a whole other book.

2. THE FIRST YEAR SUBJECTS

While it's important to realize that you'll have a lot to learn in a relatively short time, it's equally important to appreciate the nature of what you're learning. Typically, a first year student takes classes in Contracts, Torts, Civil Procedure, Criminal Law, Property, and Legal Writing. Some schools include Constitutional Law in the first year curriculum as well. This is very different from a typical college course load which probably found you juggling history, astronomy, accounting, psychology, and economics. Each one of these was a separate and distinct discipline with its own subject matter, study methodology, and specific vocabulary. Law school subjects, on the other hand, are not separate disciplines. They may be divided into discrete areas but that's primarily for teaching purposes. The way the law operates and how it's learned doesn't change because the course bears a different name.

However, some students believe that there are such major differences between subjects that they must "think" one way for Torts, another for Contracts, and yet another for Civil Procedure. This is a serious misconception. While each subject develops its own specialized body of case law and some areas are based on enacted law rather than common law, it's important to understand that the essential nature and structure of the law is consistent. Not only are there common themes and general principles in the law, but the process that's followed to analyze and resolve a legal question is fundamentally the same whether the problem sounds in Contract or Tort.

While not every student will experience law school in the same way, there are enough similarities in the process to guarantee that you'll find some value in what follows.

(a) Don't be deceived by Torts

Torts is an excellent place to start because most students tell me it's their favorite subject among the first year courses. Of course I'm only one professor and my experience is limited, but it seems to be true of all the students I ask. Torts is followed closely by Criminal Law. Interestingly, it's never Contracts and only rarely is it ever Civil Procedure.

"Why Torts?" I ask. The answer is invariably something like, "it's so clear and straightforward and easy to follow." I think to myself, "so wrong. So very, very wrong." It's none of those things but they won't realize it until the final exam when it's too late. Students are suckers for elements and they fall hard for the intentional torts. Just mention "battery"and the first year student is eager to recite the rule and show off her newly acquired legal knowledge:

> *A battery is the intentional infliction of a harmful or offensive contact with the person of another.*

The mistake is that this is not all there is to know; there is nothing straightforward or easy in assessing the "intent"required for commission of a battery or any of the intentional torts. Nor is there anything easy about other areas of Tort law but novice law students remain unconvinced – at least until the final exam.

So what's the lesson to be learned? If anything, it's to take nothing for granted. Just because it's possible to cull a rule from the cases without too much of a struggle, it doesn't necessarily follow that it's any easier to apply the rule to the facts. The study of Torts requires the same diligence and depth and precision of understanding as any other subject.

(b)   Criminal Law is more than the elements of a crime

Not surprisingly, Criminal Law is another student favorite. I suppose it's all the crime shows on television but students seem to feel a natural affinity for the subject (something I find rather worrisome!) They connect with the substance of Criminal Law as they do with Torts. However, they often mistake the relative ease with which they read the cases for what is challenging subject matter and one which intersects questions of public policy on a sophisticated and complex level.

Unlike Torts, Criminal Law requires working with all the sources of rules and not just the common law. Criminal cases involve enacted law, which can be either constitutional or statutory. Also, Criminal Law is often the first doctrinal course where students are required to consider and work within the bifurcated system of federal and state law. Although this is equally true of Civil Procedure, students often complete that course without fully appreciating the dual system of government, perhaps because the primary focus is on the Federal Rules of Civil Procedure and federal actions. Conversely, Criminal Law requires students to work with the common law, statutory law, constitutional law, and the Model Penal Code.

Working with statutory law can be a lot easier and a lot harder than you think. The easy part is that the statute gives you the black letter rule. It's right there for you to read and dissect. Which brings us to the hard part: reading the rule. Reading a rule, particularly a statute, requires attention to every single word. Often, you'll hear it referred to as "parsing"a statute.

While the same process applies to reading common law rules when deconstructing them into elements, requirements, or factors, it is especially critical here. The challenge for most beginning law students is learning to read carefully and methodically and noting such critical language as "unless," "if," "or," "and," and "only."

In addition to testing your reading skills, statutes challenge your ability to accurately paraphrase a rule. Once again, the same is true of common law rules, but here the likelihood of making a mistake is greater. It's always best to use the precise language of the rule and not substitute your own. Of course you may want to paraphrase on occasion when explaining the rule, but be very careful not to change its meaning when using your own words. Changing even one word can change the meaning of an entire rule. If you have any doubt about your interpretative ability, use the actual text. It's not plagiarism to quote the rule (that's the purpose of citation).

In addition to these sources of positive law, students must grapple with the larger philosophical issues surrounding the criminal justice system. They must consider what constitutes criminal behavior and how that behavior should be punished. They must weigh the needs of the society against the rights of the individual and not lose sight of the moral judgments made at every step along the way. Finally, they must confront a body of law that takes as its subject matter the most heinous and shameful side of human behavior and still find the fortitude to evaluate it objectively. Clearly, these are anything but easy topics calling for the simple application of crime elements but require thoughtful, rigorous, and careful study.

(c)   What to watch with Civil Procedure

Whether the professor begins the course with jurisdictional issues or the rules of modern pleading, the subject matter of Civil Procedure tends to be dense, theoretical, and hardly the stuff of a first year law student's vision of what it means to be a lawyer. I'll admit that it's hard to get excited over the more mundane questions of personal jurisdiction but there is something to be said for your first exposure to the principles of substantive and procedural due process, not to mention your first Supreme Court cases. No doubt you'll read some Supreme Court decisions in your Criminal Law class, but here they form the sum and substance of the course. As you'll see, reading and understanding Supreme Court decisions is no easy task but the effort is well rewarded, especially when you begin the study of Constitutional Law.

If reading complex Supreme Court cases isn't challenging enough, Civil Procedure is all about what its name implies: the process by which matters are adjudicated in our civil court system. Admittedly, this is abstract material so expect it to be challenging to conceptualize. This doesn't mean, however, that there's nothing you can do to help it along: you can go to court and sit in on proceedings. Process is always learned best by doing and since you're not ready for trial practice or clinical courses just yet, you have to do what you can to simulate the experience. Some Civil Procedure professors require their students to attend a court proceeding and note their observations. You don't have to be required by a professor in order to go. Be proactive. Choose a civil trial and then a criminal proceeding to get a sense of the differences. After you've witnessed live proceedings, it's not likely you'll ever confuse criminal with civil actions.

It's incredibly valuable to spend time in court even if you're not planning to be a litigator. It's one thing to read about a trial and quite another to see one. While I am a firm believer in the power of the written word and the ability to learn from books, it's often necessary to go beyond the page and engage in the activity. This is one of those times. Imagine learning to cook by only reading recipes. Or playing the piano by reading sheet music. It just can't be done.

On a very practical level, Civil Procedure introduces you to the critical concept of articulating "threshold questions." These are the questions lawyers routinely ask when assessing a new legal problem and determining the manner in which to proceed. As you'll see, there are threshold questions common to all areas of the law and then there are questions unique to a particular area. In Civil Procedure, you'll learn the basic questions to be asked by all practicing attorneys when considering litigation. For example, the following questions are the initial questions raised in determining personal jurisdiction, which is the authority of a court to render a binding decision with respect to the parties coming before it.

- Is this a matter for state or federal court?

- Does the court have jurisdiction?
  Is there subject matter jurisdiction?
  Is there personal jurisdiction?

- Does an assertion of jurisdiction comport with the requirements of due process in this instance?

(d)   The dialectic of parties in Contracts

When you read Contracts cases, you'll notice that the problems tend to be long, factually dense, and feature numerous communications and actions between and among various parties. You'll also notice a kind of "back-and-forth" where one party's words or conduct create a number of possible responses in return. Most students find Contracts challenging and it's principally for these reasons – there's a lot to keep track of and the situation is constantly changing.

Contract law is about relationships. This is in sharp contrast to Torts and Criminal Law where the problems typically concern a single act or event and it's pretty much contained. Consider, for example, a battery, a defective product, or a homicide where the primary focus is on the contemplated and executed act. Although there are often multiple and subsequent actors involved in tortious and criminal activities, there is typically a triggering and finite event from which all flows.

On the other hand, a contract may bring parties together for a single performance or endure over time and require multiple performances. Of course one could argue that there is but "one" event from which all flows in Contracts and that is the "contract." However, the difference is that the contract is but a point on the continuum in the parties' relationship which includes the formation, execution, and performance of the contract. Although the contractual relationship is often based on a single "act" such as an agreement to build a house or deliver a quantity of shoes, the dialectic of the parties makes for a more complicated situation. Each phase of the parties' relationship is fraught with possibilities for dispute: the negotiations leading up to and surrounding the final agreement, the duties and obligations involved in the performance, and the consequences which flow in the event of breach.

Nevertheless, Contracts need not present any more difficulty than the other first year courses. Once it's clear that dealing with the nature and effects of reciprocal relationships requires a more sophisticated level of analysis, it's a matter of careful reading and organized thinking.

It might be worth noting that some students are initially confused by what seems to be the several sources for Contract law: the common law, the Restatement of Contracts, and the Uniform Commercial Code. Taking a few minutes to understand the sources and organization of Contract law goes a long way in resolving the confusion.

Contract law is essentially case law. It was, however, one of the first subjects undertaken by the American Law Institute ("ALI"), a select group of judges, practitioners, and law professors, for its task of organizing the mass of case law into concise statements of the rules in the form of Restatements of Law. The Restatement of Contracts was completed in 1932. A major revision was undertaken in 1962 and the Restatement Second of Contracts was published in 1981.

As a law student, your primary concern is to know what measure of authority to give the Restatements. While its rules are the work of noted authorities in the particular subject area and shown great deference by the judiciary, the Restatements are not themselves the law. They are considered persuasive authority and therefore not binding on courts.

The Uniform Commercial Code, on the other hand, is the law. It is statutory law and some version of the Code has been enacted in every state except Louisiana. The Code is divided into 11 substantive articles. Typically, your Contracts class is concerned with Article 1, General Provisions, and Article 2, Sales. Whenever you have occasion to consider transactions involving the sale of goods, therefore, you will be working with the Code's provisions. As a result, one of the threshold questions you'll ask when evaluating a Contracts problem will be to determine whether it involves a sales of goods or services.

(e) *Legal Writing*

Every law student takes a legal writing or legal methods class. Individual programs vary by coverage and credit hours but for the most part, the goals are the same: to teach you the nature and structure of legal analysis, the tools and methodologies of legal research, and how the two work together. It is a skills-based course and you'll probably have several short written exercises before you're ready for your final assignments which typically include a legal memorandum and an appellate brief. Still, "the times they are a changing," and some programs now include more practice-based assignments such as client letters, negotiations, and Motions for Summary Judgment or Orders to Show Cause.

In any program, you will be required to write. Unfortunately, too many students find this reason enough to dislike the course. To borrow a phrase from the vernacular, "get over it." Every lawyer must know how to write clearly and competently. Even if you choose a practice area where writing is at a minimum because you're handling real estate transactions or tax work, you'll still have occasion to write client letters or office memos.

To some extent, however, student apprehension is warranted. Legal writing is different from other types of writing and even if you were an English major or consider yourself a strong writer, there is a period of adjustment. The perspective and structure for legal writing is unique but the essential requirements for good writing – clarity, integrity, and vision – remain the same. While there is general form to follow, the style of writing is individual and should reflect you. You will learn to adapt your style to the subject matter, adapting one style for persuasive briefs and another for objective memoranda.

The more you read, the better you write.
I have found the shortest distance to improve writing skills is to improve

reading skills. Reading allows you to model your writing by following the examples of what you read. In law school, each case is a paradigm for IRAC and another example of the process to be emulated. Of course this is true of learning to write in general and is hardly unique to legal writing. In fact, most of us learned to read before we could write and we learned to write by modeling our writing on what we had read.

You have many of the raw materials necessary to develop your legal writing skills in the cases you read for your substantive courses. It is up to you to use them effectively by recognizing their value beyond their role in a particular class. In addition to reading cases for the substantive rules of law, you should read them to enhance your understanding of the structure and form of legal analysis and the language and tone of legal discourse. Then model your own writing after only the best legal opinions – and you'll soon learn to recognize the best from the not-so-good. When combined with assignments and feedback from your Legal Writing class, this is by far the fastest and most efficient way to improve your legal writing skills

(f)   Property

Property is a challenging course for many of the same reasons we've discussed in relation to Contracts: multiple parties, events that unfold over long periods of time (just wait until you learn the Rule Against Perpetuities), and an incredibly rich and extensive vocabulary. Like Contracts, Property is about relationships. Here, however, it is about the set of legal relationships between persons with respect to things, both tangible and intangible. This makes for some very interesting and complicated cases, not to mention multi-layers of analysis.

Also, Property law is steeped in history, particularly English history. Understanding the historical context goes a long way in understanding public policies and legislation. If you find yourself struggling in a particular area, it may help to turn outside your law books to a history book.

B. BEYOND THE FIRST YEAR

There's an expression about law school that goes something like this: "the first year, they scare you to death, the second year they work you to death, and the third year, they bore you to death." I wouldn't say that this is entirely true although the fear factor dissipates by the second year and the material does seem more complex. The truth is that the second-year subjects are more advanced, but they are matched by your ability to engage in deeper and more sophisticated thought. Maybe this makes the second-year seem harder, but it's not. You just know what's expected and consequently your work tends to be more thorough and comprehensive.

1.   WHAT'S WITH EVIDENCE?

I don't think many would disagree when I say that Evidence is one of the most challenging subjects you'll study in law school. First, Evidence law involves both substance and procedure. As my professor made clear the first day of class, an Evidence question always involves the underlying substantive law. The Evidence problem is grounded in substantive law, whether it's a contract dispute or a murder trial. As a result, for each Evidence question, you need to know two sets of law because there's no way to analyze the Evidence problem without a thorough understanding of the relevant substantive law.

Second, the procedural nature of Evidence makes it seem highly theoretical, especially if you've never spent any time in court to see how the sequence of events unfold. Visiting a courtroom and witnessing the interactions of court and counsel and how objections are handled would be time well spent.

Third, Evidence is problem-based. If your professor teaches by the traditional case method, you'll need to supplement with problems on your own. Perhaps more than any other doctrinal course, Evidence requires practical application of the legal theory to make it comprehensible. You need to work through a problem in double hearsay and not just read about it to understand it. Plan to incorporate lots of practice problems into your study time. Multiple choice questions are an excellent source of practice problems. You can even convert them into mini-essays by taking the time to write out explanations of the correct answer.

Finally, Evidence is statute-based and you'll be required to learn the Federal Rules of Evidence and most likely the rules of your particular jurisdiction. Your professor may also require you to learn the common law and note the distinctions between all three.

Now that you can see that there will be lots to learn, you should also know that the best way to ensure that you really understand it is to follow your Evidence course with a practical course such as Trial Advocacy or Trial Practice. You'll use what you've learned and gain a mastery over the subject that is practically impossible to develop any other way.

·2.   CONSTITUTIONAL LAW

(a)   It helps to know some history

This may not be what you were expecting to hear – especially if you are one of those students who all too readily admits she has always "hated history." It will be hard for me, but I'll refrain from reciting the many reasons the study of history is one of life's greatest pleasures and explain instead why it's so useful in the study of law.

When I attended law school, I soon realized how my perceptions were colored by my understanding of American history. When my Criminal Law class discussed the moral underpinnings of criminal sanctions, I thought of the early vision of America as a "city on a hill" and wondered what shining example New York state was setting by re-instituting the death penalty. In Constitutional Law class, when the professor pointed out all the provisions pointing to slavery and strongly implied that the government sanctioned slavery, I want to shout that yes, there were provisions for slavery but what about the value of getting 13 separate entities to agree on anything. The risks were high – the Articles of Confederation weren't working and the future of the republic was uncertain. It was most likely the ability to compromise which secured the nation's future.

You cannot understand American law in a vacuum. While no one expects you to see these relationships, it's critical that you have some sense of what happened and when. Without a knowledge of American history, it's hard to appreciate the nature of federalism and the continuous struggles between state and federal authority. Similarly, without some understanding of the causes of the American Revolution, it's hard to grasp the struggle to create a centralized government and why the Bill of Rights was imposed initially on the federal government only. Or the significance of the subsequent application of the Bill of Rights to the states through the Fourteenth Amendment and the Incorporation Doctrine. There is so much more I could tell you but there's no need to belabor the point: without some sense of the nation's history, it's hard to understand the American constitutional system and its development.

Happily for some, you need not even turn to a history book to get your sense of the past. Instead, you can read novels or biographies. For a vision of early America, you can read Nathaniel Hawthorne, Washington Irving, James Fenimore Cooper or selections form Ben Franklin's Autobiography; for a glimpse into the mid -to-late nineteenth century, you can turn to the works of Emerson, Thoreau, Whitman, William Dean Howells, or Stephen Crane; for a sense of the early twentieth-century experience, you could consider Edith Wharton, Henry James, Ellen Glasgow, Willa Cather, Sherwood Anderson, Upton Sinclair, or Sinclair Lewis. There are many, many more. Choose something you find engaging and your efforts will be rewarded two-fold.

(b)   The cases are the law

I'll be direct: it's not easy to read Supreme Court cases. They are frequently dense, deal with the most intricate and challenging concepts you will ever encounter, and can be anything but models of clarity. This doesn't mean you can opt out and rely on case notes or supplementary materials. It just means you have to work harder to make sense of what you're reading. You can turn to any number of authoritative hornbooks for assistance in understanding doctrine, but when it comes to deciphering what the Court is saying, you must be able to read it for yourself.

On the other hand, reading Supreme Court cases is one of the headiest experiences you'll have in law school. You are reading the opinions of the highest court in the land and what it says is the final word. As you'll learn in *Marbury v. Madison*, the federal judiciary is supreme in the exposition of the law of the Constitution and it is the responsibility of the Supreme Court to act as the ultimate interpreter of the Constitution.

One final comment worth noting about this subject area is that you will most likely be required to learn case names. When I first heard this was expected, I was surprised and wondered how I would ever manage it. But I did and after a bit it seemed quite right to do so. The cases were the rules and knowing the name was often a shorthand for referring to the rule. Of course it required effort and I prepared my outline to reflect this need but it was well worth it. If you make it a point to learn the names as you take up and read each case, you should manage quite nicely.

C.   WHY ALL SUBJECTS ARE MORE OR LESS ALIKE

After explaining in rather great detail the differences you'll find in your law school courses, it may seem ironic to tell you now that despite the differences, they are all pretty much the same. I suppose only a lawyer could presume to make such an argument!

To clarify a bit, it's not so much that the subjects are the "same" because clearly they are not, but that there are recurring and common themes and a cohesiveness to how the law operates. Indeed, there is no doubt but that you will be climbing the learning curve continually throughout your years in law school, but the climb is primarily substantive after the first year. You will not be spending your time re-learning the basics but rather building on your foundation.

Nonetheless, you can expect each of your professors to be markedly different in teaching style, personality, and approach – if nothing else, this is one thing you can count on. However, the one attribute they share is what they demand from you: to learn the law with precision and specificity and write a well-reasoned argument based on an analysis of the relevant issues and an application of the law to the facts. This does not change according to subject or professor. It is constant because it is what the law requires. This is one of the reasons students tend to perform consistently. It is most unusual to find wide divergences between grades, although there is an occasional spike or plunge based on other factors going on in a student's life during a semester.

This information should make you realize that writing practice essays or answering multiple choice questions in one subject area is useful for others in developing your writing and analytical skills. If you can write an "A" Torts exam, you are capable of doing the same in any subject, given the same level of preparation and understanding. Accordingly, the many examples in this book are valuable even if they are not identical to what you'll see on one of your exams. The problems we discuss are universal and the approaches for resolving them are common to all.

D. MAKING CONNECTIONS

While it is outside the scope of this book to discuss specific legal doctrine, it is appropriate to indicate some of the recurrent themes you'll encounter to help you make the connections so vital to effective learning. Often as you proceed through each area of doctrinal law, you'll find it necessary to take a very narrow, focused approach because there is only so much you can assimilate at a time. Still, there is a downside: the same tunnel-vision that lets you navigate enormous amounts of information limits your consideration of other perspectives. This obscures your ability to see the major themes both between and within topics – at least not right away. Typically, these connections emerge when you study for finals or the bar exam but there's no need to wait until the end when it can assist your learning along the way.

Consider the following concepts as you work your way through reading assignments and engage in class discussions:

- The need to balance competing interests
- The tension between individual freedom and government control
- Protecting the expectations of the parties
- An abhorrence of unjust enrichment
- A disdain for economic waste
- The role of intent in imposing liability, whether in tortious or criminal activity
- The concept of foreseeability in limiting liability
- The idea of compensation for harm and the use of punitive damages to deter unacceptable behavior

These are but a few of the recurrent themes you'll encounter in the study of law. After a few months in law school, you should be able to add to the list – significantly.

CHAPTER 4:
THE COURSE OUTLINE AND
ITS RELATION TO THE EXAM

A. WHAT IT IS AND WHAT IT ISN'T

The outline is your personal rule book for a particular course with a particular professor. It's a compilation and synthesis of the legal principles, rules, case summaries, policy arguments, and examples that summarizes and explains the course material. It's your rendition of "Torts with Professor Jones." There won't be another exactly like it. There can't be – not even from another student in Professor Jones' Torts class. While it might come close, the differences in organization, emphasis, and content would be significant. That's because the outline reflects how you thought about the material.

The outline is where you make sense of the individual concepts and figure out the relationships between them. That's why to be of any practical use, you've got to be the one to put it together. This is one of the few occasions where homemade is not only better, but absolutely necessary. While commercial outlines provide the rules of law and cases and examples, they do so in a generic, one-size-fits-all kind of way that doesn't necessarily comport with how your professor taught the class. While not incorrect, they fail to capture the nuances and emphases made in class. As a result, they lack an essential ingredient for success on law school exams – the professor's voice in interpreting the rules and showing how the issues present.

B. ITS PURPOSE

The course outline serves a two-fold purpose: first, it facilitates your learning of the law because it requires that you organize and record the information for memory retrieval and understanding; and, second, it prepares you for the exam because it's where you work your way through analysis of the relevant issues you're likely to find there.

1. TO LEARN THE MATERIAL

How you perform on the exam begins here with how you learn the rules. The process of outlining facilitates learning because it requires that you organize the material in a meaningful way that allows you to remember it. In fact, a disorganized exam answer is usually the direct result of a disorganized outline. This makes perfect sense. *What you write on the exam comes from what you studied; if your study materials are incorrect, incomplete, or disorganized, it will be reflected in what you write.* And your grade reflects them both!

Memorization of the law is only the first step. When you memorize information, it's good for descriptive purposes but you need to do more than just recite the rules to solve problems. You need to know how the rules work. For that, you need to see the big picture. In reading cases and in discussing them in class, you focus on very narrow and specific pieces of information. You look at rules or elements or factors and how courts apply them in different factual settings. Outlining is where you take all the individual pieces and put them together in a way that defines the relationships between them. Your professor or upper class students may have told you during the semester that "it all comes together in the end." It does and it doesn't: it comes together for those who put it together.

The process of "putting it together" combines two quite disparate acts: it requires that you take apart the individual rules and then connect them in a way that reflects how they interact as a whole. For an outline to "work," it must do both. It's not enough to deconstruct the rules into their component parts. While this is essential to learning the individual rules, you still need to know how the rules work together in order to use them.

2. TO PREPARE FOR EXAMS

When you prepare for the final exam, you'll study from your outline and only your outline. Class notes, case briefs, and casebooks get put away: they've served their purpose. Your outline contains all you need to know and in the way you need to know it. It's organized to allow you to memorize the material. It identifies the issues likely to arise with each of the doctrines and the sequence in which you'll analyze them. Finally, the outline is your "legal playbook," containing all the moves you need to consider in response to the problems likely to come your way on the exam.

C. WHEN TO OUTLINE

You should begin your outline early in the semester and have it complete by the time you sit down to study for finals. Unfortunately, there's a tendency to avoid outlining until the very end of the semester and then race through the process. As a result, one of the primary benefits of outlining – learning over time – is lost.

On the other hand, you don't want to start outlining too soon. Ideally, you should begin outlining when you've completed a topic and then add to it, topic by topic, as you proceed through the semester. As a general rule, I recommend sitting down between the third and fourth week of class to begin the process. By this time, you've covered enough material in your readings and class lectures for outlining to be productive.

Here's where the casebook can help you determine when and where to get started. Compare the Table of Contents to your syllabus (if your professor doesn't provide a syllabus, simply rely on the reading assignments) and find where in the casebook your readings are located. Casebooks are typically divided by section and chapter so you'll know when you've completed a topic. Depending on your class schedule and how quickly your professor moves through the material, you should complete a topic every two weeks or so and therefore should be prepared to work on your course outline every other week. You may also find that your professor doesn't always begin the course on page 1 and work straight through the book. In fact, the sequence in which your professor takes up topics reflects how she structured the course and you can find this structure – even if she never says a word about it – by isolating and tracking the subject headings.

D. HOW AND WHAT TO OUTLINE

So far we've only talked in general terms about outlining, focusing on its purpose as a learning tool and how it's used to structure, record, and make sense of the course material. Now it's time to see how to create one.

1. FOLLOW A TRADITIONAL OUTLINE STRUCTURE

The first step is to use a regular outline format. You can work with either Roman numerals or a scientific numbering scheme. It doesn't matter which one you choose as long as it differentiates between levels. The structure of an outline forces you to rank concepts and identify main topics and sub-topics. Remember, the law is essentially a set of categories: each principle you learn belongs "somewhere" in the scheme which you need to create.

A failure to properly understand and define the hierarchy of concepts in your outline often manifests on the exam with difficulty in identifying and sequencing issues for discussion. There is a logical sequence to follow in analyzing a problem based on the construction of the rule and it's essential that this hierarchy be worked through in the process of creating your outline. The ranking system inherent in an outline format forces you to arrange the material in a hierarchy.

To get started in creating your hierarchy, you need look no farther than The Table of Contents in your casebook. It's written in outline form. Some casebooks include a Summary of the Table of Contents which is even better for your purposes since it contains only the main topics and sub-topics, eliminating the cases and notes. From here, you can really see the big picture.

Coordinate the Table of Contents with your syllabus to find your starting point and use it as a template to form your skeleton outline. Of course you'll need to make adjustments based on how your professor presents the material, but the Table of Contents provides the overview you need to begin putting things together. This should give you the major headings. You may want to consider a hornbook to help you identify the sub-headings. This is the real work of outlining: synthesizing the material so that you can differentiate between main and sub-issues. Don't be afraid to go outside your casebook and class notes for help in this regard. Most of us need the help to be found in hornbooks. A hornbook will explain the material in a way that is incredibly valuable in helping you understand it.

Once you have a sense of the main topics and sub-topics, you can begin to fill in the pieces to provide substance and meaning. Of course the only way for this to make sense is to see an example where we begin with a general topic and add sub-topics. Then you'll see how the outline takes shape as we fill it in with definitions, cases, and examples.

Consider the following example. As you can see, it has identified a main topic, "Bases for avoiding the contract," and listed two sub-topics, "Incapacity" and "Defects in the bargaining process." The first sub-topic is further divided into two bases for finding incapacity. More bases will be added to the second sub-topic at a later time. Right now, this reflects what's been covered in class and a good point to begin outlining because the first sub-topic has been completed and enough of the second has begun to provide a sense of the whole.

> I. Bases for avoiding the contract
>   A. Incapacity of the parties
>   1. Age (infancy)
>   2. Mental competency
>   a. Drugs
>   b. Alcohol
>   B. Defects in the bargaining process
>   1. Mistake
>   a. Unilateral mistake
>   b. Mutual mistake
>   2. Fraud /misrepresentation
>
> **Outlining Main Topics and Sub-topics**

2. ORGANIZE BY RULE

The organizing principle of outlining is the rule, not the case. While you learn the rules case by case, when it comes to outlining, you strip everything away and all that remains are the rules: definitions, elements, factors, exceptions, and defenses. These are your building blocks.

Be prepared to ask and answer the following questions for each principle you include in your outline:

- What is the rule? How is it defined?
- How does it work? Under what facts or circumstances would it be likely to occur?
- What does it require? Are there any tests or factors which must be met?
- Are there limitations to the rule?
- What is the consequence of applying the rule?
- What happens to the parties as a result?
- Is there a change in their position and what is it?

3. PROVIDE DEPTH, DETAIL, AND SPECIFICITY

Next, your outline must be written in sufficient detail to allow you to learn the rules with specificity. While an outline is abbreviated by nature, you can't afford to be overly cryptic. If your outline makes only general statements, then you'll learn only in generalities and you're defeating the very purpose of outlining. On the other hand, you can't get so bogged down in detail that you lose sight of the big picture. The goal is to include sufficient detail without diminishing the outline's utility as a study tool. The issue becomes one of balance: how do you achieve specificity while avoiding useless minutia? What's necessary to really "know" a rule?

There are two basic considerations when learning a rule: first, you must be able to define it fully and completely; and second, you must thoroughly appreciate how it operates. In addressing student questions about what to put in their outline to accomplish these tasks, I've developed the following checklist to guide them.

---

1. Define the rule

   Provide detail and context:
   - Are there elements? Factors? Tests? Conditions?
   - When does it apply?
   - When does it arise?
   - How is it used?
   - Applications / examples?

   Identify limitations:
   - Are there exceptions? / Limitations?
   - Are there defenses?

2. Identify the consequences of applying the rule
   - What happens if this rule is applied?
   - What is the likely result, effect on the parties, outcome to the dispute?

   Checklist for Defining the Rule

(a) Define the rule

As always, the starting point is a basic definition. But the definition is just a starting point. It's far from all you need to know or write in your outline or on the exam. You must flesh out the basic definition with sufficient detail to provide context to allow you to learn the rule in its entirety. As the checklist indicates, you must consider whether the rule breaks down by element (usually in Torts and Criminal Law) or by factor (typically Contracts, Constitutional Law and Property, to name a few). In each case, you need to define and explain each of the elements or factors.

Learning a rule also means that you know when and how it will arise from the facts. For example, in addition to defining "incapacity" in our outline, we must explain how the concept is implicated and when it applies. Let's consider what we would add to our outline to provide context and meaning.

I.   Bases for Avoiding the Contract

Parties can avoid legal obligations even when they have satisfied the requirements for contract formation, i.e., although the technical requirements of formation have been met – offer, acceptance, and consideration – there are ways to avoid the deal.

      A.   Incapacity of the parties
         Legal capacity of both offeror and offeree is essential for contract formation. If parties lack legal capacity, they cannot give the required legally binding mutual assent.

         1.   Infancy: one type of incapacity based on age.
            By statute in most states, a person under the age of 18 (21 under the common law) has the capacity to incur only void-able contractual duties until the beginning of the day before the person's 18th birthday.

Caption for Box 3: Adding Context and Meaning

Naturally, every rule demands separate treatment because each rule "breaks down" differently. Some are composed of elements; others are assessed by evaluating factors or tests. Moreover, for every "general" rule you'll learn, there'll be exceptions or at least limitations on its reach and application. By using the checklist as you approach a rule for inclusion in your outline, you'll be sure to consider all the possible qualifications.

Let's return to the capacity example. Although we've written some basic definitions, including one for infancy, there's more to include because there's more we need to know about the rule. We need to consider whether there are limitations or exceptions to the general rule regarding infancy. It just so happens that there are both and we'll take them up in the next section dealing with the legal effects of rules.

(b)   Identify the consequences of applying the rule

This step is essential and the one most frequently absent from student out-lines and exam analysis. Failure to consider the consequences of a rule tends to manifest in the application portion of the exam essay – not necessarily as a conclusory or cryptic analysis, but one that fails to link to the probable out-come. You can avoid this result by addressing the following questions with respect to each rule you include in your outline:

■ What happens if a court finds this rule applicable? What actions will it take?

■ What is the likely result/outcome/effect? Where does it leave the parties?

What is the effect of minority on the contract? We wrote that an infant incurs only voidable contractual duties. This statement is critical to our understanding because it allows us to determine the parties' duties and obligations if one of them was a minor at the time of contract. But is it enough to know that a minor incurs only "voidable contractual duties" or is more necessary to understand how the principle operates?

You need to know what is meant by "voidable," how and by whom the contract would be rendered voidable, whether it is voidable under all circumstances (what if the contract has been fully performed?), and whether all contracts are voidable. These are critical questions and must be addressed in your studies and, consequently, in your outline.

---

1. Infancy: One type of incapacity based on age.
   By statute in most states, a person under the age of 18 (21 under the common law, 18 under the Rest. § 2d.) has the capacity to incur only voidable contractual duties until the beginning of the day before the person's 18th birthday. Can avoid the contract even if fully performed on both sides. The other party is bound, for him the contract is neither void nor voidable.

   a. Effects of infancy: there is a contract if the minor takes no further action but it can be avoided if the appropriate steps are taken on the infant's behalf.

   b. An infant may disaffirm a contract (the whole not merely parts), by words or conduct, either before or after a reasonable time upon reaching majority by:

      • Asserting minority as a defense in action

      • Bringing an action to set aside the deal or to recover benefits conferred

   c. Ratification: the infant's manifestation of intent to be bound by the agreement made upon reaching majority. Ratification ends infant power to contact. Can be by words or conduct such as performance of the contractual obligation or accepting the other party's performance under the contract

   d. Exception for *necessaries*

      A transaction for necessaries is not voidable. However, there may be liability in restitution for their reasonable value, but not the contract itself. What types of things are necessaries is a question of law

   e. Checklist questions (developed in special chart to follow)

4. INCORPORATE "CHECKLIST OF LEADING QUESTIONS"

An essential part of outlining is transforming the rule descriptions and requirements you've summarized into analytical tools. As you know, it's insufficient to restate rules you've memorized on the exam; instead, you have to use them to solve the problem. Figuring out how to use the rules is accomplished during the outlining process.

Your task is to take each component or requirement of the rule and turn it into a question. In doing so, you're creating the sequence of questions which must be answered to determine whether and how the rule applies in a given situation. In other words, you are using the structure of the rule to direct your inquiry with respect to a given set of facts.

This is a lot easier to show than to explain. For example, let's see how this works with the rule regarding incapacity. We've stated the general rule that a minor can incur only voidable contractual obligations. If we are to "use" this rule, we need to identify the "checklist" questions to be asked when applying this rule. We start by framing the overall issue,

> *Can this party can avoid a contract because of incapacity based on age?*

This, in turn, leads to the first question:

1.   Was the party a minor at the time of the transaction?

This is the threshold question. If the party was not a minor at the time of contract, then your inquiry ends here because incapacity based on age would not be available as a basis on which to avoid the contract.

On the other hand, if the party was a minor at the time of formation, then you proceed to the next question:

2.   Was it a transaction for "necessities"?

Typically, this is the more detailed analysis and leads to the following sub-questions to determine whether it is or isn't a necessity. Although the issue of whether it is a necessity is a question of law, you'd still need to make an assessment on the exam and proceed.

> a.   *Is the contract for food, shelter, clothing or other such basic items typically found necessary for the maintenance of life?*

Assuming that the transaction involved a "necessary," the next question is:

> b.   *What is the quantity, quality and reasonable value of that necessity in light of the infant's social status and situation in life?*

The necessity exception is a typical exam question because it is a basis for holding the minor liable whereas the general rule is that she can avoid the contract. But even here the waters are murky: if the minor has entered into a contract for a necessity, she is only liable for its reasonable value and this liability is deemed in restitution and not on the contract. Hence, the following question: assuming a necessity, is the minor liable in restitution for its reasonable value? Understanding this principle in full means dealing with the three bases of promissory liability: contract, reliance, and restitution.

After dealing with the question of necessities, you'd want to consider whether the infant took any actions to disaffirm or ratify the contract:

3.   Upon reaching the age of majority, has the infant engaged in conduct so as to ratify the agreement either through words or conduct?

Alternatively, has the infant taken any actions which can be construed as disaffirming the contract?

These questions belong in your outline so you can become fully familiar with the structure of the rule. They are the ones you'll ask on the exam if you encounter a problem dealing with this topic. Having identified the relevant questions when studying, you'll move quickly through your exam analysis.

---

e.   Checklist questions:
   Can this party can avoid a contract because of incapacity based on age?

   1. Was the party a minor at the time of the transaction?
   2. Was it a transaction for "necessities"?
      a. Is the contract for food, shelter, clothing or other such basic items typically found necessary for the maintenance of life?
      b. What is the quantity, quality and reasonable value of that necessity in light of the infant'is social status and situation in life?
      c. Assuming a necessity, is the minor liable in restitution for its reasonable value?
   3. Upon reaching majority, has the infant engaged in conduct so as to ratify the agreement either through words or conduct?
   or
      Has the infant taken any actions which can be construed as disaffirming the contract?

   Including Checklist Questions

This covers the basic material to include in an outline regarding infancy as a basis for avoiding a contract: the general rule, its limits, and the consequences of its application. One further consideration is to include practical examples. Such examples show how the principle works. They might come from class or ones you think of on your own. Practicing problems is the best way to see whether you've learned the material. Creating your own hypotheticals tests your understanding and is the best preparation for the exam. Here you might want to consider the following questions:

> *What if a 17 year-old television star purchased a limousine to use for personal appearances, trips to the television studio, school, and the mall? Upon her 18th birthday, could she avoid the deal? Could the dealer claim it was a "necessity"?*

5. WHAT ABOUT CASES?

By now, you may be wondering whether cases belong in an outline and if they do, how they're used. The answer is that they have a place, but exactly what it is depends on the subject and professor. Typically, you won't need to know case names for exams. That's one of the surprising things about law school — the individual cases turn out not to be so very important. Of course, there are exceptions. One is if your professor tells you that you need to know them or refers to particular cases as "seminal" cases. Then you'll include them in your outline and learn their names and holdings. On the exam, you'll cite the case name in support of a rule or analogize the facts of the problem to the case you've read. Sometimes, professors ask specific case-based questions to show whether you've read and understood the material. Then there's no way to avoid knowing the cases. Second, if you take courses which rely on Supreme Court cases, then you most certainly need to know the cases. How could you take Constitutional Law, Civil Procedure, and Criminal Procedure and not expect to know case names and holdings? Here, the cases are the rules. Finally, if you find that cases help you recall the rules, then a brief summary explaining how the rule was applied to the facts in the case will be useful in your outline.

For more detailed information and specific examples, refer to the outline excerpts in the section, "How Substance Determines Style."

6. INTEGRATING CLASS NOTES

A chapter on outlining would not be complete without discussing the role of class notes. As we noted at the beginning of the chapter, your outline should reflect what you learned in the course and it should do so in the way your professor presented the material. Capturing your professor's tone in an outline requires that you take good class notes.

(a) Good note-taking begins with good listening skills

The ability to listen is important to the general task of learning but it's vital to learning the law. Not only is it essential to every step of the law school learning process, but it's essential to every task associated with the actual practice of law.

Going to class and listening to your professor is the single most important step in the learning process. Your professor speaks the language of the law and your job is to listen very carefully – not only to what is being said, but to how it is said. Pay strict attention to vocabulary and write down every legal term of art, especially if your professor mentions it more than once. Your goal is to learn to speak the language like one of the "natives."

(b) What notes to take

Class notes should create a snapshot of what occurred in class on a particular day, allowing you to relive exactly what was covered that day in terms of the cases discussed, the questions asked, and the comments made. Your notes should even have a particular voice – that of your professor.

Since you're not expected to make a transcript of each class, what should you write?

- Any points, questions, and observations the professor makes about the cases. Strive to capture how your professor "thinks" about a case, which is quite separate from the basic information you already have in your case briefs.

- All the questions the professor asks in class. With some professors, all you get are questions. It's a big mistake to overlook them while waiting for "answers" that are not likely to come. *Here, the answers are in the questions.* Trust me. The answers you're looking for are in the questions that the professor asks of you and the material. Your job is to be learn to ask the same types of questions. Soon you'll be the one asking the questions, finding the problems in the case, and the inconsistencies in the court's reasoning.

- Every hypothetical and example. This is the stuff of which exams are made. Consider every hypo a potential exam question and write it down as well as any variations. Professors are known to present one problem and then keep changing the facts. Write it all down.

- Comments relating to policy, legal theory, and doctrine. These comments let you know how your professor thinks about the law.

- Everything written on the blackboard. Law professors are traditionally so "low-tech" that even writing on the blackboard is a major event. So when it happens, you can be very sure it's important. Write down every word.

- Legal terms. Since your job is to learn the language of the law, make sure you write down the words, phrases, and legal terms of art associated with the topics as they are discussed.

- Steps of analysis; tests; standards. This is not the same as the "black letter rule." That's in your casebook, the hornbook, and every outline in the bookstore. What you want is the way your teacher presents the rule to you and the way she works through the sequence of analysis. Listen for such signal language as *"there are two questions to be asked"* or *"the patterns to look for are."* Soon you'll be able to detect when your professor is about to give you the gift of analysis. Write it down.

DO'S AND DON'TS

<u>Don't</u>:   Rely on your memory to reconstruct class lectures.

<u>Don't</u>:   Waste time and effort to rewrite basic rules that are in the cases and already in your case brief. Instead, listen for how your professor breaks down a rule into elements or provides steps of analysis and write that down — this is unique to your professor and not to be found elsewhere.

<u>Do</u>:   Strive to make your notes a "re-creation" of all that was discussed in class on that day, but not a transcript. Focus on what's unique and can't otherwise be found in a casebook or hornbook.

<u>Don't</u>:   Spend time rewriting your notes.

<u>Do</u>:   Go over your notes promptly after class and fill in any missing words. Reading what you wrote will prompt your memory and you'll be able to fill in missing words and complete sentences.

Taking Notes in Class

(continued on next page)

Don't: Use your computer to take notes unless you are a sufficiently expert typist to keep up with the professor.

Don't: Use the computer if it will distract you.

Do: Rely on your longhand — especially if you're going to be writing your exams. You need the practice and to develop your stamina.

Do: Practice good organizational skills: date your notes, begin each day's notes on a new page, keep class notes separate from case briefs and outlines.

Do: Focus on legal language. Pay particular attention to legal phrases, terms of art, and concepts — especially the ones the professor repeats several times.

Do: Write the hypos the professor presents in class. These are additional examples offered to illustrate some portion of the rule. Be sure to follow and include the analysis.

Do: Treat hypos like mini-exam questions and write down all hypotheticals.

Do: Write down any summary or overview the professor presents. It's a guide to how the professor sees all the pieces fitting together.

Don't: Rewrite your case briefs after class.

Do: Annotate your case briefs during class discussions. Make sure you've dissected the case properly by:

- Stating the relevant facts

- Identifying the correct issue

- Correctly articulating the rule

- Correctly identifying the court's rationale

Taking Notes in Class

(c)   What about typing?

I'm often asked whether I think students should type their class notes. The answer is "it depends." It depends on whether you can type well enough to keep up with what's going on in class. It depends on whether you're easily distracted by the computer and all its "other" capabilities. It depends on whether you'll be typing or writing your final exam.

Generally, I recommend students try writing their notes in good, old-fashioned longhand and here's why. In my experience, typed notes tend to be the most incomplete and cryptic. They may "look" good, but they say little because the student may not be a sufficiently proficient typist to keep up with class discussion and instead settles for "buzzwords." Conversely, students who type well often seem to think they must type everything they hear and end up with a transcript of the class, including basic information readily available in the case book. What they lose in trying to type every word is the opportunity to really listen and think about what's going on in class. When you write, you know you can't possibly capture everything that's said, so you tend to think more before you write which is itself a filtering and learning process.

If you decide to use your laptop to take class notes, one thing consider is to have your case briefs available in hard copy. This avoids a problem I've seen occur repeatedly: I'll call on a student to discuss a case and she starts switching between screens to find the brief. While I doubt any professor expects an instantaneous response, the delay is often significant while the student locates the case and then tries to find her place in it.

You'll also want to avoid the following situation: you become so engrossed in navigating between notes, outlines, case briefs, and other software support programs in trying to respond to a question from the professor that the point of the question is lost entirely in the wake of the search.

Some students handle these problems by incorporating their case briefs, study notes, and class notes into one document. Unfortunately, that simply presents a problem of a different type: when everything is mixed together, it's hard to tell where case briefs end and notes about them from class begin. Of course, there's a solution to everything and one student told me that she types in different colors to separate her work from class notes. I suppose this is one approach but it seems to make the task of note taking more complex than need be.

Another reason in favor of writing over typing is that it develops the stamina required for exam writing. If you're not going to be typing your exam, you'll need to be able to write for long periods of time, which can be anywhere from three to four hours at a stretch. Maybe more. Taking your notes in class every day prepares you for writing exams.

Further, you should consider how easily you become distracted in class. Computers can be very tempting diversions when you're bored. But you can't afford distractions in law school and anything that interferes with your concentration must be eliminated. For many students, writing their notes keeps them focused in a way that typing does not.

Whether you write or type your notes is a purely individual choice and comes down to a matter of what best suits your needs and abilities. There is no one-size-fits-all approach and sometimes what works for one class may not work for another. You need to be flexible and aware of your own learning style. Since the goal of taking notes is to capture everything of importance that's going in class, it just makes sense to do so in the way that's most effective and efficient for you.

There is one final point worth noting: just because you've typed something doesn't mean you have a finished work product. You still need to review your class notes to edit, organize, and integrate them appropriately into your outline.

(d) The connection between class notes and the exam

How you write your notes may be just as important as what you write. While it's easy to see how the substance of your notes relates to exam performance, it's not quite so easy to see how their form would affect it as well. But it does. If your notes tend to consist of one-word buzz words, short phrases, and bulleted points, then there's a strong likelihood that the same brevity will appear in your exam answers.

The "fix" is relatively simple: take every opportunity to think and write in complete sentences. With practice, it will become automatic. Professors speak in full and complete sentences. Endeavor to do the same. Answer questions in complete sentences when called upon in class and write in complete sentences when you take notes. If you don't have enough time to complete every sentence during class, go back later while the thoughts are still fresh in your mind. Not only will this reinforce the material covered in class, but it will improve your writing and consequently your exam performance.

7. PUTTING IT ALL TOGETHER: HOW THE PIECES FIT

(a) Completed excerpt

I.   Bases for Avoiding the Contract

Parties can avoid legal obligations even when they have satisfied the requirements for contract formation, i.e., although the technical requirements of formation have been met — offer, acceptance, and consideration — there are ways to avoid the deal.

A.   Incapacity of the parties

Legal capacity of both offeror and offeree is essential for contract formation. If parties lack legal capacity, they cannot give the required legally binding mutual assent.

1.   Infancy: one type of incapacity based on age.

By statute in most states, a person under the age of 18 (21 under the common law; 18 under the Rest. §2d) has the capacity to incur only voidable contractual duties until the beginning of the day before the person's 18th birthday.

a.   Effects of infancy: there is a contract if the minor takes no further action. But it can be avoided if appropriate steps are taken on infant's behalf.

b.   An infant may *disaffirm* a contract (the whole, not merely parts), by words or conduct, either before or after a reasonable time upon reaching majority by: (*Bowling v. Sperry*: contract for sale of car avoided by minor)

- Asserting minority as a defense in an action

- Bringing an action to set aside the deal or to recover benefits conferred

c.   *Ratification:* the infant's manifestation of intent to be bound by the agreement made upon reaching majority. Ratification ends infant's power to avoid the contract. Can be by words or conduct such as performance of the contractual obligation or accepting the other party's performance under the contract.

d.   Exception for *necessaries*: a transaction for necessaries is not voidable. What types of things are necessaries is a question of law but typically include food, shelter, clothing, etc. Whether something is a necessity in a particular situation is a question of fact tied to the party's social position.

e.   Checklist questions

Whether this party can avoid a contract because of incapacity based on age?

1.   Was the party a minor at the time of the transaction?

2.   Was it a transaction for "necessities"?

a.   Is the contract for food, shelter, clothing or other such basic items typically found necessary for the maintenance of life?

b.   What is the quantity, quality and reasonable value of that necessity in light of the infant's social status and situation in life?

c.   Assuming a necessity, is the minor liable in restitution for its reasonable value?

3.   Upon reaching majority, has the infant engaged in conduct so as to ratify the agreement either through words or conduct?

or

Has the infant taken any actions which can be construed as disaffirming the contract?

Completed Outline Excerpt

(b)   In comparison

Our outline on infancy works by breaking the rule into a hierarchy of questions to be asked, thus allowing it to be used to guide you through analysis of a problem. It passes the test for any outline by answering these questions:

- Does it provide a definition and thorough explanation of the rule, including all of the relevant exceptions, limitations, and defenses?

- Can you use it to analyze a problem by leading you through the relevant questions?

The following excerpt is based on a student outline on the same topic. Does it pass the test?

I.   Avoidance of Contracts
Defenses that affect assent can render a contract voidable. Other defenses may render a contract void. In a voidable contract, the innocent party may enforce the contract, but the contract cannot be enforced against him. If a contract is void, neither party can enforce the contract.

Voidable contracts may be ratified by the party with the power to avoid the contract once the reason for such avoidance, such as minor age, no longer exists.
   A.   Capacity to contract.
      1.   Infancy (Rest. §14)
         Minors – those less than 18 years old in most states may disaffirm a contract except for necessaries (typically food, shelter, clothing).

         A minor can avoid contractual obligations for a reasonable time upon reaching the age of majority. However, if he fails to disaffirm within a reasonable time, the contract is binding.

         Bowling v. Sperry: case of returned car.

                                                            Student Example

---

This example shows that simply following an outline format won't guarantee a structured outline. While the excerpt adheres to outline form, the structure necessary for understanding the rule is missing. There are no "checklist" questions to guide an analysis involving the rule; there are no definitions or connections between concepts to allow for true understanding. The language lacks precision and, while terms of art are referenced, they are not fully defined.

This type of outline is all too common. It takes up the task of outlining but falls far short of the mark. Typically, the student is completely unaware of its deficiencies until receiving a poor exam grade and begins the search to find out why. In working with students, we find that it usually comes down to the outline: if the rule was incorrect or incomplete when studying, there was little chance it would come out right on the exam.

(c)   Where it all came from

I wouldn't be a bit surprised if you were thinking that the excerpt looks so professional that it's something you couldn't possibly do yourself. But you could and here's why: each part of the outline proceeded from the guidelines we defined and if you follow them, you'll achieve the same result.

- We began with the hierarchical structure in the casebook's table of contents.

- We filled it in with information from our class notes, case briefs, and the explanatory notes in the casebook.

- We took the pieces, thought about how they worked together by asking the questions in our checklist, and created a logical, orderly structure which now works for us when we study.

(d)   How it works on the exam

I'm sure you're also thinking this is great in theory but takes an awful lot of time and effort. Surely, there must be an easier way. There isn't: you must figure out how the pieces fit when you're studying because there just isn't time on the exam. That's when solid preparation really pays off. Let's see how your outline on incapacity would work for you on the exam. Consider the following hypothetical:

On April 15, 2005, Amy entered into a contract with the KIDZ Channel to star in a new television series. She would be paid $1.5 million to appear in all 22 episodes of the season.

Production began in June and by August, Amy was tired of the routine and the television studio. She lost interest in the series and began showing up late for work without learning her lines.

The KIDZ Channel threw a surprise party for Amy's 18th birthday on September 15, 2005 and invited all her friends and family. Amy was delighted. Once again, she was excited about the series. The next day and for the following two weeks, Amy reported promptly for work. She knew her lines, behaved professionally, and stayed late three nights in a row to master a particularly difficult dance routine.

On October 5, Amy's enthusiasm came to an end. She had enough and called KIDZ and asked to be let out of the contract. What result?

Sample Question

This question could appear as one issue among several in a long fact pattern or as an individual short answer question. In either case, you'd proceed readily and efficiently through the problem by summoning to mind the relevant checklist questions from your outline. After framing the issue, *"whether Amy can avoid the contract she entered as a minor when for two weeks upon reaching majority she performed her contractual obligations,"* you'd be ready to write:

Amy was a minor when she entered into the agreement with KIDZ on April 15 because she was only 17. The general rule is that a minor has the capacity to incur only voidable contractual duties until the beginning of the day before the person's eighteenth birthday. Therefore, she could either ratify or disaffirm the contract upon reaching her 18th birthday on September 15.

The question is whether Amy engaged in such conduct upon reaching her 18th birthday so as to ratify the agreement either through words or conduct. *[This sentence is a translation of the first of our checklist questions. Here it's been turned into an issue statement to begin the analysis.]* Amy's behavior could be seen as ratifying the contract because after her 18th birthday party, she continued to perform her obligations under the contract. For the next two weeks, she reported for work, knew her lines, behaved professionally and even stayed late three nights to learn a dance routine. This conduct might be considered ratification of the agreement.

On the other hand, two weeks might be too short a period of time to terminate the power to disaffirm. The question is whether Amy could still disaffirm given these actions. *[This sentence is the second checklist question and used here to consider the alternative argument.]* Amy performed for only two weeks following her birthday and within three weeks asked to be let out of the deal. Three weeks upon attaining majority is a relatively short time given the length of the contract, a television season. She performed for the months of June, July, August, and half of September before her 18th birthday and only two weeks thereafter. Consequently, two weeks of performance subsequent to turning 18 may not be sufficient to terminate her power to disaffirm. In this case, Amy could avoid further performance under the contract.

Sample Answer Using Checklist Questions

This is where and how your preparation really pays off: you're able to write a solid exam answer well within the given time constraints by following the analytical steps you've learned from your outline.

E. COMMERCIAL STUDY AIDS

The best and most useful study aids are those you create yourself. There is simply no substitute for your own efforts. However, there is value in some of the materials you'll find in the bookstore – you just have to choose them carefully and use them correctly. And you certainly have lots to choose from: there are study aids to guide you through every step of your legal education – from composing admissions essays to writing bar exam essays. Some of these will be very helpful. Some won't. The following suggestions are intended to help you make appropriate choices.

1.   INTRODUCTORY MATERIALS AND HORNBOOKS

If you haven't already done so, I'd suggest reading one of the books that introduce you to the law school experience. They provide a pretty good idea of what to expect. However, most of what you read won't fully resonate until you've been in class a while and living the life of a law student.

Once classes have begun, you'll find hornbooks very useful. They explain the law and are written by experts in the field. I'd ask the professor for a recommendation. Chance are very good she'll recommend the hornbook she uses and you'll soon be hearing "familiar" language in class discussions.

Still, a word or two about hornbooks is in order. They must be used appropriately to be effective. They're not meant to be read like novels, where you begin on page one and work your way through to the end. No doubt you'd learn a lot, but you'd never complete your work. In law school, you're constantly working against the clock which means that you can only consult so many resources to help you prepare for class and learn the material. Here's where hornbooks can really help: use them to read about a topic and acquire a general understanding before you read the assigned cases in your casebook. You'll find the case reading proceeds more easily and efficiently when you have a context for understanding what you're reading. Still, reading a hornbook is not a substitute for the work of reading the cases themselves. You must engage with the actual words of the court and learn to make sense of them yourself. No one can do this for you.

You'll also turn to hornbooks when you require additional explanations for the more challenging and complex legal principles. The cases don't give themselves up easily to understanding – you often need an outside assist. Next to your professor, the most reliable source for this kind of information is a hornbook – and they're readily available whenever you have a question.

2. GENERAL STUDY AIDS

As even a quick perusal around the bookstore will show, there are volumes devoted to helping you with just about every one of your law school tasks. There are aids for briefing cases, writing outlines, and organizing legal research. In addition to books and flash cards, there are audio tapes and software programs. Multiply these options by the number of courses you're taking per semester and it's easy to see how it adds up. That's why before you invest your time and money, you should know what they can and cannot do for you.

Study aids are only supplements. They're neither short-cuts to learning the material nor substitutes for your own thinking. Unfortunately, their ready availability makes them seem an attractive alternative to the long hours and hard work needed to sort, synthesize, and otherwise thoughtfully engage in the course material, but they're not. Nothing is. But while they're no substitute for your own work, they can be of assistance if used appropriately. For example:

- Hornbooks can explain topics and concepts in greater depth than goes on in class thus helping you develop a more thorough understanding of the material.

- Outlines can provide a general framework to use in creating your own course outline. You can adapt the structure and incorporate the material you've covered in the specific manner in which you're professor presented it, including the particular use of vocabulary and structure of analysis.

- Law summaries can help focus your thinking in preparing your own summaries of the rules.

- Case summaries can help you digest cases and aid in the preparation of your own case briefs. But once again, they're not substitutes for writing your own case briefs. Each professor stresses something different in analyzing a case and you must adapt your case brief to meet the needs of the classroom.

- Study aids with hypotheticals and suggested answers can provide much needed practice in answering questions. When studying, it's critical to combine substantive review with practical applications to see how the issues will arise. The more problems you practice answering – and especially in writing – the more prepared you will be for the actual exam.

3. THE SOFTWARE FACTOR

It's probably fair to say that there's a software program available to help you with just about every law school task, from downloading case books to automatically generating course outlines. While I'm in favor of using technology to improve the speed and ease with which we perform our jobs, the danger is that the veneer of technology can seduce you into thinking that manipulating text is analyzing law. Copying is still copying, whether it's high tech computer downloading or page by page photocopying. Once again, it's okay to use these tools if you realize that they are just that and nothing more – tools to help you organize the task of learning but not the act of learning itself.

F. HOW SUBSTANCE DETERMINES STYLE

In creating your outline, you need to consider form as well as substance. Different subjects lend themselves to different formats; different learning styles do so as well. Although it's a safe choice to follow the general outlining scheme we've illustrated, other models can make your outline work "visually" as well as "substantively." For example, tables, flowcharts, and timelines can present material in a way that allows you to see relationships between concepts that might not be so readily apparent from a typical line-style format. For many, charts facilitate the learning process by organizing the material visually and illustrating the links between the "if, then" scenarios so common in legal analysis.

Outlines can be tables and charts, purely text, or a combination of both: you get to decide. What must be common to all is the presentation of the material in an organized, logical manner that allows you to learn it specifically and accurately – for practice and for the exam.

1. BASIC OUTLINE FORMS

As we've seen from the example on incapacity, the basic outline form is text-driven and hierarchical. While useful for summarizing the material, it has limitations. Words alone are not always sufficient to let you see the relationships between concepts and navigate the sequence of questions necessary to resolve legal questions. Sometimes flowcharts and tables can be a more effective means of presenting the material.

2. CHARTS, TABLES, AND TIME-LINES

The hierarchical nature of flowcharts is an almost perfect fit with the hierarchical structure of legal analysis. While all good outlines function as roadmaps by organizing and linking the course material in a meaningful way, flowcharts have a unique advantage: they arrange the material visually, allowing you to see relationships between concepts which might not otherwise be clear.

Flowcharts need not be fancy: paper and pencil and your own thought process is often all you need. Text, boxes, and arrows are sufficient to identify and show the links between concepts. What's critical is how you put the pieces together and the process of putting them together.

For example, in addition to completing a typical "word" outline for Contracts, I organized all the general principles graphically in a Contracts time-line or continuum. By physically displaying the relationship between concepts, it was easier to see when and in what context certain issues would arise.

3. EXCERPTS

(a) Contracts time-line

The charts opposite are excerpts from the Contracts time-line. The first provides an overview of the main headings and the second is an examination of the formation phase only. It is a topical outline that shows the "place" each principle occupies in the overall structure of the subject. This type of overview is helpful to get a sense of the big picture and let you see the "forest for the trees."

Please note that the terms and category delineations represent but one way of looking and thinking about Contracts law; they are not definitive. The chart is meant as a way to begin looking at the parts to make sense of the whole. Some topics transcend "categories" and would appear in more than one. For example, "good faith" is an implied term of every contract and figures in all phases of contract enforcement and performance. Consequently, it might be included under several headings. The goal is to make a chart that reflects your understanding of the material in a way that is meaningful to you. It will reflect your thinking on the subject as well as how your professor presented it (see opposite page).

(b) Constitutional Law chart of concepts and cases

In addition to time-lines, tables can be very effective study tools, allowing you to arrange substance in a visually memorable manner. They can be adapted for all subjects because they are incredibly flexible. Of course, their effectiveness as a study tool depends on your knowledge of the material, organizational skills, and computer proficiency.

The following excerpt is from a Constitutional Law outline. It is Part One of the Due Process outline. Part II, which would follow, would be cases involving the topic of Personal Autonomy: Abortion, Intimate Relationships, Right to Refuse Medical Treatment, Right to Die. The entire course was outlined in this format and made the concepts and cases of Constitutional Law clear and easy to study when it came time to prepare for finals. I should know because it was my outline.

FORMATION	AVOIDING THE DEAL	PERFORMANCE	BREACH/REMEDIES
Do we have a deal?	We have a deal but,	Who has to do what and when, or maybe not	Someone failed to perform when required, now what?
Mutual Assent + Consideration			
Offer Acceptance Bargained-for Exchange	Incapacity Illegality Misrepresentation Unconscionability	Parol Evidence Rule Interpretation Conditions Good Faith	Anticipatory repudiation Breach Substantial Perfomance Damages

Excerpts of Contracts Time-line

FORMATION
DO WE HAVE A DEAL?

MUTUAL ASSENT + CONSIDERATION

Offer +

Objective test
"Master" of offer
Contractual Intent
Definiteness
Price quotations
Preliminary Negotiations
"Reward" offers

Acceptance

Power of Acceptance
Counter-offer
Mirror-image rule
"Battle of Forms"
Unilateral contract
Bilateral contract
Irrevocable offers
  • Option contract
  • "Firm offers"

Bargained for Exchange

"Peppercorn Theory"
Benefit/detriment
Mutuality of obligation
Illusory promises
Past consideration
Gift promises
Moral obligation
Promissory estoppel
Modification/pre-existing duty

Defenses to formation:
  • Misunderstanding
  • Statute of Frauds

Additional formation concepts:
  • Implied-in-fact contract
  • Implied-in-law or quasi-contract

Close-up on Formation

As you'll notice, the format is based on a table but plays with its form to incorporate additional text at the beginning of each topic. Each section begins with a summary of basic doctrine, applicable tests, and definitions and is followed by case support. This makes the connection between cases and principles clear and aids in the memory process by a clear visual depiction of the relationship. The case support includes the relevant facts, holding, and reasoning of each case – the essentials of a case required for analysis. I recommend this format for any course that is case-sensitive.

CONSTITUTIONAL LAW – PRINCIPLES AND CASES

Section 2   ***Protection of Personal Liberties under the Due Process Clause***

The Ct determines that there is substantive due process protection for FUNDAMENTAL RIGHTS. The word "liberty" in the due process clause of both the 5th and the 14th Amendments offers special constitutional protection for privacy, personal autonomy, and some family relationships. S Ct applies the Constitution to protect these rights against the power of national and state legislatures.

SUBSTANTIVE DUE PROCESS PROTECTION FOR FUNDAMENTAL RIGHTS

1. Fundamental rights: will get strict scrutiny

2. Non-fundamental rights: will continue to get rational basis scrutiny

TEST FOR RATIONAL BASIS SCRUTINY

- Must be a rational relation between a legitimate state objective and the challenged regulation (P has burden of proof)

- Applies to non-fundamental rights - Ct generally defers to the legislative judgment

TEST FOR STRICT SCRUTINY

- There must be a compelling state interest, accomplished through narrowly tailored means. Means-end fit must be very close so that the means are "necessary" to achieve the end. Only if the govt entity imposing the restriction can show that the limitation is both necessary and narrowly tailored to serve a compelling govt interest will it be found constitutional

- Applies to fundamental rights - few statutes meet test of showing compelling interest that can't be achieved in a less burdensome way

TYPES OF RIGHTS:

Due process right (substantive/procedural) - issue deals with an individual being denied a liberty

Equal protection right - issue deals with similarly situated persons not being treated similarly; a regulation separates into classes (gender, racial, etc).

Determine what classification to determine what type of scrutiny is required.

Is it fundamental?

Is it general?

CASE	RULE OF LAW
Section 2	**Protection of Personal Liberties under the Due Process Clause**
Meyer v. Nebraska (1923) Right of parents to make choices for the education of their children.	S Ct struck down a state law which prohibited the teaching of foreign languages to children during the first 8 yrs of school. Ct held that "liberty" as used in the 14th Amend included many rights, not just the freedom from bodily restraint. This included the right of the individual to contract, to acquire useful knowledge and to enjoy those privileges essential to the pursuit of happiness. Also includes the right of parents to make choices for the education of their children.
Pierce v. Society of Sisters (1925) Right of parents to educate their children where they want.	S Ct struck down a state statute requiring children to attend public schools, thus preventing them from attending private and parochial ones. Court held that parents have the liberty to direct the upbringing and education of children under their control.
Skinner v. Oklahoma (1942) Right to procreate.	S Ct invalidated an OK statute which provided for involuntary sterilization of persons convicted three times of felonies showing moral turpitude but which did not apply to white collar crimes such as embezzlement. Ct held that marriage and procreation are fundamental rights.
Griswold v. Connecticut (1965) Questions concerning reproductive issues in a marital relationship are a matter of privacy bet married couples. This is the first case dealing with and creating a fundamental right of privacy. Bill of Rights provides certain guaranteed rights. Penumbra theory is that stemming from the B of R there are other rights. A right emanating from a right which already exists. Connecticut law forbade the use of contraceptives, making it a criminal offense.	S Ct found that there are specific guarantees in the Bill of Rights (corresponding with several amendments) which have penumbras (shadows, emanations*) that help give those guarantees life and substance. Hence, various amendments in the Bill of Rights create zones of privacy. The right of married persons to use contraceptives falls within these penumbras. *Ct claimed that the 1st Amend, by its protection of the freedoms of speech and the press, has emanations which create a penumbra - it is this penumbra which protects the freedom of association, a freedom not explicitly mentioned in the Constitution. The 4th Amend's ban on unreasonable searches has a penumbra which protects privacy interests as do the 3rd, 5th, and 9th Amend. Together, these Amends establish a zone in which privacy is protected from govt intrusion. This privacy right is inherent in the marital relationship; thus the fundamental right to marital privacy is created.

FAMILY AND MARITAL RELATIONSHIPS

Moore v. City of East Cleveland Right of a family to live together; Powell relied on nations's history and tradition in finding support for the extended family to receive protection. Ct found a fundamental right of privacy in family living arrangements.	Ct struck down a zoning ordinance which allowed only members of a single family to live together. The ordinance's definition of a family was a restrictive one which prevented P from living with her 2 grandsons who, having different parents, were first cousins to each other. A 4-Justice plurality opinion found that the right of members of a family, even a non-nuclear one, to live together was a liberty interest, and that state impairment of that interest must be examined carefully. Although the state claimed its interest was in preventing overcrowding, traffic congestion, and burdens on schools, these interests were only marginally advanced by the ordinance. Using a heightened level of scrutiny, the Ct held that such interests did not warrant the intrusion upon a family's privacy.

CASE	RULE OF LAW
Loving v. Virginia (1963) S Ct first recognizes right to marry as a fundamental right, protected under the liberty interest in the due process clause of the 14th amendment	Court struck Virginia's anti-miscegenation statute which prohibited a white person from marrying anyone other than another white person. In terms of the fundamental right to marry, the Court said: "The freedom to marry has long been recognized as one of the vital personal rights essential to the orderly pursuit of happiness by free men." The Court stated that marriage is one of the "basic civil rights of man, fundamental to our very existence and survival." Thus, a state determining who a person can/cannot marry deprives that person of liberty without due process of law.
Zablocki v. Redhail (1978) Right to marry is fundamental; substantial interferences with that right will not be sustained merely because the state has a legitimate interest and the means used are rationally related to that interest.	P attacked a Wisconsin statute requiring any parent under a court order to support a minor child not in his custody meet 2 requirements before being permitted to marry: 1. Payment of all court ordered support and 2. Show that the child was not and would not become a public charge. Ct struck down the statute in that the right to marry was a fundamental one and that a direct and substantial interference with it should be subjected to a strict level of scrutiny. The state interest was not compelling and could be met with less restrictive devices. Ct noted that where a regulation had some effect upon the ability to marry but did not significantly interfere with that ability, only a mere rationality test would be used.
Michael H. V. Gerald D. (1989) No fundamental right for a child to maintain a relationship with a biological parent. This interfered with the more fundamental right of the family.	Ct would not let illegitimate father bring action to seek rights of paternity although they did not preclude such a possibility if the biological relationship were combined with ongoing parent-child contact. Issue was whether the state awards substantive parental rights to the natural father of a child who was conceived outside but born into a marriage where there is a legal father, when that natural father wishes to raise the child. Ct found that biology alone did not confer a fundamental right. However, five justices seemed to agree with the proposition that "although an unwed father's biological link to his child does not, in and of itself, guarantee him a constitutional stake in his relationship with that child, such a link combined with a substantial parent-child relationship will do so."

PART 2: PERSONAL AUTONOMY

G. WHY YOU MIGHT NEED MORE THAN ONE OUTLINE

Even if you've created a detailed outline that includes all the relevant rules, elements, limitations, and exceptions with respect to a particular subject, you'll benefit from making one or both of the following types of outlines as well.

1. AN ANALYTICAL OUTLINE OF "LEADING QUESTIONS"

This outline consists solely of the sequence of questions necessary to guide you through analysis of a problem. If you recall, we included "checklist questions" as the final element in outlining a principle of law where we identified each component or requirement of the rule and turned it into a question. By isolating and consolidating these checklist questions, you form an analytical outline – and one which is far easier to memorize.

Consider the following example. In Contracts, you learned that the parol evidence rule may bar the introduction of extrinsic evidence to contradict or even supplement a term in a written agreement. Your outline would contain this rule and lots more – the rationale for the rule, its application and limitations, and perhaps even reference to the differing views of Williston and Corbin. All this is necessary to learn and understand the context and dynamics of the parol evidence rule. However, general statements are not particularly helpful when it comes to analyzing a problem:

Carly and Simon decided to combine their talents and formed Shuzzies, Inc., a shoe manufacturing company. Carly would design the shoes and Simon would be responsible for business operations. Each party contributed $50,000 to start the business.

Carly planned a line of extravagant evening footwear that would appeal to celebrities. She knew they would be expensive to produce but her goal was to become shoemaker to the stars. Simon, on the other hand, was practical and planned a product line that would appeal to teenagers.

On January 25, 2001, Carly and Simon signed a written agreement that provided in relevant part:

> *Upon written request by either party, Shuzzies shall, within sixty days of receipt of such request, re-purchase the interest of the requesting party at the original investment cost of $50,000.*

By March 2003, when Carly still wasn't designing sandals for celebrities because Simon insisted on sneakers for teenagers, Carly decided it was time to pursue her dream. She made a written request on Shuzzies for it to buy-back her interest pursuant to the agreement. Simon then reminded Carly that before the agreement was signed, the parties had orally agreed that the buy-back provision would only apply if the business was making a profit on the date of the request. As of March 2003, Shuzzies had not yet made a profit. For this reason, Simon told Carly that the business would not buy back her interest.

Carly duly commenced an action against Shuzzies for breach of contract, seeking to recover her $50,000. At trial, Carly's attorney objected when Simon sought to testify about the oral agreement limiting the buy-back provision. The court overruled the objection and permitted the testimony. Was the court's ruling allowing Simon's testimony concerning the oral agreement correct?

Contracts Hypothetical

Using checklist questions to answer an exam question

Assume that identification of the issue presents no difficulty: you see that the parol evidence rule is in question because there's a writing and Carly is seeking enforcement of an oral agreement. However, the next step isn't so easy: how to write a logical and efficient analysis given the time constraints of the exam.

Here's where studying from an analytical outline is so essential – you would have already identified the relevant questions to be asked in answering a parol evidence problem. Now all you'd do is use that sequence of questions to guide your thinking through the facts.

The following are the checklist questions you'd rely on from your outline to lead you through an analysis, beginning with the general issue:

1.   Is evidence of the prior oral agreement barred by the parol evidence rule?

2.   Is the agreement integrated or unintegrated?

3.   Did the parties intend the writing to be a final expression of their agreement with respect to the terms it contains even if it was not intended as a complete expression of all the terms?

4.   Assuming the agreement is integrated, is it totally or only partially integrated?

     a.   Even if the agreement is a total integration, is this the type of collateral agreement that under the circumstances would naturally have been omitted from the writing? If so, then the parol evidence rule would not bar its admission as long as it does not contradict the main agreement.

     b.   Assuming this is a partial integration, is this an additional or contradictory term?

With these questions as your roadmap, you're ready to get to work.

> *Comment: As you read through this answer, note that the italicized sentences are the "checklist questions" translated into issues appropriate for the problem. You should also note that the essay follows the general IRAC structure.*

Whether the court was correct in allowing Simon's testimony regarding the parties' oral discussion of the buy-back provision depends on whether it is barred by the parol evidence rule. This rule determines the provability of prior or contemporaneous oral discussions when the parties have a written agreement. Here, the parol evidence rule may bar introduction of the parties' oral agreement regarding a limit on the buy-back provision because it relates to a term in the writing.

Whether Simon can introduce such evidence, we need to know whether the agreement is integrated or unintegrated. Where an agreement has been reduced to writing which the parties intend as the final and complete expression of their agreement, evidence of any earlier oral or written expressions is not admissible to vary the terms of the writing. If the parties had such an intention, the agreement is said to be "integrated," and the parol evidence rule bars evidence of prior negotiations for at least some purposes.

To determine whether the agreement is integrated, we need to ask whether Carly and Simon intended the writing to be a final expression of their agreement with respect to the terms it contains even if it was not intended as a complete expression of all the terms. If the writing appears thorough and specific enough to be taken as a final agreement on the terms it contains, then the agreement is considered integrated with respect to those terms. Here, it seems that the agreement is integrated because it expresses their intent regarding buying out of the business. It provides the method by which it would occur, "upon written request," who could exercise the right, "either party," and when the money would be disbursed, "within sixty days."

Assuming the agreement is integrated, the next question is whether it is totally or only partially integrated. If the writing is a final expression of the parties agreement and complete with respect to all of its terms, it's a total integration and cannot be contradicted by any type of evidence nor supplemented by consistent (non-contradictory) additional terms. A partial integration is final as to the terms it contains but not complete as to all the terms so it may be supplemented by consistent additional terms, but cannot be contradicted. It's possible this was a total integration because it includes all one would expect to find in an agreement to buy out of a business such as the need for a written request, the amount to be paid, and the notice to be given. Therefore, evidence of the parties' prior oral agreement would be barred.

Even if the agreement is a total integration, it is questionable whether the oral agreement was the type of collateral agreement that under the circumstances would naturally have been omitted from the writing. If so, then the parol evidence rule would not bar its admission as long as it does not contradict the main agreement. In this case, it might not be natural to include mention of a company's financial profitability in a provision which simply outlines the procedure for re-purchasing the original interest.

On the other hand, if the parties intended that the only way the buy-back provision could be exercised would be if the company were in the financial condition to afford it, then they would certainly have included it in the writing and if it were not there, the court should not imply it.

Assuming, however, that this is a partial integration, the next question is whether this is an additional or contradictory term. Even if the writing is only partially integrated, extrinsic evidence of terms contradictory to one of the integrated terms is not admissible. Here, none of the terms regarding the buy-back deal with the issue of profitability. Instead, they specify written notice, a period of sixty days for Shuzzies to act on the request, and the specific amount of $50,000. Therefore, a term regarding profitability could be seen as additional. However, since the profitability term expressly limits or modifies the buy-back provision, it could be seen as contradictory and thus inadmissible.

The court's ruling was incorrect because evidence of the oral agreement was barred by the parol evidence rule.

Using Checklist Questions to Write an Exam Answeer

You should identify checklist questions for each of the general principles of law covered in your course because each is a potential exam issue; by structuring your studying around such questions, you can effectively "pre-take" your exam. With some thought and effort, it's easy to determine the major exam topics for each of your courses and come to the exam having studied the appropriate checklist questions. Once you read the specific exam question, you can rely on the analytic formula and proceed to the facts.

2. A SUMMARY OUTLINE

You'll want to condense your course outline to just a summary of key topics in the days right before the exam. The "fully-loaded" outline is too long and detailed for final exam preparation. It has helped you learn the law, but now it's crunch time and reducing your outline to a list of core topics is critical for final review purposes.

By narrowing your outline to its essential points, you accomplish the following:

- Organize your thinking

- Finalize a framework for the overall structure of the course

- Create a topic checklist for issue-spotting on the exam

Using a summary outline for final review

To see how this works, consider the following Sales outline. It shows how one outline can serve two purposes: by defining the main issues in the form of leading questions, it incorporates the checklist questions of the analytical outline with the brevity of a summary.

SEQUENCE OF ANALYSIS FOR A SALES PROBLEM

The following framework of questions moves from one issue to the next as if you were answering a hypothetical that raised every possible issue covered in the course:

1. Do the provisions of Article 2 apply?

    Is it a sale of goods or services? Is it a hybrid? If so, are goods the predominant purpose?
    Are one or both of the parties to the agreement "merchants"?

2. Was there an agreement or "bargain of the parties in fact"?

    A. Do we have an offer and acceptance?
    B. Do we have a dispute over contract terms because of additional or different terms in the acceptance, i.e., "battle of the forms"?

3. Have the parties, by agreement, attempted to limit the scope of their bargain?

    Are there disclaimers or limits on warranties, remedies, or the statute of limitations?

4. What are the terms of the agreement?

    Do we need to use "gap fillers"? Is it an output/requirements contract or exclusive dealings?

5. Would the agreement survive a Statute of Frauds charge?

    Does an exception apply: specially manufactured goods, admissions, goods paid for and accepted, or received and accepted?

6. What effect is to be given to the writing? Is there a parol evidence problem? If so,

    • Is the agreement integrated or unintegrated?
    • Assuming the agreement is integrated, is it totally or only partially integrated?

7. Has there been a modification to the agreement? If not a modification, could it be a waiver?

8. Can performance be excused by a "failure of presupposed conditions"?

9. Performance

    A. Did seller "tender" the goods to the buyer?
    B. Has buyer "accepted" the goods?

      C. Has buyer "rejected" the goods? Was it a "rightful" rejection?

      D. Does the non-conformity "substantially impair the value of the goods" to buyer so as to allow a revocation of acceptance?

      E. Does seller have a "right to cure" the nonconforming tender or delivery?

10. Risk of Loss: have the goods suffered damage or has there been a loss? If so, who bears the risk of loss? Has it passed to buyer or is it still with seller or a bailee?

11. Did buyer breach?

      A. By wrongfully rejecting the goods?

      B. By wrongfully revoking acceptance of the goods?

      C. By failing to make a payment due on or before delivery?

      D. By repudiating with respect to a part or the whole contract?

     Ask (1) was repudiation by statements? (overt communication)

         (2) was repudiation by conduct? (an action)

         (3) was repudiation by failure to give adequate assurances?

     Was it breach of an installment contract? Can buyer reject an installment?

         (1) Is it non-conforming, and

         (2) Did the non-conformity substantially impair the value of that installment, and

         (3) Can seller cure the non-conformity?

     If there was a breach of an installment, was there a breach of the whole?

12. What are seller's remedies for buyer's breach?

      A. Can seller pursue an action for the price?

      B. Can seller resell the goods and recover the difference between the resale price and the contract price and any incidental damages less expenses saved as a result of the breach?

      C. Whether the goods have been resold or not, can seller can seek damages for the difference between the market price at the time and place for tender and the unpaid contract price?

      D. Is seller a lost volume seller?

13. Did seller breach?

      A. By repudiating?

      B. By failing to deliver?

      C. By tender of delivery which fails to conform to the contract (perfect tender rule)?

14. What are buyer's remedies for seller's breach?

      A. Does buyer have a right to specific performance or replevin?

      B. Does buyer have a right to cover?

        • Is buyer entitled to incidental damages?

        • Is buyer entitled to consequential damages?

         (1) Was the loss caused by the breach?

         (2) Was the loss the result of "general or particular requirements and needs" of buyer "of which seller at the time of contracting had reason to know"?

(3) Was the loss one "which could not reasonably be prevented by cover or otherwise"?

(4) Was the loss proved with "reasonable certainty"?

15. Warranties: can buyer claim breach of warranty?

A. Did seller made some warranty, express or implied?

B. Was the warranty breached?

C. Was the breach the cause of the damages sought?

Was there a disclaimer of warranties?

Was the disclaimer unconscionable?

Does the seller have a defense to the warranty?

A. Did buyer misuse the goods or fail to follow directions for use?

B. Should buyer have discovered the non-conformity before use or
assumed the risk by using goods with a known non-conformity?

C. Did buyer accept the goods and fail to give proper notice?

D. Is the suit barred by the statute of limitations?

E. Is there privity?

H. OUTLINING FOR OPEN-BOOK EXAMS

Most students think that open-book (and take-home) exams are easier, but they're
not. They require the same preparation as closed-book exams, perhaps even more
because the professor's expectations for an organized and legally precise exam
answer are higher. All this means is that your outline is still vital for success and you
need to create it with the same diligence and effort as if you were taking a closed-
book exam.

Since an open-book exam allows access to your study materials, you'll want
to make the most of this opportunity. Here's what to consider in preparing an open-
book "friendly" outline:

- Be sure to include checklist questions for every likely exam topic.
- Organize your outline to find what you're looking for quickly and easily.

There's no easier way to waste precious writing time on an exam by looking
through your notes. Organize your outline to find what you need quickly. Use tabs
to find topics easily and consider flowcharts or checklists to lead you through the
material.

- Never rely on your outline for law you should have memorized.

Students often waste time on open-book exams looking through outlines for law they should have committed to memory. The outline is only back-up; you still have to learn the law to complete the exam in a timely manner.

I. GAUGING YOUR OUTLINE'S EFFECTIVENESS

The true measure of an outline is how well it works for you in learning the material. One way to gauge its effectiveness is your performance on the final exam. However, you can't afford to take chances and leave it until then to find out if it has any deficiencies. You need to know while you still have time to do something about it. This is yet another reason why taking practice exams (a subject we discuss in the next chapter) is so essential to the study process – it lets you see just how well you've learned the law and where, if at all, you've gotten it wrong.

HERE'S HOW IT WORKS

If you find you've answered a practice question incorrectly, either an essay or multiple choice question, you need to return to the place in your outline where you covered that topic. The outline should allow you to figure out the right answer and help you understand why your original answer was incorrect. If you can't do this, then your outline is deficient. Now you must go back to your original sources – class notes, casebook, and hornbook – to figure it out and rewrite that section of your outline accordingly. Don't despair: you need to know if you don't understand something now, while you are studying, so you can fix it before the final. That's the whole point of including practice exams in your study routine.

There's final bit of advice I need to give you about outlining: don't let yourself become obsessed with the form of the outline at the expense of its content. The emphasis should never be on format and getting it to "look" right. What's important is that it "works" right and the only way to know this is by using it to solve problems. There is no one right way to make an outline. It's critical not to let making the outline become an end in itself, distracting you from its true purpose and yours – learning the law.

CHAPTER 5: PREPARING FOR LAW SCHOOL EXAMS

A. GETTING EXPERIENCE

One theme that has been constant throughout this text is that there are no tricks for mastering law school exams, only the solid understanding of legal principles and basic knowledge of core substance that comes from hard work. Still, hard work alone will get you only so far – you also need to know how to work smart and what work to do. Studying to learn the material is one activity; practicing with it in preparation for the exam is quite another.

It's not enough to memorize and understand elements and rules without some idea of how the issues present and will be tested. Exams vary greatly in their format, composition, and emphasis. Taking an essay exam is quite different from taking a multiple-choice exam. Unless you have some idea of what to expect and practice applying what you know in the context of the particular format, you will not be able to perform as well as you should on exam day. How you prepare for each of your exams will therefore vary according to the type of exam you'll take.

This is as true of a law school exam as any other. Just imagine showing up for a driving test without ever having driven a car. Even if you could identify all the parts of the engine and the indicators and controls on the dashboard, this doesn't mean you could actually drive the car. You would have needed actual time "behind the wheel" to develop the particular skill of driving no matter how well you knew its theory of operation.

Here's where experience plays a significant role in your success. A large part of experience is simply having done something before. And having done it before, you get a pretty good idea of what to expect in the future. The same is true for exams. You need experience in taking exams to know what to expect from them and from your own performance. The only way to get this type of experience before the actual exam is to practice from simulated exams.

B. LEARNING FROM PAST EXAMS

There is a method to learning from practice exams and you may be surprised to discover that it's not just about sitting down and answering the questions. That's what you'll do on exam day but not when you're studying for the exam. The difference is between just answering the questions and using the questions to learn. One of the most important things you can keep in mind as you study is that the only test that counts is the one you take on exam day. All the rest is preparation.

There are two phases to the preparation process: the first involves what goes on during the course of the semester and the second concerns what happens in the weeks and days leading up to the final exam. This chapter will examine the "when" and "how" of each preparation phase.

C. WHAT TO DO DURING THE SEMESTER

1. BEGINNING ON DAY ONE

If you've followed the suggestions in the chapter on outlining, you've already performed several of the activities involved in preparing for law school exams: you've read and briefed the cases, listened to what your professor said in class, taken careful notes, organized the material into a course outline, and practiced problems in each subject area as you've completed it. If it seems like I'm saying that exam preparation begins on the first day of class, then you're absolutely right – it does. And it continues, day by day, as you add to and build on your knowledge base. This type of learning, which is learning over time, allows you to retain information, especially the type of detailed and complicated information demanded by the study of law.

If it also seems that I'm saying that "cramming" the night before the exam is not an effective study method, then you're right once again. While it might have worked for you in the past, it's not likely to do so now. Certainly there are some students who can pull it off, but for most of us, it's not a method likely to produce an "A" grade. If you're lucky, cramming can give you a rudimentary knowledge of the rules but not the depth of understanding necessary for solid exam performance. That only comes with mastery of the subject matter, something which doesn't happen overnight.

2.   THE "HOW" OF LEARNING OVER TIME

In addition to sequencing your outlining as you proceed daily and weekly though the semester, it's essential to incorporate practice problems and feedback into your study plan. You have several options and you should try to incorporate each of them into your study plan.

(a)   Practicing problems

You should practice answering hypotheticals on individual topics as soon as you've covered them in class and integrated them into your outline. Never wait until you've completed the course and you're studying for the final exam. Working with rules as you learn them by applying them in the context of new factual situations is the most effective way to find out whether you truly understand them while you still have time to find answers to questions that naturally arise as you learn new material.

You can find problems in this book, review books, exams on file in your law school's library, and you can create them yourself. This will give you experience in answering questions, but you still need feedback on what you've written. Some questions will have sample answers for you to use to compare to what you've written; unfortunately, most will not. In this case, use the chapter on forensic IRAC to learn how to evaluate your own work objectively to assess its strengths and weaknesses.

(b)   Using professors' exams on file

While we'll discuss using released exams with respect to preparing for the final exam, it's also an effective means for learning along the way. You should answer exam questions your professor has on file and ask to have them evaluated. You just have to be more careful in selecting your problems to choose ones which test the material you've covered so far since you haven't completed the semester. A quick perusal through the exam should indicate the topics you're capable of handling at any given point.

While it's unlikely your professor will review an entire exam (although possible), she'll certainly give you feedback on individual questions. In my experience, most students fail to take advantage of this option yet it's the best possible source of instruction with respect to learning the material and what to expect on the exam.

(c)   Making the most of mid-terms

If you're lucky, you'll have a mid-term. You're probably wondering how this could possibly be a good thing, so I'll tell you. First, it forces you to confront the material well before the end of the semester. For students who tend to leave everything for the last minute, this is an excellent wake-up call. Second, a mid-term gives you an idea of what to expect on the final, both in terms of depth of coverage and style of question. This is valuable for all students, but especially for first year students who have as yet no experience with law school exams. Third, it provides another grade for the course besides the final examination. Finally, it gives you feedback from your professor on exactly what you're doing right and where you're going wrong. However, a caveat is needed here: you'll probably have to meet with your professor to get this kind of feedback since professors typically don't write much (if anything) on your exam. But a mid-term gives you this opportunity and it's up to you to take it.

3. MEETING WITH YOUR PROFESSOR

One-on-one time with your professor is invaluable because it provides a rare opportunity to get the professor's individualized attention. It's also an incredible learning experience and essential to the development of your oral and written communication skills. Students meet with their professors for various reasons, but the following are the most likely to involve specific appointments:

- To discuss questions you have on the material after you've been unable to resolve them on your own or in a study group.

- To get feedback on essay questions you've answered.

- To review a quiz or mid-term.

Sadly, too many students fail to realize the full potential of meeting with their professors primarily because they do not prepare adequately. Yes, it's true: you must prepare properly if you expect to get something from the meeting. Since the time with a professor is limited, the meeting must have an agenda and set goals. For example, you can't go to see your professor about your mid-term grade, sit back in the chair, say something like, "I don't see why I got a C. Explain it to me," and expect a productive exchange. Instead of assuming the burden for trying to determine where you might have gone wrong in your studying, understanding of the material, or analysis of the problem, you've placed it all on the professor to figure out for you. This is guaranteed not to work for either of you. You'll leave the office feeling frustrated and, more than likely, your professor will see you in a less than favorable light for not assuming your responsibility.

Consider the following suggestions before meeting with your professor:

- Ask to see your exam *before* the scheduled meeting. This allows you time to review the exam question and, even more important, consider what you wrote in response. Often you'll be able to identify your own mistakes. Some may result from nervousness and ineffective time management; others may come from carelessness in reading the question or the facts. Typically, these are not problems your professor can solve but might require time with the Academic Support Professional in your school. On the other hand, if you find mistakes in your understanding of the material because you can't see why your answer failed to receive full credit, then you have something to discuss with your professor. Prepare specific questions about the substance of what you've written and the structure of your analysis of that problem.

■ Ask whether there is a sample answer you can read before meeting to review your exam. Sample answers are terrific learning-tools, whether student- or professor-written, because they provide something with which to compare your work. Still, this only works if you're willing and capable of being totally objective about your writing. As you may have realized, this is the most challenging part of the exercise and the most critical to your development: you have to be objective about your work and read exactly what you've written, not what you wish you'd written, or what you think you've written. The words have to stand on their own. After all, this is what the professor has read, and only what she's read. There is no side-bar explaining what you meant to say, only the words that you've written. To learn how to be objective and assess your own work, refer to Chapters 8 and 9.

■ Identify problems in the form of specific questions. For example, instead of saying, "I just don't get remedies," formulate a precise question such as, "I'm not sure when a party may recover consequential damages." Of course this requires that you make an effort to figure things out on your own before going to the professor, but it's an effort that will be well-rewarded: not only will you learn the material more effectively because you've actively engaged with it, your professor will see a hard-working, thoughtful student intent on mastering the material. Finally, by defining a specific problem, you have given your professor a starting point and focus for discussion.

D. WHAT TO DO AT THE END OF THE SEMESTER

The last weeks of the semester should be spent completing your reading and your outlines. Then when classes are finally over, you're ready to focus solely on memorizing the rules and acquiring the deeper understanding of the material needed to do more than just issue-spot an exam. Instead, you'll be able to identify problems, analyze the facts, and explain your answers with sophistication and a nuanced knowledge of the law.

Now that it's "crunch-time," here's what to do:

1. FINALIZE YOUR COURSE OUTLINE

If you've been unable to do so earlier, you should strive to complete your outline within a day or two of the last day of class. Completing the outline means you've covered all the material in the course and have a good sense of how the pieces fit. Typically, this is when it "all comes together." The sooner you complete this task, the sooner you can get down to the real job of studying which requires memorizing and practicing what you've learned.

2. CREATE YOUR SUMMARY OUTLINE

As we discussed at the end of the previous chapter, you'll want to create a condensed version of your course outline to use during the final review period. Reviewing your outline to reduce it to its essential points is itself an effective study method because it requires you to consider the whole course and identify the main topics and the sub-topics. For some, it's not until all the descriptive narrative and illustrative examples are stripped away that the relationships and connections between concepts become clear. For these students, a summary outline is especially important.

3. TAKE PRACTICE EXAMS

One purpose of taking practice exams is to make the whole process of reading and answering the questions so automatic that you'll follow it instinctively on exam day. Another purpose of practicing exam questions – lots and lots of them – is so that you'll over-prepare. By doing everything you can possibly do to learn and over-learn the material, you'll approach the exam in the optimum position for success. Not only does it help to minimize anxiety to know that you've done everything you can to prepare, but it pretty much assures that you've seen how most if not all of the issues are likely to arise.

At this point in your preparation, it's time to practice complete exams. You're ready to see how all the individual issues are likely to appear together. Now is also the time to start working on your timing: learning to budget your time and working within that time is the only way to ensure that you'll complete the exam – or come as close as possible to answering every question. Your goal is to answer as many questions as possible, as completely as possible.

(a) Find your baseline

For your first couple of practice exams, don't worry about the clock. You just want to see how long it takes you to complete an entire exam. This is your *baseline*. Don't be surprised or disheartened if it takes longer than the allocated time. This is normal the first time you approach new material and writing an entire law-school exam is a completely new experience for many of you.

Even if it's not your first set of final exams, you'll probably benefit significantly from getting a better sense of how you use your time. Once you've established your baseline, you can concentrate on improving your timing through practice.

(b)   Simulate exam conditions

A timed practice session should be as close to actual exam conditions as you can get. It's essential to include several timed sessions in your study plan because you need to know how you perform under the pressure of time constraints.

Consider each practice exam a dress rehearsal by writing your essays within what will be the time parameters on the exam. If you're working with your professor's released exams, follow the guidelines identified for the individual questions. If they are not available, calculate your own time allocations based on the overall length of the exam. Refer to Chapter 6 for guidelines on allocating your time.

Exactly how many exams you need to practice is an individual matter. A general recommendation would be to answer a sufficient number to feel comfortable with the format while completing the entire exam within the prescribed time.

4.   LEARN TO RECOGNIZE YOUR PROFESSOR'S VOICE

By working with your professor's questions, you become accustomed to her specific use of vocabulary in addition to becoming familiar with the types of facts that invoke certain rules. Working with past questions provides knowledge of the structure, substance, and style of your exam and gives you a pretty good sense of what to expect. As we discussed earlier, some professors provide sample answers, either student essays or suggested analyses. By reviewing and analyzing released exams and sample answers, you can target your energies and gain a universe of experience in seeing how the topics come together and what is expected of you in response.

Of course there's no guarantee that just because your professor followed a particular exam format in the past, it will be replicated on your exam. Still, while question structure may vary, language and presentation generally remain the same.

As you review past exams, consider the following:

(a)   Do you need to know and use case names?

Ordinarily, the professor will tell you whether you need to include references to case names in your analysis, but it never hurts to see what happens in actual practice. Even if your professor says it's not necessary to cite them, quite often you'll find that the "A" paper includes such specific references.

(b)   Do class discussions end up on the exam?

There's a very good chance you'll discover that your professor likes to present hypotheticals patterned closely after cases you've read and discussed in class. Typically, this includes all the "what if" scenarios that flew around the room when the professor changed the facts of the case and asked you to speculate on the results. Here's the big payoff if you've taken careful notes in class: you've captured the professor's interpretation of the cases and you're ready to work with it in answering the question. This is also where your ability to analogize and distinguish case facts plays a critical role in your analysis.

(c)   Are there signals in the professor's specific use of language?

When you read your professor's exams, you should detect a pattern in the use of particular vocabulary. Your ability to identify such vocabulary is critical and only practice with actual questions gives you this familiarity. Very often, the difference between a correct and incorrect answer turns on the meaning and significance attached to particular language in the fact pattern. Words are signals and it's just as important to be attuned to the signals in the language of the questions as in the rules.

(d)   Do you need to know "magic words"?

Students often believe that a professor is looking for special language in an exam answer and if only they knew what it was, they would be the lucky recipients of "A" grades. Students refer to these as "magic words."

This is dangerous thinking because it makes it seem as if you need to perform tricks to master the material and heck, if you're no magician, you don't stand a chance. But the words aren't magical ones to be divined – they are the words of the court or the statute and well within your grasp. They are also the words your professor used in presenting the material to you.

(e)   Why do I find some professor-written sample answers confusing?

Although they are undeniably the best possible resource for understanding the questions and specifically for seeing how your professor would resolve the question, some professor-written sample answers can be present difficulties for students trying to learn by example. This is because students are still novices and professors write like the experts that they are.

The challenge for students is two-fold:

- If the answer is a seamless weaving together of rule and fact, the student has a hard time following the steps in the analysis because she's looking for conformity with the IRAC structure and it doesn't seem to be there.

- If the answer is just a series of bullet points of what should be covered in the answer, the student is often left trying to figure out exactly how it would actually all come together in an essay.

The best approach is to accept the sample answer for the wonderful gift that it is and then get to work using it. First, compare the sample to your own answer to make sure you've identified the correct issues and analyzed them fully and appropriately with respect to the relevant law. Now you're ready to make additional use of the sample as follows:

- If your professor has provided an actual written answer, then take the opportunity to read it carefully from beginning to end, noticing the structure as well as the substance of the argument. Observe the full and complete treatment given to one issue before moving on to consider the next. Note the use of transition language to lead the reader from one topic to another, letting you know exactly what to expect and making it easy for you to follow.

- If the sample answer is simply a list of points you should have covered in your answer, then use them to review your answer to make sure it's complete substantively. This type of answer key won't help in showing you how to connect the thoughts into a fully-formed, structured essay but it allows you to verify your issue-spotting skills.

- Further, you might consider turning to Chapter 7 at this time and read about working with the IRAC structure of legal analysis. Your professor's sample answer is probably an excellent example of how to write an analysis without reliance on the obvious words, *"the issue is"* and *"under the rule."* While you may need to rely on such leading language to help you structure an analysis, it's not necessary and can be abused. However, simply because the words are not used does not mean that your professor hasn't identified the issue. You just need to read carefully for the meaning in the words.

E. DIFFERENT TYPES OF EXAMS CALL FOR DIFFERENT TYPES OF PREP

While a general objective of all exams is to test your knowledge of the substantive law, certain exam formats emphasize some skills over others. For example, essay exams focus heavily on reading comprehension and writing skills. Long, involved fact patterns with multiple parties test organizational abilities in addition to the other skills. Single-issue essays seek to determine your responsiveness to the question which is another means of testing your ability to follow directions and maintain focus. Finally, multiple-choice questions test your knowledge of the substantive law, reading comprehension skills, and legal reasoning skills.

Refer to Chapter 7 for the precise steps to follow in answering each type of exam question. Here you'll find detailed descriptions and learn exactly how to approach and respond to a question from the initial read to writing the answer. It's the process you'll follow on exam day and the one you'll follow when you practice. The only difference will be the matter of timing. How long it takes to answer a question during practice is not your primary concern. Timing is the last part of the preparation process, not the first.

In contrast to defining the specific steps you'll take to answer a question, the following discussion explains the inherent differences in exam formats and how they necessarily impact your study approach.

1. ESSAY EXAMS

Essays test your ability to identify legal issues, engage in legal reasoning, and write in a logical, lawyer-like manner. The ability to think and write critically is a fundamental lawyering skill and heavily tested on law school exams and the bar exam. There is no escape from having to demonstrate your competency in this area.

Law school essay exams vary in length, style, and format but essentially fall into two categories: the hypothetical with multiple issues and/or parties and the short answer question. The former tests your ability to organize and the latter your ability to focus.

(a) The multi-issue hypothetical
- Requires full IRAC treatment

As you'll discover in the next chapter, each issue and sub-issue forms the basis for a separate and complete IRAC analysis. Preparing for this type of question, therefore, requires that you actually practice writing in the IRAC structure and working your way through one detailed analysis after another. You need to see what it means to "analyze" an issue in light of the relevant law and facts. Further, you need to see how to transition from one issue to another. It's one thing to talk about it and quite another to do it. Even if you've completed a Memorandum or Brief for your Legal Writing class, writing an exam-type analysis is different in terms of structure, style and emphasis. The last thing you can afford to do is wait until exam day to make this discovery.

- Why it challenges your organizational skills

Open-ended inquiries such as "analyze fully" present a true test of your organizational skills. It's your responsibility to identify the issues and decide on an organizational scheme. More than any other type of exam question, the fact-laden hypothetical tests your ability to remain in control as you move from analysis of one issue to the next.

Since only clear, organized thoughts can give rise to coherent, comprehensible answers, you'll want to organize your thoughts into an outline before you actually write. An outline for an exam essay is little more than a list of the rules of law you've identified from the issues raised by the fact pattern but if you've never outlined an exam before, you'll need practice to develop this essential skill. You'll also want to practice with different organizational approaches to see which is more appropriate for different kinds of questions.

(b)   The short answer question
■ Relies on "CRAC"

A short answer question is "short" because it's narrow and issue based: it asks you to come to a conclusion by answering a particular question. This can prove troublesome for two reasons: first, because it asks you to come to a single conclusion, it tests your ability to marshal the law and the facts and argue for only one appropriate outcome. This probes your ability to reason through a series of legal principles to arrive at a logical conclusion based on an application of the facts to the law.

The second problem is that students tend to "kitchen sink" their essay answers. Not only is it inappropriate in this case, but it can and does lead to lost points and wasted time.

■ Why it challenges your ability to be precise

This type of question asks you to do what most law students have the most difficulty in doing: answering a direct question with a direct answer. When you're asked to adopt a position, you can't equivocate and write around the answer. Your professor has written the question to support a particular outcome. Your job is to identify it.

Since the question typically identifies the issue for you, you can move immediately upon answering the question to incorporating the rule into your analysis of the facts. This is how your answer follows a "C,R/A,C" format.

There's no doubt that it takes practice to learn to write these types of answers. I've just indicated what's involved and informed you of the need. Chapter 7 takes you through the process step-by-step but you must allocate the study time in your schedule to accommodate it.

2.   MULTIPLE-CHOICE EXAMS

In addition to testing your knowledge of the substantive law, multiple-choice exams test your reading comprehension and reasoning skills, ability to work quickly and efficiently, and capacity to remain focused and in control as you move from one question to the next.

Studying for objective style questions is not the same as studying for other types of exams. It requires not only that you memorize the rules of law but that you fully understand them. If you don't know the rules with precision and specificity and truly comprehend how they fit together, you won't be able to find the issue in the facts, apply the rule, and select the best answer from among the answer choices in the short amount of time you're given.

There are significant differences in law school multiple-choice questions and as you may have guessed by now, the differences are pretty much professor-specific.

Once again, your plan must be to incorporate plenty of practice questions into your study routine to get a sense of what they are like. After you've completed an area of the law and reviewed your notes, you're ready to go to work on answering multiple-choice questions.

Refer to Chapter 7 to learn how to read and reason your way through multiple-choice questions and for practice with actual questions; refer to Chapter 9 to apply forensic IRAC principles to incorrect answer choices and identify the flaws in your reasoning.

The following discussion outlines the different types of questions and explains how to work with them.

(a)   Bar-exam style

Some professors model their objective questions after the Multi-State Bar Exam ("MBE") In this case, you can practice with the actual released bar exam questions and get a very good idea of what to expect. The questions are available from the National Conference of Bar Examiners and you can order released questions from their web site at www.ncbex.org. You can also find plenty of simulated bar exam questions in commercial sources and it's valuable to work from them as well.

(b)   Teacher-specific

There are some professors who write their own material. Unfortunately, they tend not to release their questions because they use them over and over again. If you've ever tried to write an objective question, you'll find that it's not an easy task so their reluctance is understandable.

Professor-written questions are not always analytical but sometimes require straightforward, specific knowledge of the material as covered in class. Once again, there's no substitute for attending class and paying attention to discussions.

You have a number of options:

- Pay extra attention to your class notes: the words spoken in class find their way back in the form of exam questions. No matter how "objective" your professor tries to be in writing the question, it's certain to reflect your professor's voice and how the material was presented.

- Work with questions from other sources. Simply because your professor doesn't release questions doesn't mean that alternate sources aren't available and useful. Working with objective-style questions is helpful whatever the source because you need to develop your reading comprehension skills. Careless reading is often the reason behind an incorrect answer choice and only practice will let you know if you have reading problems.

(c)   How to study from the questions

The more I work with students, the more I realize that they don't know what it means to study from questions. Instead of learning from them, students are constantly testing and grading themselves. Certainly the instinct to "answer" the question and see if you've gotten it "right" is instilled in the educational process early on, but here it's more of a hindrance than a help.

The following is a fairly typical study session:

> *Amy, the law student, sits down at a table in the library and commences to answer as many multiple-choice questions as she can in 60 minutes. At the end of the hour, she checks her answers and tallies her score. Then she "does" another round of questions, once again tallying the number of correct responses at the end of the session. After a couple of hours and "doing" about 65 questions or so, she's ready to call it a day. She packs up her books and commends herself for studying so hard. What did she learn?*

Let's say she answered half of the questions correctly.

- Does this mean she "knows" 50% of the material?
- Can she be sure that the correct responses were "right" for the right reasons?
- Does she know why her incorrect responses were wrong?
- Did she select an incorrect answer choice because she didn't know or failed to identify the controlling rule of law?
- Did she identify the correct rule but apply it incorrectly to the facts?
- Did she misread the call-of-the-question?
- Did she misread the facts?

Sadly, Amy probably doesn't have a clue to any of these questions. But unless she can answer them, the hours she's just spent "doing" questions were pretty much a waste of time.

This approach doesn't work because while you may have "answered" questions, you've not learned to "analyze" questions. And you must know how to reason through a question to arrive at the correct answer choice. Not only is this process essential to arriving at the correct answer, but you must be aware of how you've reasoned through a problem so you can go back and examine that thought process should you make an incorrect choice.

What you need to do is *learn how to learn from the questions*. For example, it's not cheating to look up the rule to help you work through an analysis of the question. This is learning through repetition and reinforcement. The process of going back to your outline and reviewing what you've written to help you work through a specific problem is learning in context. It also exposes any errors or omissions in your outline since if it's not helpful in answering the question, then it's likely to let you down on exam day as well. It's preferable to find out now and fix the problem.

(d)   What it means to "do" questions

Now that I've told you what not to do, it's time to explain what you should do. There are two parts to this discussion: the first is to learn how to answer multiple-choice questions and the second is to learn how to practice them.

For detailed instructions on how to answer a question, refer to Chapter 7. The following is just a summary of the steps you'll follow. Chapter 7 explains each step in detail and provides examples. You will:

(1)   Read actively from the call-of-the-question or "stem" and then to the fact pattern

(2)   Find the issue in the fact pattern

(3)   Move from the issue to articulation of your own answer

(4)   Translate your "answer" to fit an available "answer choice"

The other part is learning the right way to practice. Here's how to do it:

(1)   *Select a group of questions from the specific area of law you've just reviewed. For example, if you've just finished studying strict products liability, you'll select questions in this area.*

By practicing groups of questions in a particular area of the law, you can:

■ Identify your strengths and weaknesses

If you consistently answer questions dealing with a particular rule incorrectly, this means that you need to return to your notes and review that topic more thoroughly before attempting more questions. You simply don't know the law well enough.

■ Begin to see patterns in the facts

When you practice questions of a particular type together, you can see their common characteristics and realize that there are only so many variations of a fact pattern with respect to a single legal issue. This lets you become familiar with the way particular topics are tested. As a result, your comfort level increases as do the number of correct answer choices.

■ Become familiar with the way language is used

In addition to becoming familiar with the types of facts that invoke certain rules, by working with groups of questions in a particular area, you also become accustomed to the way vocabulary is connected to the rules. Very often, the difference between a correct and incorrect answer choice turns on the meaning and significance attached to particular language in the fact pattern. Your ability to identify such words is critical and only practice with questions will provide the opportunity to gain this familiarity.

(2)   Answer a question and immediately check your response.

By checking your choice right after you've selected it, the fact pattern is still fresh in your mind and, hopefully, so is your reasoning for choosing that answer. Getting immediate feedback on your analysis of the question serves two functions: first, it reinforces your understanding of the rule if your answer choice was correct; and second, it allows you to assess quickly the flaw in your reasoning if your answer choice was incorrect.

For detailed procedures on how to work through incorrect answer choices, refer to Chapter 9. It explains how to recreate your thought process and retrace your steps to find the flaw in your analysis. Until you know why you select wrong answer choices, you can't make the necessary corrections. That's why it's essential – absolutely essential – to answer only one question at a time. If you try to work with groups of questions, you won't recall what you were thinking with respect to any one question and it will be impossible to recreate your thought process.

(3) The timing factor.

To time or not to time? That is so often the question. Students frequently ask me whether they should time themselves when they practice exams. My answer is invariably, "it depends." Consider this: does an athlete set world records during practice or during the competition? How quickly you can "race" through the questions during your practice sessions is of no particular value. What matters is what you learn when you practice and how you ultimately perform on exam day.

During your practice sessions, you're concentrating on learning the law, how the professor tests that law, and how language is used to phrase the questions. If this is your goal when you practice multiple questions (or any part of the exam), then how long it takes you to read and answer the questions is not the issue. Rather, it's whether you absorbed anything meaningful from the practice. It doesn't matter how long it takes you to answer a question, but whether you answered the question correctly and did so for the correct reason. I can practically guarantee that once you become comfortable with the process of analyzing the questions, your speed in answering them will increase automatically.

It never hurts to include a few timed sessions in your practice routine but there's no need to do so until shortly before the exam. Remember, you always operate at optimum speed during the exam because of the adrenaline flow.

3. OPEN-BOOK AND TAKE-HOME EXAMS

Because open-book and take-home exams allow access to your study materials, rote memorization is not the issue but the need for proper preparation remains essential. Even if it's a take-home exam, you're still working under time constraints and the last thing you need to do is learn the material as you race the clock to answer the questions. What this means is that you should plan to prepare much as you would for a closed-book exam.

There is one small difference: you should pay equal attention to prepping your study materials so they too are exam-ready. This topic is covered in the chapter on outlining so we don't need to discuss it again here. Although you still need to learn the material, you can rely on your study aids for some help during the exam. You just need to be able to find what you're looking for without wasting valuable exam time.

A word or two about take-home exams is in order. Some of us actually prefer in-class over take-home exams for the following reasons:

- Completing the exam in three hours instead of overnight or days imposes limits we often find hard to impose on ourselves.

- Writing in school and under exam constraints places everyone on a level playing field.

- Professors have higher standards for take-home exams. They are far more forgiving of writing errors and organizational defects on in-class exams. Let's be honest: they expect more when you have more time to complete a task.

F. THE STUDY GROUP

I can't think of a single lawyer movie that doesn't include a scene or reference to the law school "study group." From *The Paper Chase* to *Legally Blonde*, it seems everyone who goes to law school must join a study group to do well. Like most things in the movies, they're not necessarily true: you don't need a study group to succeed in law school although some of the skills developed in such groups are useful.

Learning to listen to what your classmates say in class and in study groups is a vital step in learning how to work with others. Much of law school learning is collaborative in nature and this requires that you respect what others have to say by listening carefully when they speak. In law practice, you'll be expected to be a team player and get along well with others. This applies not only to the members of your firm but also to outside firms, agencies, and offices. Your work will often require you to collaborate with others in structuring deals, negotiating contracts, settling disputes, and a myriad of other activities. In order to be an effective member of the team, you must listen carefully to hear what others have to contribute.

1. DO YOU NEED A STUDY GROUP?

Not everyone needs a study group or has the opportunity to participate in one. If you're a part-time evening student, there's precious little time to get together with other students after finishing your own work. It would be nice but quite often it's just not possible. Although the journey might be a little lonelier for you than for those who find their way into happy and productive groups, there's no reason to think you won't make it through law school.

On the other hand, there are students who work well with others and the problem-solving nature of legal questions lends itself nicely to discussion and debate. If you're one of these students, you'll want to form a study group soon after arriving in law school. The focus will be on finding compatible study mates and ensuring that the group functions effectively. A successful study group just doesn't happen: it takes commitment, effort, and serious work.

2. SIZE MATTERS

Successful groups are usually composed of a minimum of three members and no more than six. Three allows for the diversity of skills and aptitudes necessary for a solid group dynamic and learning experience. With numbers over six, the group becomes too large to function efficiently because there's a tendency for small group conversations and disruption. The goal of the group is to get together to review the material, not to socialize. With larger numbers, it becomes harder to control "the chat factor."

3. ACHIEVING GROUP PRODUCTIVITY AND EFFECTIVENESS

For a study group to work effectively, every member of the group must be invested in the success of the group. This means that it's a "one for all and all for one" type of thing where each member is committed to the successful experience of every other member.

If you choose to set up or join a study group, be prepared for the following:

(a) To be supportive of each other in learning the material.

(b) To be respectful and engage in appropriate behavior. You must be willing to listen to others and accept differing viewpoints.

(c) To do your own work and neither "free load" nor "show off." The "freeloader" is one who lets others do the work, contributes little or nothing of her own, and still wants to reap the benefits. Naturally, this causes resentment for the other study group members who rightfully won't want to continue sharing their work product. "Show-offs" are just as damaging. They like to dominate discussions and use the group to show off their knowledge. The antidote is self-monitoring. You must be responsible for your own work and hold every other member equally responsible. Setting clear rules from the beginning is key and defining penalties for non-conformance is essential.

(d) To create a safe haven from the usual competitiveness of law school. The study group should be a place where you feel free to share openly and ask questions without fear. This requires a high level of trust but goes a long way toward eliminating the social and academic isolation felt by so many to be a part of the law school experience, but certainly need not be.

CHAPTER 6:
EXAM-TAKING BASICS

A. DIFFERENT PLANS
FOR DIFFERENT TYPES OF EXAMS

There are three basic exam formats: the closed-book, the open-book, and the take-home exam. Most of the following discussion is appropriate for the closed- and open-book exam. The take-home varies the greatest but mostly with respect to budgeting your time.

B. BEING IN THE MOMENT

No matter how much you've studied, how many practice exams you've taken, and how carefully you've outlined and considered what's likely to be tested, once you get to the exam, you must be prepared to let go and "be in the moment." This means that you respond to what the professor asks of you and not what you want to tell the professor you know. Professors craft exam questions to test you on the material you should have mastered in class; if you turn questions around or avoid answering the ones that are asked, you're thwarting the professor's agenda and substituting your own. Trust me – there's no better way to ensure a poor grade than to ignore what's asked of you. By answering the professor's question, you'll be showing what you know.

Now let's talk about the "exam zone." If you've prepared properly and you're willing to surrender to the professor's questions, this moment will come. Like a "runner's high," it's a feeling that there is only "the now." It's where you're on auto-pilot and your training has taken over. You've connected with whatever it was you were working to achieve: for the athlete, it's that connection of mind and body that allows for peak performance; for the law student, it's that command of the material that lets you see the issues in the facts and connect it with the rule and allows you to write with clarity and cogency. Your thinking and writing come together – it flows because you flow.

The first rule of exam taking and reaching the exam zone is that you must know the law to write the law. There is no substitute for knowledge of the law. You must know the rules with specificity both to identify the legal problems presented in the facts and to write a comprehensive answer that gets points. The second rule is to let go of a prepared script and respond to what comes your way.

Now we're ready to get down to exam basics.

C. WHAT TO DO THE NIGHT BEFORE

If I've managed to convince you of anything at all, it should be that learning the law is not solely about memorization. Consequently, last-minute cramming and all-nighters don't do much good. In fact, they're probably counter-productive because they leave you too exhausted to perform optimally on the exam. Instead, aim for a quiet evening and a good night's sleep. Don't spend this time with your study group or fielding last minute questions from classmates. If you've been doing what you should have been doing all semester, you're ready for the exam. More than ready. Now you need to get your rest so you'll perform at your best.

D. WHAT TO DO THE DAY OF THE EXAM

1. FOR DAY STUDENTS

In the morning, enjoy a healthy breakfast – you can't concentrate when you're stomach is growling – and plan to arrive at the test site with time to spare.

2. FOR EVENING STUDENTS

If you won't be taking your exam until evening, getting through the day can be a challenge. The anxiety and the waiting are the problems: I know because I was an evening student. But there are some things you can do to make it less stressful and the time productive. Here's what I recommend:

■ Make every possible effort to be home on exam days even if you've managed to get this far without taking off time from work. You must be free from distractions so that all you have in your head is the law. You simply can't do this if you're at the office; despite your best efforts, something always comes up at the last minute.

■ Pace yourself during the day so you're not tired at exam time. Review your outline in the morning, have lunch, and then address the topics you feel you must look at one last time. This is more for your peace of mind than anything else. You're not about to learn something new at this time. It's just a matter of keeping what you know in your head so that it will flow from your pen.

■ Since you lose your dinner time when you sit for evening exams, it's best to eat lunch later in the afternoon and make it a good one. You might opt for a small snack before the exam but don't go for anything that might upset your stomach or put you to sleep – absolutely no turkey sandwiches or ice-cream!

3.   FOR EVERYONE

Now that it's time to go to the exam, make sure to do the following:

(a)   Bring all of your supplies with you. Have enough pens that actually write, markers or pencils if you use them, and your exam number. You might consider a watch or small clock so you can see the time without having to look up. If you must bring something to eat, make sure it's exam-friendly – no noisy candy wrappers.

For an open-book exam, make sure you have the materials you're allowed to bring to the exam in the precise form the professor has specified. Be attentive to page limits and format requirements. You don't want your materials confiscated during the exam – or worse.

(b)   Consider earplugs if you are easily distracted by noise around you.

(c)   Allow yourself sufficient travel time to the test site. Ideally, you want to arrive about an hour before the exam so you can acclimate yourself. There's never a problem in being a bit early – only in being late.

(d)   Upon arrival, go directly to a quiet study area where you'll be alone. This is essential. The anxiety level during exam time is so high it's palpable. Even if you're not one of those students prone to extreme stress, it's hard to ignore the tension at these times. It's best to remove yourself from that environment and stay away from anyone and everyone who adds to it. This goes for your friends as well. You don't want to be cornered by well-meaning classmates with last minute questions. My friend and I had an agreement about pre- and post- exam times: we'd spend this time together under the condition that neither of us would discuss anything about the exam. It worked beautifully: just being together amidst the surrounding swirl was reassuring and we could calm down.

E. IMPLEMENTING THE METHOD

It's finally arrived. Your blue book is on the desk in front of you and you're told to begin.

What follows is a step-by-step approach for taking the exam. It's a blueprint you can follow to guide you through practice sessions and then implement on test day. Following this plan saves time and prevents anxiety: if you know exactly what you're going to do, and practice the routine sufficiently, it becomes second nature. On exam day, you can count on the routine to take over and prevent you from freezing up. You'll soon be in the "exam zone."

1. THE MOMENTS BEFORE THE EXAM

While the proctors are handing out the exam materials, sit calmly and do not think about anything or anyone else. Do not worry about other exams – past or future. You can't do anything about them but you can do something about the one you're taking right now. It requires and demands your full and undivided attention.

2. WHEN TOLD TO BEGIN AND THE NEXT TEN MINUTES

These are critical minutes for setting the pace and tenor of your exam experience. You want to start smoothly, work efficiently, and above all, remain focused and calm. Here's how to do it:

You can skip the following step if you're taking an open book exam and you're allowed to bring annotated materials or your outline in with you.

(a) Write down what you're afraid you'll forget

If you're worried that there's something you're likely to forget during the course of the exam, write it down on scrap paper. It only takes a few minutes and it buys peace of mind. For example, I would write down elements and definitions that I was sure I'd forget in the heat of the moment. Also, I would list the general topics covered in the course to use as a checklist against exam questions to see whether I'd considered all the possibilities. This would come in handy if I had trouble spotting issues. Just remember to look at your notes during the exam!

(b)   Scan the exam

Take a quick look through the entire exam to get an overview of what you're facing. Note the number of questions and the overall composition of the exam. A general sense of the exam is necessary to let you plan your time and keep focused by knowing what you'll be expected to do. For example, if you see that all the questions are targeted and specific, then it is not an issue-spotting exam and you won't what to waste mental energy going down paths you won't need to address.

So ask:

- Is it all essay?

- Are there multiple choice questions?

- Are there short answer questions?

- Is it a combination of any of the above?

3.   ALLOCATING YOUR TIME

Learning to budget your time and working within that time is the only way to ensure that you'll complete an exam. You want to divide your time in accordance with the way the professor has allocated the points. The most points deserve the most minutes. And you should think about it in terms of minutes.

Typically, a three-credit course is a three-hour exam which translates into 180 minutes. Sometimes your professor will give you a suggested time limit per essay. Alternatively, you may be given a point value and then you can use that to allocate your time. In either case, you'll make a timetable on your scrap paper and refer to it throughout the exam to keep you on track. The cardinal rule is never to "borrow" time from one question to answer the other. Stay within the timetable you've defined.

For example, consider the following schedule based on a three-hour exam composed of two essays and 25 multiple choice questions. You are told that essay one is worth 25 points, essay two is worth 50 points and 25 multiple choice questions complete the remaining 25 points. Assuming the exam begins at 9:00 a.m, the following would be your schedule:

9:00 - 9:45	Essay one (25 points translates to 45 minutes)
9: 45 - 11:15	Essay two (50 points translates to 90 minutes)
11:15- 12:00	Multiple choice questions

If you prefer, you can begin with the multiple choice questions and then proceed to the essays. The sequence in which you take up the questions doesn't matter in the least; what matters is that you make it perfectly clear to your professor which question you're answering.

This schedule completely eliminates your need to think about the clock during the test. All you do is look at the piece of paper and the time. You'll know exactly where you're supposed to be throughout the exam. But remember, the schedule only works if you follow it. You have to move on when your allotted time has run out on a question. Otherwise, you'll shortchange the other questions.

F. THE TAKE-HOME EXAM

The primary concern with the take-home exam is time management. Just because you have more time doesn't mean you have time to waste. You must plan your time as carefully as you would an in-school exam; you just have the bonus of some flexibility.

It's essential not to procrastinate and leave the exam until the last minute. While there's definitely more time for a take-home exam, there's never enough time. So be sure to use your time wisely. Consider point allocations in deciding where to begin and how long to devote to each question. Read the questions and decide the order in which you will answer them. Make a schedule and stick to it.

Finally, make sure to take the exam in a suitable environment. It's amazing how easy it is to be distracted when you don't have a ticking clock and the controls of a formal test environment.

G. MASTERING ANXIETY

1. WHY SOME ANXIETY IS A GOOD THING

A little anxiety can be a good thing before an exam. Some anxiety is absolutely normal and very necessary. It's useful because the adrenaline ensures that you'll operate at peak performance. It helps to keep you focused. The problem occurs when it interferes with your performance.

One student told me that she was so afraid of exams that she decided to calm herself before exams with relaxation techniques. The problem was that they worked so well and she was so relaxed that she never finished the exam. She was so mellow that it took her more than half an hour after the exam had begun to function at full capacity. Since this would never do, we changed her pre-exam routine to include a quiet period where she read some final review materials to keep focused on the task to come. This allowed her to maintain her composure and proceed without delay when the exam began.

2. PREPARATION IS USUALLY THE ANSWER

There's one sure answer to the test-anxiety question and that's preparation. You must go into the exam room knowing that you've done everything possible to prepare. In fact, you've over-prepared. It's the best way to provide the confidence necessary to ward off the usual exam jitters.

Preparation is essential for another reason with respect to anxiety. If you think about it, and you're willing to be absolutely honest with yourself, you'll realize that you're most anxious when you know you haven't really learned the material. This can be for any of the following reasons:

- You short-changed a particular subject in terms of the study time you devoted to it.

- You knew there were topics you didn't fully understand but never did what you needed to do to clear up the gaps in your knowledge.

- You acquired a general understanding of the subject but never went beyond that to gain specific knowledge, i.e., where you committed the rules to memory so as to be recalled upon demand.

- You never answered any of your professor's old exams to practice how the topics might be tested.

In these cases, your anxiety is not so much about taking the exam as it is about being unprepared and exposed by a poor performance. On the other hand, if you've thoroughly prepared by following the approaches outlined in this book, you'll be in position to find the "exam zone." Whether you call it "auto-pilot" or "muscle memory," what happens is that your preparation will take over and you'll respond to the questions as you've trained yourself to do.

3. SOME ADDITIONAL APPROACHES

For most students, over-preparation is sufficient to calm pre-exam jitters and any remaining stress tends to disappear once the actual exam gets underway. But for some, the anxiety does not dissipate and can be debilitating. In these cases, the following suggestions might prove helpful:

- Recall past experiences of success. You've taken tests all your life and you've done well or you wouldn't be in law school sitting for exams right now. Just think of all the college exams you've taken and the LSAT itself. These were tough exams and you managed quite nicely. There's something to be said about the value of past experience – if you've done it before, you can do it again.

■ Remember it's only an exam. In the general scheme of things, it's still just an exam. It doesn't decide your entire future, one way or the other.

■ Conjure a "negative" role-model. This worked nicely for me. I knew several people from high school and college who had gone to law school and were living full and productive lives as lawyers. I had not considered them particularly exceptional. So whenever I became nervous, I thought to myself "if so-and-so could do this," then most certainly so could I. It worked like a charm. I'm sure you can think of someone from your life who can serve as your own negative role model. Just never tell them.

CHAPTER 7: TAKING THE EXAM

A. EXAM-TAKING IS PROBLEM SOLVING

Law school exams are all about solving problems. The only difference between exams is how the problems "present" and how you provide the solution. Essay exams require you to write and explain your answers while short, objective-style questions require you to match your thinking to one of the answer choices.

While each type of exam requires solid knowledge and understanding of the rules, there is decidedly more leeway with essay questions. Here you can score some points even when you've taken a wrong turn if you provide a thoughtful and well-reasoned analysis of the issues and legal principles involved. On the other hand, there's no such option with multiple choice questions. Your answer is either right or wrong. But look at the bright side – the correct answer is literally right in front of you.

B. THE GOOD THING ABOUT ESSAYS

The way I see it – and the way you should see it too – is that the essay, more than any other type of exam question, presents the greatest opportunity for you to succeed. The reason is simple: when you write, you're the one in control. Unlike a multiple choice question where you have to match up your analysis of the problem with one of the set answer choices, essay questions afford a relatively high degree of flexibility. While there are definite limits determined by the issues set up in the facts, you can sometimes take a slightly different path and still accrue significant points.

Think of essays as your *opportunity to converse* with your professor and show with every word you write that you have mastered the material covered in the course. Mastery is demonstrated by reasoning in a logical, lawyer-like manner and using the *language of the law*. Presumably, after reading all of the cases during the semester, you sound something like a lawyer. When your professor reads your essay, there should be "a scintilla of evidence" to show that you've attended the class.

C.   THE DIFFERENT TYPES OF ESSAYS

Law school essay exams vary greatly in length, style, and format but they are very similar when it comes to what they require from you – a demonstration of your ability to problem solve. You'll find two general types of essay questions:

- The hypothetical with multiple issues and/or parties

- The short answer question

Each seeks to test your problem-solving skills and knowledge of the substantive law. However, each does so in a slightly different way and thus requires a slightly different approach. We'll look at each type of essay separately, beginning with the traditional issue-laden fact scenario.

Once you're familiar with the basic structure and substance of essay questions, we'll consider the possible formats. As we noted in an earlier chapter, the most common format is that of the closed book exam. It's the one you're most likely to encounter in law school and certainly when you take the bar exam. In fact, some professors claim that they give closed book exams to prepare their students for the bar exam. In any case, a closed book exam requires that you know the material "cold" – that you come into the exam with all the material clearly understood and memorized. On the other hand, "open book" and "take-home" exams allow access to certain materials, so rote memorization is not the issue. But you're still expected to understand the rules and apply them thoroughly.

The discussion that follows is appropriate for all types of exams; the slight modifications necessary to accommodate the different formats are discussed individually.

D.   THE MULTI-ISSUE HYPOTHETICAL

A fact pattern may be as short as one paragraph or as long as several pages. It may feature one, two, or a dozen parties. And it may take place over the course of an hour or be years in the making. It doesn't matter. Your task is always the same: to address the question that is asked of you through a solid explication of the law and the facts. What changes is your focus and your organizational scheme.

The following is a summary of the steps to be taken in answering an essay question. We'll be looking at each step in detail – lots and lots of detail – but review the steps before proceeding to get a sense of what will be covered.

Summary of steps:

After allocating your time for the exam as discussed in the previous chapter, you're ready for the first question.

I. Read the question

A. Begin with the call-of-the-question.

B. Read the fact pattern "actively":
   (1) Identify the sub-area of law and note any legal relationship between the parties.
   (2) Circle amounts of money, dates, locations, quantities, and ages.
   (3) Note the words "oral" and "written."
   (4) Be perfectly clear about *who is doing what to whom.*

II. Outline your answer

A. Organize ideas into an outline based on a consideration of the relevant issues.

B. For each issue, compile the building blocks for the rule of law by considering, as appropriate:
   (1) the general rule
   (2) elements/factors
   (3) exceptions to the general rule
   (4) distinctions/limitations
   (5) defenses

III. Write the essay

A. Begin with identification of the issue: whether or not you use such language as *"the issue is whether,"* include the word *"when"* in your issue statement to ensure that you include the relevant facts.

B. Introduce the rule of law with, *"Under the* [state the controlling law: common law, federal rule, state-specific statute, etc.].

C. Follow the hierarchy of concepts by
   (1) Moving from the general to the specific
   (2) Defining each legal term of art

D. Introduce your analysis with *"Here"* or "In this case."

E. Use *"because"* throughout your analysis to make the connection between rule and fact.

F. Match each "element" in your rule of law with a "fact" using "because" to link the two.

G. Conclude and continue: offer a conclusion with respect to the issue and repeat the process where each issue and sub-issue forms the basis for a separate IRAC analysis.

E. IMPLEMENTING THE APPROACH

1. READING THE QUESTION

Before you can write an answer, you have to read the question. How you read the question determines exactly what you will write. Many of the mistakes made in answering a question begins with a misreading of the question. Do you really want to lose points when you know the rules but simply misread the question?

(a) The first read

Note that this section is entitled the "first read." That's because you'll need to read a question several times before you're ready to write. Each reading of the question accomplishes a different task. The purpose of the first read is to acquaint you with the general story, the parties, and the type of question.

(1) Begin with the call of the question.

Always begin your reading with the interrogatory at the end of the question. The interrogatory, or "call-of-the-question," lets you know what is required of you. This informs your subsequent reading of the fact pattern and ensures that you read "actively" for the information you need.

• *If you're reading Example 1, begin with "Analyze fully."*

• *If you're reading Example 2, begin with* "Has Ben incurred this liability and if so, on what basis?"

■ *Example 1:*

Dan asked Ben for some advice. Dan met a woman online and they had been e-mailing each other for a few weeks. They met for the first time last week and Dan thinks he is in love. But there is somehing odd about Cindy because she insists on wearing a scarf around her neck – all the time. She even wore one when they went swimming. Ben agreed that this was odd behavior and suggested maybe she was hiding something.

Dan decided he had to know what was under the scarf. He offered to make them dinner for their next date. He prepared an 18 pound turkey for the two of them, hoping the turkey dinner would put Cindy to sleep and he could sneak a peek at her neck. After eating half the turkey, Cindy fell asleep on the couch. Dan carried her into the bedroom and placed her on the bed. He drew the blinds and closed the door. He went over to Cindy and started to untie her scarf. It was in a knot secured with a gold pin. Dan was all thumbs – he had trouble untying the knot and then he stuck Cindy with the pin. Before he could get the scarf off and while he still had his hands around her neck, Cindy awoke, looked around the darkened room and started to scream, "Where am I and what are you doing to me?" Dan stammered "You fell asleep on the couch and I moved you in here to make you more comfortable. I thought you were choking on a turkey bone, so I was untying your scarf." Cindy replied, "Let me out of here." Dan stood aside as she ran out the door.

Now Cindy is threatening a lawsuit. She claims she can no longer eat turkey for fear of falling asleep and when she does sleep, she has nightmares about having her neck exposed. Dan wants to know if Cindy has any viable causes of action against him. Analyze fully.

■ *Example 2:*

While Sam was home with a cold, he developed a recipe for a caffeine-free latte that soothed his sore throat and opened his nasal passages. The next day, Sam brought a cup of the latte to his friend Ben because he had a cold too. Immediately upon drinking the special brew, Ben exclaimed, "Sam, you've cured me. I can breathe again!" Then Ben said, "You could make a fortune with this latte." Sam responded, "You know Ben, I was going to call my attorney. I am thinking about patenting the recipe and maybe going into business. But I am too sick to go out. Why don't you go and meet him for me so we don't waste any time. Let me know what he says."

Ben agreed and met with Sam's attorney, Mr. Greene. Ben informed Mr. Greene that his friend and developer of the latte was unavailable for this meeting. The attorney advised that they move immediately to patent the latte because recipe theft was common. Ben hesitated a bit and finally said, "I suppose Sam would want to protect his recipe. Go ahead and do what you have to do." The attorney drafted the papers for Ben's signature. Mr. Greene said that the fee was $5000 for the work he had done and he would require another $5000 to set up the business. Ben said, "Sam will send you a check."

Sam could not believe that Ben signed papers and Sam now owes $10,000. "Well, just forget it. I only told you to meet with him. I didn't tell you to sign anything." Mr. Greene files the papers and sent a bill to Sam for $10,000. When Sam refused to pay, Mr. Greene brought suit against him. Has Sam incurred this liability and if so, on what basis?

(2) *Determine whether it's a "general" or "specific" style essay or some combination of the two.*

These are the two basic essay styles and the call-of-the-question lets you know which one you're facing. An essay is either a general, open-ended question where you must raise and identify all the possible issues or it's a narrow, issue-based problem where you must come to a conclusion by answering a specific question.

A "general" style essay will leave the question open-ended. The following are particular law professor favorites:

- *"Analyze fully."*
- *"Identify all possible claims and defenses. Explain fully."*
- *"What result?"*

On the other hand, a "specific" essay will present a precise question to be answered:

- *"Was the court correct in granting Plaintiff's motion for summary judgment?"*
- *"Did the Surrogate correctly admit Ben's will to probate?"*
- *"Did Amy violate her good faith obligation?"*

Sometimes you'll find a hybrid: you'll be asked to answer a specific question but to do so you'll have to engage in a complex analysis of several issues and sub-issues to arrive at the answer. In this respect, there's not much difference between the two styles of exam questions except that even in this case you're asked a specific question which you must address.

It's pretty easy to see that Example 1 falls into the general category because it asks that you "analyze fully."

Example 2 appears to fall into the "specific" category because it asks you to address a very specific question – "Has Ben incurred this liability?" However, it then adds, "if so, on what basis?" which turns the problem into a hybrid where you must engage in the same sort of open analysis as a general question and still be sure to resolve the specific question asked of you.

(3) *Skim through the problem, spending no more than a couple of minutes to acquaint yourself with the general story and the parties.*

(4)   Re-read the call of the question to set your focus.

(b)   The second read

Now you can read the question more slowly and focus on the information relevant to your task. For example, if you're asked to evaluate court rulings, you'll go and find those rulings in the fact pattern and use them as a framework to inform your reading. Similarly, if you're asked to evaluate constitutional issues on behalf of a particular party, you'll read the facts with an eye toward framing arguments from that party's perspective.

(1)   Read the fact pattern "actively."

"Active reading" means that you search for and identify the following:

■ *The sub-area of law*

When you walk into your exam, you know whether you're about to take an exam in business organizations, constitutional law, or contracts. But these are still wide open categories and you must narrow it to specific sub-topics. For example, you'll ask one set of questions if the parties are involved in a transaction involving a sale of goods and another, quite different series of questions, if the parties are performing a construction contract. A critical component of reading actively is reading in context; on exams, it's your job to provide the context.

■ *The legal relationship between the parties*

While we don't care about much about the names of parties except to keep them straight in our answer, we care very much about the legal significance of parties' relationships. The nature of the relationship is often of major significance to a resolution of the problem.

For example, look for such significant relationships as husband/ wife, attorney/client, buyer/seller, landlord/tenant, employer/ employee, parent/child, and teacher/student, among others. Professors use such relationships to test your ability to note distinctions in how the law treats such relationships. Here, you may be dealing with fiduciary duties, different standards of care, and additional obligations imposed by law.

Note: Instead of underlining or highlighting key language, write the words which characterize the relationship in the margin, i.e., "merchants," "landlord/tenant," etc. The key is for you to concretize your thinking in language. If you highlight, you won't necessarily recall what it meant and you'll have to reread the passage to recall your thoughts. In effect, you'd be doing the same thing twice and wasting valuable time.

■ *Amounts of money, dates, locations, quantities, and ages*
Be sure to circle dollar amounts, dates and times, quantities of items, jurisdictional information, and any ages if they appear in the fact pattern.

Imagine if you fail to make note of the time sequence of events in a contractual relationship. Your analysis of the offer, acceptance, and requirements for performance may be way off. The same is true for transfers of property. Dates also signal statute of limitations problems. On the other hand, ages are generally tied to a statutory issue (consider statutory rape) or a standard of care (fiduciary duty) while money and location information tend to indicate jurisdictional thresholds. Reading carefully assures that you won't miss critical signals.

■ *The words "oral" and "written"*
These words figure prominently in contract, property, and evidence questions. They signal potential issues with the Statute of Frauds, enforceability of promises, transactions with respect to land, and even admissibility of certain kinds of evidence. Be sure to circle the word as soon as you read it. Also, note language that signals a writing or oral conversation i.e, a letter, a fax, or a telephone call. It's so easy to overlook a single word as you read through the problem. For want of a word, whole essays may be lost!

(2) **What "active reading" does not *include***
■ *Adding facts to the problem*
Unless you are told to do so specifically by the call of the question, you are never to add your own facts. Occasionally, you may find an exam question that asks you to identify additional facts necessary to resolve the problem. Here the professor has crafted the question to require the addition of specific facts. It's part of the test to see if you know what is necessary to complete an analysis. However, in most cases, you are given all the facts you need to use and should use only those facts.

■ *Making assumptions.*
Never make assumptions. This will lead you astray and into dangerous exam territory. On the other hand, an assumption is not the same as a logical inference, which often must be made from the facts you're given. When working with a set of facts, you may need to draw factual inferences and connect these inferences to the dictates of the rule. But remember that inferences are not assumptions.

For example, if the facts of your problem indicate that

> *"It was the end of December in New York at 7:00 p.m. when Dylan smashed a window and entered Ben's house"*

you should infer this to be a "nighttime" event. This is the logical inference to be drawn from the facts. The logical chain of inferences is that since it was the end of December, it was winter, and since it was winter in New York, it would be dark at 7:00 p.m.

■ *Never confuse your parties.*

As you read and most certainly before you write, make absolutely certain that you are clear about *who is doing what to whom.* You don't want to confuse the actors. After all, your professor will not be able to intuit that you meant to conclude that "Dan is not guilty of manslaughter" when you actually wrote "Ben."

2.   ORGANIZE YOUR THOUGHTS

Only clear, organized thoughts can give rise to coherent, comprehensible answers. Accordingly, after you've completed your second read, and before you write your answer, you must organize your ideas into an outline based on a consideration of the relevant issues. Resist the impulse to start writing immediately – it doesn't matter what others around you are doing – it's worth the few minutes it will take to think through the problem and plan your response. While you won't have time to write the type of detailed outline you may be used to preparing for a research paper, this doesn't mean you can afford to skip the process entirely. If you take the time to organize your thinking and draft an outline around the relevant issues, you'll have the beginnings of an "A" essay.

(a)   Set up a working outline

An outline for an exam essay is a list of the rules of law you've identified from the main issues in the fact pattern. There's no need and no time to do any more than write a rules-based outline. This is sufficient to prompt the string of associations that should be in your head. Facts are not included in your outline because they are already in the problem.

Let's see how this works. If we write an exam outline for Example 2, it would look something like this:

> Define Agency
>
> Define/discuss the types of authority
> 1. Actual (relationship between Principal and Agent)
>   a. Express
>   b. Implied (inherent)
>
> 2. Apparent (agent with respect to third party)
>
> ***Outline for Example 2***

This is more than enough information to guide you through a thorough explication of the issues involved in this problem. Thinking through a problem in this manner allows you to develop your analysis in its proper order – from the initial question regarding agency through a discussion of the concepts of authority. The outline assures that your answer will be well-organized because it leads you through the issues and sub-issues as they naturally unfold. As you write, you'll refer to each point, using it to prompt your thinking and develop each point fully.

While a more complicated problem would require a longer outline, it would not require a more complicated outline. The more time you devote to writing the outline, the less time you have for writing the answer – which is, after all, the only writing to receive a grade.

(b)   Use sub-headings

The purpose for using sub-headings is as much for the writer as it is for the reader. They promote organization – both of thought and expression. Your choice of sub-headings should be simple and direct. Often, you need look no further than the topics identified in the interrogatory, i.e., "Motion for Summary Judgment," "Identification of Damages," "Easement by Prescription." Examples of additional sub-heading topics include parties and causes of action, i.e., "George v. ABC Company," "Buyer's Remedies," "Jon's Available Defenses."

(c)   Find the issues

The challenge in drafting an outline – and writing a solid exam answer – lies in identifying the legal issues. All the outline represents is a list of the relevant rules you've discerned from the issues. Each issue becomes a focal point around which you'll write your analysis.

Consequently, you must identify the issues before you can even write a rule outline. I know I've said this many times before but it bears repeating here – the issues are the legal questions raised by the facts. And you must know the law to find the issues because you won't see the legal question in the facts if you don't know the law.

On exams, the issues come from one of two possible sources, depending on the particular form of the essay. For example, in the specific-style essay, you'll use the interrogatories to guide your articulation of the issue while in the general-style essay, you'll need to ascertain the issues directly from the fact patterns.

Let's see how this works.

(1) Finding issues in the specific-style essay

Consider the following hypothetical:

One pleasant Sunday afternoon, Jerry was taking his dalmatian, Spot, for a walk to the pet shop to buy him some treats when he heard the shattering of window glass from the pet store and the ringing of the store's alarm. Jerry stopped to make sure that Spot hadn't been hurt by any flying glass. When he looked up, he saw a woman running out of the store, carrying a box of pet toys and treats. Spot began to chase the woman for the treats and Jerry took off behind him. Before Spot and Jerry could reach the woman, she accidentally ran into Sam, a pedestrian, knocking him against a lamppost where he fell and severely injured his head. The woman ran away, but she dropped the box and all the toys and treats spilled onto the street.

Spot stopped running to eat the treats and Jerry called an ambulance. Sam thanked Jerry. Jerry waited with Sam until the ambulance arrived. Sam insisted that Jerry come with him to the hospital and since Jerry wouldn't leave Spot, they all went in the ambulance together. There the doctor told Sam, who was conscious, that his condition was serious because the fall caused bleeding in his brain, and that Sam would require immediate surgery. Just before losing consciousness, Sam thanked Jerry and Spot for their help and told Jerry that the woman who knocked him down was Cindy, a woman he once dated and has never gotten over him. Sam's final words to Jerry were, "The doctor said my condition is serious, and surgery is necessary to save my life. Don't let Cindy get away with this." Despite surgery, Sam died later that night from the injuries he sustained when Cindy ran into him.

Cindy has been indicted by a grand jury for burglary and felony murder. At Cindy's trial, Jerry testified to the pertinent foregoing facts, and began to testify to Sam's statement to him in the ambulance. Over the objection of Cindy's attorney that Sam's statement to Jerry constituted inadmissible hearsay, the court permitted Jerry to testify to Sam's statement. Was the court's ruling correct?

Following our paradigm, we begin by reading the interrogatory. Here the call of the question is simply:

"Was the court's ruling correct?"

With an interrogatory like this, the precise issue in controversy is not explicit and requires a multi-step analysis to identify it. Let's think through, step by step, how you would proceed after completing your reading of the entire fact pattern:

- Return to the court's ruling at the end of the fact pattern:
  "The court permitted Jerry to testify to Sam's statement."

- "Translate" to yourself exactly what the court must have concluded about that statement to allow the testimony into evidence. Here's where legal analysis is required on your part *because the issue is not,*

  "Whether the court was correct in permitting Jerry to testify to Sam's statement."

This is merely a restatement of the question and not a statement of the issue in controversy.

- How do you find the issue? This is the critical step. You must engage in legal analysis and find the controversy behind the ruling by asking yourself:

  "What must have been the court's theory in allowing the testimony?"

- To figure this out, you must determine the factual basis for the legal controversy behind the ruling from the fact pattern.

Here you find in the sentence prior to the court ruling that Cindy's attorney had objected to admission of the statement on the grounds of inadmissible hearsay. Consequently, when the court overruled the objection and permitted the testimony, it had to be because the court found the statement either not to be hearsay or to be admissible on the basis of some exception to the hearsay rule. Now we have something like:

  "The issue is whether the court was correct when it allowed testimony of an out-of-court statement and whether that testimony was admissible based on one of the exceptions to the hearsay rule."

- At this point, you've identified an issue suitable for essay writing purposes. However, you should refine it to determine precisely which hearsay exception is in controversy. This ensures that your analysis and articulation of the rule will be on point. As you know, there are many exceptions to the hearsay rule. Your job is not to list and analyze them all; rather, you must focus your discussion on the particular exception raised by the facts of your problem.

- To determine the specific hearsay exception, re-read the paragraph which contains Sam's statement. Now the facts will have particular significance to you because you're looking for those facts which fit the elements of a hearsay exception.

■ You determine that Sam's statement might be considered a dying declaration. This leads to a more complete articulation of the issue:

> *"The issue is whether the court was correct when it found Sam's statement to be a dying declaration, an exception to the general rule against hearsay, and therefore admissible."*

■ From this issue, you're ready to draft a working outline:

1. General rule for hearsay

2. Dying declaration exception

(A list of the elements required for a dying declaration would follow and complete the outline)

Note: The specific elements for a dying declaration provide a mini-outline where each element forms the basis of its own IRAC analysis and guides your application of the facts.

As you can see, finding the issue is a backward process, beginning with the question you're asked and working back, step by step, to the specific legal question put in controversy by the particular facts.

With practice, you'll find that your ability to articulate a specific issue from a general statement will become instinctive. Not only is this a valuable skill for the purposes of the exam, but one which you need in practice as well. After all, when your adversary calls out "Objection!" during your questioning of a witness, you need to know the basis for the objection in order to oppose it.

(2) Finding issues in the general-style essay

In this case, we'll work with Example 1. Once again following our paradigm, begin by reading the call-of-the question:

> *"Dan wants to know if Cindy has any viable causes of action against him. Analyze fully."*

Such general-style questions as "analyze fully" or "discuss all claims" present a test of your organizational skills as well as your knowledge of the substantive law. The challenge lies in your ability to cover the relevant issues with the requisite level of detail without going astray. Whether you decide to organize your response around the parties or the causes of action, you'll want to choose your organizational scheme and use it to focus your thinking and your writing.

As we did before with the specific-style question, let's think through the problem, step by step, after reading the entire fact pattern:

■ *Example 3: Issue Identification*

Dan asked Ben for some advice. Dan met a woman online and they had been e-mailing each other for a few weeks. They met for the first time last week and Dan thinks he is in love. But there is something odd about Cindy because she insists on wearing a scarf around her neck – all the time. She even wore one when they went swimming. Ben agreed that this was odd behavior and suggested maybe she was hiding something.

Dan decided **(this word signals "intent")** *he had to know what was under the scarf* **(the intended act is to look under the scarf)**. *He offered to make them dinner for their next date. He prepared an 18 pound turkey for the two of them, hoping* **(another word signalling "intent")** *the turkey dinner would put Cindy to sleep* **(he intended to put Cindy to sleep, which is not by itself tortious conduct although strange)** *and he could sneak a peek at her neck* **(but looking at her neck while she's asleep might be since she didn't seem to want anybody looking at her neck while awake)**. *After eating half the turkey, Cindy fell asleep on the couch. Dan carried her* **(the act of picking her up might be battery but not assault because she was not aware he was coming at her because she was asleep)** *into the bedroom and placed her on the bed. He drew the blinds and closed the door* **(this might indicate intent to confine)**. *He went over to Cindy and started to untie her scarf* **(here's an indirect contact by touching the scarf)**. *It was in a knot secured with a gold pin. Dan was all thumbs – he had trouble untying the knot and then he stuck Cindy with the pin* **(another indirect contact via pin)**. *Before he could get the scarf off and while he still had his hands around her neck* **(here's a direct contact around her neck – and it could also be a confinement)**, *Cindy awoke, looked around the darkened room and started to scream, "Where am I and what are you doing to me?"* **(Might be assault because she's indicated awareness because she screamed and asked what was going on)**. *Dan stammered "You fell asleep on the couch and I moved you in here to make you more comfortable. I thought you were choking on a turkey bone, so I was untying your scarf." Cindy replied, "Let me out of here."* **(Possible confinement because she asked to be let go)**. *Dan stood aside* **(he was in her way if he had to stand aside to let her pass showing possible physical confinement, but the fact that he stood aside to let her pass may indicate a lack of confinement because he did not use any physical restraint, direct or indirect, to keep her in the room and prevent her escape)** *as she ran out the door* **(the door was not locked and she was not prevented from leaving)**.

Now Cindy is threatening a lawsuit. She claims she can no longer eat turkey for fear of falling asleep and when she does sleep, she has nightmares about having her neck exposed **(seems to be suffering emotional distress)**. *Dan wants to know if Cindy has any viable causes of action against him. Analyze fully.*

- Since the interrogatory presents an open-ended query, it's our responsibility to find the issues.

- Although the interrogatory asks only whether Cindy has any viable causes of action against Dan, we must consider Dan's defenses as well. It's part of evaluating the strength of Cindy's claim to determine whether there are viable defenses.

- It's easy to decide on an organizational scheme because we've been asked to discuss possible causes of action and our reading of the problem indicates that we're dealing with intentional torts. We'll identify the torts and use them to create an outline. Each tort will become a sub-heading when we write the analysis.

- We're ready to spot issues in our second reading of the hypothetical. To give you a sense of what you should be thinking during your second read of the problem, I annotated it in Example 3 (opposite) to show you my thoughts as I read to spot the issues. My thoughts are indicated in parentheses using bold font. While you shouldn't expect your thinking to mirror mine, you should stop at the same points and raise similar questions.

- After spotting the issues, you're ready to set up an outline. It's relatively simple because it's a list of the intentional torts but there's a twist: you need to identify the several possibilities for each tort. This problem is relatively complex because there isn't just one possible assault, battery, and confinement but several of each. This is one of those rare cases where your outline will reference "facts" for each tort to prompt your response.

- Consider the following working outline:

---

1. **ASSAULT – DEFINE**
   - *When he tried to untie her scarf*
   - *When she awoke with his hands around her neck*

2. **BATTERY – DEFINE**
   Intent: include substantial certainty

   - *When he fed her turkey to put her to sleep to untie her scarf*
   - *When he carried her into the bedroom*
   - *When he untied her scarf*
   - *When he stuck her with a pin*
   - *When he had his hands around her neck*

3. **FALSE IMPRISONMENT – DEFINE**
   - *When he put her in a darkened enclosed room*
   - *When she awoke with his hands around her neck*

4. **INFLICTION OF EMOTIONAL DISTRESS – DEFINE**

   Outline for Example 1

- The facts are no more detailed than necessary to guide you to the specific incident – the briefer the better because there's no value in rewriting facts. And no facts are necessary for emotional distress because there's only one instance to write about. Finally, the incidents are listed in the order in which they occurred because working sequentially is usually a good way to stay organized.

Note: This example is probably more detailed than you would write on the exam but I've had to be explicit so you could follow it.

This hypothetical features another typical problem for students: *the multiple use of the same set of facts*. On exams, as in practice, the same set of facts may be implicated in a number of different causes of action. Of course, this is not the problem. Rather, it's when the writer believes (quite erroneously) that if the facts are used for one cause of action, they cannot be used for another – as if they could be used up!

The way to overcome this problem is to block out all thoughts of other torts while concentrating on one. This allows you to analyze the facts appropriately with respect to that tort (or whatever the cause of action) and not interfere with your analysis when you move on to the next and proceed to work with the same facts but with respect to a different cause of action. Keep them separate in your head and separate on the paper. This is why an outline is so important – it puts you in control by setting your agenda.

The secret to writing a successful answer for this type of essay is to organize your response. Use subheadings to separate "causes of action" from "possible defenses." While it may appear easier to answer this type of question as opposed to the specific-style model where you have to engage in some preliminary deduction to find the issue, you must be careful nonetheless to keep your analysis on-point and fact-driven. The issue may well be whether Dan committed a battery but the battery occurred within a particular set of circumstances. Your ability to keep your response tied to the facts of the problem will ensure that you complete your analysis in a focused and timely manner.

(3) "Issue spotting" vs. "issue creation"
Never discuss issues that are not in controversy. Not only is it a waste of precious time, but it indicates that you're unable to distinguish between what is relevant and what isn't – and that's a serious problem. It's simply wrong to discuss something that's not in controversy.

There are a couple of ways you can end up writing about non-issues. One way, and perhaps the most common, is the tendency to write everything you know about the topic without regard to the question asked – and without regard to whether there are any facts to support the discussion. This is referred to as "kitchen sinking." Just because you're writing "law" doesn't mean that it's correct to do so. While you might write a perfectly correct statement of the rule, if it's not necessary to address a legal question raised by the facts, your discussion is irrelevant. This kind of regurgitation of all you know is never appropriate. In court, it would be deemed frivolous. It would be a waste of the court's time and resources; your professor sees it the same way.

The question is how do you avoid going down that road. The answer lies in the facts: they are your guide. There must be a factual basis to support a discussion. Sometimes, however, it's hard to distinguish when there is a sufficient factual basis to support an argument and when there isn't – in many cases, it's a judgement call. Do you raise the question and then dismiss it, or do you leave it alone altogether? How do you know what to do?

While there are no "bright line" rules to follow, you're on safe ground if you rely on the "straight face" test – if you can't make the argument without laughing at your own tortured and twisted sense of the facts, then you have to let it go. This doesn't mean that you don't consider all the arguments. It's just that you don't commit them to paper unless they show a shred of credibility. A credible argument is one that is grounded in the facts. It's perfectly acceptable if your analysis fails to support an overall finding but you must have some legitimate basis on which to raise the question.

Consider the following hypothetical* and the case of the student who found a claim in emotional distress:

Scarlett O'Hara has lived in New Orleans, Louisiana, for the past 50 years. For a number of those years she has had an on-again, off-again relationship with her neighbor, Rhett Butler. Last week, as news spread of a hurricane developing in the Carribean, Rhett decided to take a long deferred trip to Las Vegas to sample the gambling at Harrah's. He urged Scarlett to leave town too, but she declined.

As predicted, the aptly named Hurricane Tara made landfall in New Orleans, wreaking havoc. While the water in Lake Charles stared to rise, Scarlett was mildly concerned for her safety, but when a couple of levees near her home were breached, she realized it was time to leave. By the time she had put together the possessions she thought she could carry, the water was up to the top of the steps leading into her house.

Scarlett, knowing that Rhett was out of town and certainly not in need of his boat, decided to take Rhett's canoe, which he kept on the porch of his house. She waded across the waist-high water in the street and dragged the boat back to her house, where she loaded her few possessions and set out for dry land.

After paddling for some time, she encountered another neighbor, Ashley Wilkes, who was standing on a deck on the top floor of his house, from which he had an unobstructed view across the city. He called to Scarlett that the water level around their respective homes seemed to have stabilized, and he suggested that she join him in his home, which he assured her had ample provisions for at least a month.

Welcoming his offer, Scarlett steered towards the steps in front of Ashley's house and, reaching them, climbed out of the boat, which at this point had sprung a leak from a small gash in its side. Scarlett managed to drag the canoe up onto the porch beside her, then she fell to the floor and began to weep.

Identify and analyze the intentional tort claims suggested by these facts.

(*Courtesy of Dean Nicola Lee)

I've done my best to read the problem the way the student must have read it to find a claim in emotional distress. And there's only one way to do it: ignore the facts and consider only the call of the question which asks for "intentional tort claims." But this isn't how the process works. You can't ignore the facts and simply proceed to identify every intentional tort you covered during the semester and then concoct an argument to make it fit. This is not "issue spotting": it's "issue creation" and not something you're supposed to do.

The facts of this problem do not lend themselves to the question of emotional distress. You're not given enough to work with to question whether Scarlett has suffered emotional distress when all you're told is that she "began to weep." Even a cursory run-through of the elements in your head should immediately dispel the notion that you have anything to discuss. On the other hand, if the facts had indicated that Scarlett fell to the floor and began to weep and never stopped for six months – unable to work, unable to sleep, unable to eat – you might have something to consider since she seems to be in distress. But even here, you can't make a claim when there is no tortfeasor. Scarlett's "distress," if any, was weeping because of the hurricane. Who's the defendant? How can you bring an action without a defendant? Sometimes you really have to take a step back and look at the big picture.

3.   WRITE YOUR ANSWER

Now that you've read the problem and created an outline based on the rules, you're ready to write. Your goal is to demonstrate mastery of the material. How do you convey this message? By using the language of the law in the format and structure of legal analysis – and by following exam instructions down to the very last detail.

Follow instructions

Before you demonstrate your analytical skills with what you write, you'll want to show that you can follow basic directions. It may not seem all that important to you, but if your professor asks you to write on only one side of the paper or skip every other line, then you must do so. If page limits are defined, then you must observe them. If you're asked to assume a role – law clerk or judge – then be sure to play the part. If you're asked to draft a memo, begin your response with a mock memo heading. If you're asked to reach a conclusion, then by all means answer the question. In addition to your knowledge of the substantive law, your ability to read and follow directions is a vital lawyering skill that is being tested on the exam.

(a)   What is this thing called "IRAC"?

IRAC stands for the basic "Issue, Rule, Application, Conclusion" structure of legal analysis. It's commonly used by law professors to explain to their students the process of applying the law to the facts. At its core, it's an organizing principle – a way to help structure your thinking and your writing – nothing more.

Still, it's enormously useful and while it won't guarantee an "A" paper, students who learn to structure their analyses and write well tend to receive good grades.

I would be remiss if I didn't tell you that some of your professors will object to IRAC and insist that you refrain from using it on their exams. They have reasons for feeling as they do, since like anything else, IRAC can be abused. But it has also been wrongly accused: the objection is not so much to the concept but to a tortured application.

IRAC is a tool to aid in the organization of analysis, not a formula. Each problem is different and will proceed from a different issue based on the question that is posed in the facts. Unfortunately, some students twist their analysis to fit a set structure without using their judgment to consider the following:

What is being asked?
By whom?
And in what context?

All this means is that you must use your judgment when you answer a question. IRAC is not always an appropriate fit. It depends on what you're asked and how you use it. For example, an IRAC structure is not useful in the following situations:

- To make policy arguments

- To evaluate competing theories or rules

On the other hand, even where IRAC is an appropriate fit, you don't want to make the mistake of using it improperly. For example:

- Expressing all the issues in the problem in one paragraph, all the rules in another, and finally all the analysis in a third. This is a serious abuse and one that professors find most objectionable. And rightly so. It shows that the student has no real understanding of the nature of analysis but is simply following a formula. IRAC doesn't work this way.

- Labeling the essay answer with the words, "issue," "rule," "application," and "conclusion." I've seen this done a variety of ways and can't decide which is more appalling. In one case, the words are written right along side the paragraphs. This must mean that I can't read for myself what is written in the paragraph and need little signposts along the way. Or maybe the words just don't make it on their own to let me know that I'm reading the issue or factual analysis. Either way, it's an insult to the reader and an abuse of the process. In other instances, the writer dispenses with such usual writing conventions as paragraphs and transition sentences and divides the answer up into IRAC sections. Once again, the writer is demonstrating rigid adherence to a convention rather than true understanding.

Note: I have heard of instances where the professor has asked students to label paragraphs and if these are your instructions, then be sure to follow them. However, this is the exception rather than the rule.

■ Treating each part of IRAC "equally" on an essay where writing one line of rule automatically equates to writing one line of analysis. IRAC is not a one-to-one relationship. That would make it a formula and it's not. Thinking about and using IRAC in this manner is what's dangerous.

As always, there is no substitute for good writing and one characteristic of good writing is that it addresses its audience and the particular task. So while IRAC is not a formula and there is no one way to write an exam answer, it's also true that there's no real way to avoid the essential IRAC elements when composing a basic legal analysis: you must apply rules to facts ("R" before "A") after you've identified the legal question at issue ("I"). That's just what lawyers do.

(1) Why it's all about the "legal question"

Your ability to find the legal question in the facts is the single most important element in the analysis because you need to know enough law to find the issue. It's not enough to master the substantive rules of law: you need to know when a particular rule is implicated by the facts. This is the critical connection: if you miss the issue, whether or not you know the rule doesn't matter – you never get to the rule if you don't see the issue.

Even after you've identified the issue, it remains a critical factor in the development of your discussion. Faithfulness to the legal question as you proceed allows you to distinguish between relevant and irrelevant facts and avoid being led astray. Further, it ensures that you'll be on the right path in your analysis, leading to an essay that connects the rules with the questions presented rather than one that rambles and follows a "kitchen sink" approach.

(2) The "rule of law"

The issue leads you to the statement of the rule needed to resolve the issue. The general "rule" to follow when writing the "rule" is to include a sufficient discussion of the law to provide an adequate context for your analysis of the facts in controversy. That's because your analysis of the facts will not make sense unless you have first identified the rule which determines the legal meaning to be attributed to those facts.

(3)   Application, not recitation

Once you've identified and explained the controlling rule, your next task is to examine the inferences and implications of each fact in light of the rule. The analysis or application is the heart of the discussion. As you write your analysis, you'll work from your articulation of the rule to guide your application of the facts. Here your statement of the rule provides a blueprint to follow for your discussion of the facts.

(4)   Conclude and continue

Finally, you're ready to offer a conclusion with respect to the issue. Typically, there is no right or wrong answer – there is only a logical analysis based on the rule and the facts which lead to a reasonable conclusion. Then you are ready to repeat the whole process for the next issue you identify where each issue and sub-issue forms the basis for a separate IRAC analysis.

While IRAC will never cover for a lack of knowledge nor substitute for an absence of analysis, you can use it as tool for organizing your thinking and your writing. Think of it as a supporting scaffold (or training wheels) to ensure that the necessary steps are followed. Once the process becomes instinctive, then the props can be discarded. But until then, you have something to rely on to guide you through the process.

(b)   How it's actually done

This is the where most books would leave you to your own devices. After describing the basics of IRAC, you'd be given some hypotheticals and told to practice the process by writing out answers. However, a vital piece in the process is still missing – that is, how to do it. It's one thing to tell you to write an answer – and quite another to show you how it's done. Sometimes, you need to be shown exactly what to do.

(1)   Writing the issue

In writing the issue, it helps to think of it as the first question in a series of questions you'll need to consider. Typically, the answer to one question depends on the answer to another, and most likely, still another. Consequently, when you write "the issue," you are simply starting the chain of associations that you'll develop in the course of your analysis.

For example,
*"Whether the contract is enforceable **depends on whether** it falls within the Statute of Frauds when performance cannot be completed until September."*

From this statement, it's pretty clear that the question of the contract's enforceability depends on whether a writing will be required to satisfy the

Statute of Frauds which in turn raises the question whether the contract falls within the one-year rule.

- It's also helpful to use the "whether, when" construction to lead you to connect the legal question with the specific facts in controversy.

> *"Whether the contract falls within the Statute of Frauds when Ben's employment was to commence seven weeks after the making of the contract."*

> *"Whether Sam violated his fiduciary duty to the partnership when he purchased the property for his own use."*

This method of building the issue relies heavily on the specific facts you will work with to analyze the problem. It doesn't state all the facts, but isolates the key ones and provides a path for you to follow.

Once again, some professors might not want to see this language – "the issue is whether" or any such blatant issue-type language. You can achieve the same result with other words – consider using "Did" or "Can." In any case, don't get fixated on language. Follow your individual professor's instruction and realize that either way, you achieve the same result: identification of the legal problem.

Still, you can always use the following language to guide your thought process and then strip away the words when you write.

Begin with,

> *"The issue is whether,"*

identify and state the legal conclusion you want the court to reach,

> Don *committed a battery,* (or an *offer was made,* or the *court can assert personal jurisdiction*)

then connect to the "relevant" facts (the relevant facts being those facts which will determine the outcome),

> *when* he pushed Pam even though he knew she was in no danger of being hit by the bicyclist (or *when he said,* "would you buy my watch for $500 in cash on next Tuesday?" or *when* the defendant conducted business in the forum state, had an office and a full-time staff, and paid state taxes.)

When you use either of these two approaches to formulate a working issue, you avoid overly general issue statements. Remember: an issue is rarely if ever such a general statement as:

> *"The issue is whether there was a contract."*

Instead, look to identify the underlying facts which make it questionable whether a contract was formed:

> *"The issue is whether a contract was formed **when** the acceptance stated additional terms."*

Or

> *"The issue is whether the buyer can enforce its requirements contract with the seller **when** the buyer doubled its requirements after two months."*

Having identified the question in controversy, you're ready to move on to the rule of law.

(2) Stating the rule of law

Your discussion of the applicable law is an essential part of your exam answer: it lets your professor know that you have identified the legal problem (in many cases you can avoid or compensate for an incomplete issue statement if you go directly to the relevant rule) and it shows that you know the law. While your job on an exam is not to regurgitate the rules or provide lengthy treatises, you are supposed to discuss the relevant rules in a manner sufficient to analyze the problem and to do so in a concise and coherent manner.

For the purposes of instruction, I've separated the "rule" section from the "analysis" section of the essay – although the preference and your goal is to weave together discussion of rule and fact. This allows for greater efficiency in exam writing since you're combining analysis of the rule with the facts as opposed to dividing these tasks. Not only is it more efficient, but it produces a smoother writing style. Still, it may be easier (and safer) to keep them separate until you achieve the level of mental and written fluency where you can blend rule and fact analysis effectively and transition between thoughts without loss of either substance or reader.

Writing the rule consists of two parts: first, writing enough of the rule, and second, writing the rule in a logical order.

- Write enough rule

By now I know that you're asking yourself:

> *What is enough rule?*
> *How do I know how much rule to write?*
> *Isn't there such a thing as too much rule?*

The general rule about writing the rule is to write enough law to provide the context in which you will analyze the facts. The rule and the facts are inextricably linked. Your analysis of the facts will not make sense unless you have first identified the rule which determines the relevance of those facts. You must use the facts of the problem to guide your discussion of the law.

For example, if your issue is whether the parties intended to form a partnership when there was no written agreement, then a sentence such as,

"A partnership is defined as an association of two or more persons to carry on as co-owners a business for profit."

is insufficient as your entire statement of the rule of law. What's missing are the factors or criteria needed to evaluate intent and conduct. You need to prepare a foundation on which to base an argument as to why the parties' conduct either did or did not evidence the intent to form a partnership. Without identifying the relevant criteria, you have nothing to guide your analysis. You have no basis on which to offer a judgment. You would have to add something like the following,

"A partnership may be based upon evidence of an agreement between parties, either express or implied, to place their money, effects, labor, and skill in business with the understanding that profits will be shared."

Now you have identified objective factors you can use to assess the parties' conduct. First, you've indicated that intent may be express as well as implied, thereby establishing that a partnership may be found absent a writing. Second, by setting forth such concrete factors as money, labor, and skill, you have a basis against which to measure the facts you're given in the hypothetical. Finally, you've identified the importance that the sharing of profits plays in a partnership. By providing tangible indicia of partnership, you've set up a context in which your evaluation of the facts will have legal significance.

Another example of an incomplete statement of the rule might read something like this:

"A battery occurs when there is the intent to cause a harmful or offensive bodily contact or touching" (use the precise language your professor used in class – it will vary).

A discussion of the legal meaning of intent is completely missing from this statement. As you know, the concept of intent is critical when analyzing any of the intentional torts. Also absent is an adequate explanation of what constitutes a "harmful or offensive" touching. You can imagine the professor looking through the exam booklet and wondering where something like the following statement of the rule was to be found:

"A battery occurs when there is the intent to cause a harmful or offensive bodily contact or touching. To show intent, one must prove either that the defendant desired to bring about the wrongful physical contact with the person of another or that the defendant acted with purpose or knowledge to a "substantial certainty" that a contact would result or there is transferred intent from another intentional tort. A harmful contact is one that causes pain or bodily injury. An offensive contact is one that is offensive or damaging to a reasonable person's sense of dignity. Further, the plaintiff need not have actual awareness of the contact, which may be direct or indirect, at the time it occurs in order for a battery to result."

After reading this paragraph, you should see that the first sentence – "a battery occurs when there is the intentional infliction of a harmful or offensive bodily contact" – would be but the first sentence in your rule statement. No doubt it is a very important sentence because it forms the foundation from which you build the rule of law: it just couldn't be the only sentence.

Consider the following guidelines for building a rule statement:

1. Note your immediate response after you've completed reading the entire hypothetical. Typically, it will be the specific rule, element, or exception to the general rule needed to answer the question in controversy.

   For example, when you read a question in the context of a sales hypothetical that asks:

   "Whether Buyer can cover when Seller tells him that he 'might not be able to perform' a week before the scheduled performance is due."

   there is a very strong likelihood that you will immediately form an answer in your head that concludes something like this:

   "No, Buyer does not have the right to treat Seller's words as an anticipatory repudiation and go into the market and purchase substitute goods because the words were equivocal and just expressed doubt. This was not an anticipatory repudiation."

   With this response, you've identified the basic principle you need to analyze the legal question. But that's all you've done and you'll need more. A reference to the relevant rule is just a starting point.

2. Write "anticipatory repudiation" in your rule outline. It's the first block in building the rule of law.

3. Now consider the following building blocks for constructing a solid statement of the relevant rule:

(a)   Elements:

Even if you've identified a specific element of a rule as the one in controversy in your problem, you still need to include a general statement identifying all of the elements.

For example, suppose your issue is whether a party's possession of property was uninterrupted for the statutory period to satisfy a claim in adverse possession. While the heart of your analysis will be this question of continuous possession, you will preface your analysis with a general statement identifying the basic elements required for a cause of action in adverse possession: actual and exclusive possession, hostile to the true owner, notorious and open, and uninterrupted for the statutory period. Then you will focus on the element or elements in controversy. The point is that even though only one or two of the elements may be in dispute, you need to identify all of them to provide context. (While you will also need to offer a brief statement as to why they are not in dispute, this part will be addressed in the analysis section.)

(b)   Definitions:

You can build on a general statement of law by writing a definition for each of the legal terms of art you've identified. A basic definition can be written in a sentence or two. What you must do is avoid going beyond the scope of the question and writing a treatise on rules not in controversy. Let the facts of the problem be your guide.

Consider the earlier anticipatory repudiation example. Here you would need to define the principle with something like this,

> *"If either party to an executory bilateral contract, in advance of the time set for performance, repudiates the contract by words manifesting her apparent intent not to render the performance she had promised, the other party may treat such anticipatory repudiation as a present, material breach of contract and bring an immediate action for the entire value of the promised performance."*

This is an excellent starting point but wholly inadequate for a thorough evaluation of the relevant language. To analyze whether the words "he might not be able to perform" rise to the level of an anticipatory repudiation, you would have to define the type of language that qualifies by explaining what would be sufficient to "manifest [an] apparent intent not to perform." For example, you would need to add to your earlier definition that

> *"An express repudiation requires a clear, positive, and unequivocal refusal to perform."*

Now you have a standard against which to judge – clear, positive, and unequivocal.

(c) Exceptions to the general rule:

If, on the other hand, you've identified an exception to a general rule as the critical factor for your analysis, then go back and identify the general rule. You want to begin your discussion with a statement of the general rule before turning to the specific exception brought into controversy by the facts of the problem. A statement of the general rule provides the much-needed context for understanding the exception.

Exceptions to the rule are the stuff of which law school exams are made. In fact, you can pretty much count on your exam questions to force you to deal with exceptions because that's where the problems typically arise in the real world. If everything were clear and could be answered by reference to a "general rule," there would be little need for attorneys!

(d) Distinctions:

Often you will have a problem where the state law differs from the federal rule and common law from the statutory law. It's often appropriate to note such distinctions to show your understanding of how application of one rule as opposed to the other yields a different result.

To illustrate, consider the common law's "mirror image rule" and the Uniform Commercial Code. Under the common law, an acceptance must conform to the precise terms of the offer. Any variation is deemed a counter-offer and terminates the offeree's power of acceptance. On the other hand, an acceptance may be found even if it "states terms additional to or different from those offered" when it involves a sale of goods.

■ Write the rule in its logical order

There is a "natural" order to writing the rule which is based on a hierarchy of concepts. This means that when you draft the rule statement, you work from the general to the specific. Your analysis should begin with a statement of the general rule and then move to the exception, not vice versa. The general rule provides a context for understanding and appreciating the role of the exception.

For example, suppose your problem requires you to evaluate a challenge to a federal expenditure brought by a taxpayer and the question turns on whether the taxpayer has standing. Since the general rule is that a federal taxpayer lacks standing to raise a constitutional challenge to federal expenditures, then surely you are dealing with one of the exceptions. Consequently, before you identify the exception and evaluate its merits, you must preface the discussion with a statement of the general rule.

- Define each legal term of art

   When your statement of the rule contains a legal term of art, your next sentence should be a definition of that term. This is one of the easiest ways to go about building a complete statement of the rule in a logical and methodical manner. The sentences flow almost effortlessly because one statement leads naturally to the next.

   Assume that you have the following issue to address:

   > "Whether Sam has incurred liability for the contract with Mr. Greene depends on whether an agency relationship can be found between the parties."

   We begin with a basic definition of "agent" and follow through with definitions related to the concept of authority. Identification of one term leads smoothly to discussion of the next. Note that the legal terms of art are in bold-face type.

*"An agent is one who consents to act in a fiduciary relation on behalf of another, the principal, and is subject to the principal's control. An agent can act with either **actual** or **apparent authority**. **Actual authority** is the authority to act in a given way on a principal's behalf if the principal's words or conduct would lead a reasonable person in the agent's position to believe that the principal had authorized him to act. There are **two types of actual authority**: implied authority, which comes in conformity either with law or the general business customs of a particular trade, and **express authority**, which is the power that the principal has conferred directly upon the agent. **Apparent authority**, on the other hand, is an agent's authority to act in a given way on a principal's behalf in relation to a third party if the words or conduct of the principal would lead a reasonable person in the third party's position to believe that the principal had authorized the agent to so act."*

   While other terms of art are implicated in the basic definition of "agent" – most notably "fiduciary relation" – it is important to address one concept at a time and develop it fully before moving on the next.

- Use precise language

The language of the law is precise and your use of it must be equally precise. You must use the language of the court or the words of the statute and you may not substitute your own.

Suppose your exam question requires that you evaluate a state's basis for jurisdiction over a nonresident defendant and your discussion centers on an evaluation of the defendant's "minimum contacts" with the forum state. In the course of your discussion, you'll use such specific language as "volitional and beneficial," "continuous and systematic," and "fair play and substantial justice." This language comes from Supreme Court cases and it's "the law." You're expected and required to use it – just as it is. Paraphrasing is not acceptable so you just have to learn it.

(3)   Application = Rule + Fact

The analysis or application portion of your essay is the heart of the discussion. Here your job is to examine the legal significance of each fact in light of the rule of law. The difficulty for most students lies in distinguishing between reciting the facts and analyzing them. Just stating the facts, even if they are the facts relevant and material to the point you are trying to make, does not equate to analysis. The professor won't give you credit for merely restating the facts in the problem – after all, she knows the facts quite well since she wrote them!

How you set up the rule now drives the structure of the analysis. Your statement of the rule provides a blueprint to follow for your discussion of the facts. Work from your articulation of the rule to guide your application of the facts. Match up each element/factor you've identified in the rule with a fact, using the word "because" to make the connection between rule and fact. This ensures that you write facts "plus" the significance of those facts.

Think of writing the application portion of your analysis in terms of a formula:

Application = Rule + Fact, where "+" is "because"
(A = F + R)

Consider the following examples to see how this works:

(1)   Deb's actions could be considered "procedurally unconscionable" *(rule)* ***because*** (+) she used her knowledge and position "as a well-known music agent to pressure Ann, an amateur musician," into signing the contract on the spot *(facts)*.

(2)   Ann could claim the process was "procedurally unconscionable" *(rule)* ***because*** (+) Deb "did not give Ann any time to read the 20-page, closely-typewritten document and refused to allow her to review it with an attorney" *(facts)*.

(3)   Sam the shareholder can "pierce the corporate veil" *(rule)* of Carl Corp. ***because*** (+) Carl was "the sole shareholder and freely intermingled funds, used corporate funds to pay both corporate and

personal expenses, maintained only one set of accounting books, and never held any corporate meetings" *(facts)*.

(4)   The court can determine a "reasonable price" *(rule)* **because** (+) the fair market value of the air purifier has been determined to be $7800 *(facts)*.

■ *Use signal words*

Use the word *"Here"* to introduce your analysis. It acts as a signal to the reader, letting her know that you've moved from your statements of rule to the specifics of the problem. When you get bored, you can always use *"In this case"* but there's little need to worry about boring your professor. Whatever you do to make your professor's job easier by providing clear transitions will be greatly appreciated.

■ *The importance of "because"*

Analysis is the weaving together of the rule that you've identified and the facts from the hypothetical: the word "because" is the vital link between the two. If you realize that an exam question is always asking you to explain "why," then you'll see that you must answer with "because." It's that simple.

Here's how it works: with respect to each rule you've included, ask yourself *why* you relied on that particular rule. This forces you to say *"because...."* Using this leading language will help focus your thinking and lead you to be direct in your writing. Remember, if you can articulate the "why" of the rule and connect it with "because," you're well on your way to writing an analysis and not just a series of statements.

You'll find that you can also make use of the words "as" and "since" – they serve the same function as "because."

For example, many students overlook the obvious statement,

*"This was a contract for the sales of goods **because** paper is a good,"*

but such a sentence is essential to a solid analysis because it completes the nexus between your statement that the Uniform Commercial Code governs transactions involving sales of goods and your facts which discuss the sale and delivery of paper.

Consider the following examples of how "because" works to change recitation to application:

What not to write:

While Pete the police officer was giving Dan a sobriety test, he noticed that Dan fit the description of an eyewitness to the robbery, giving the police officer probable cause to arrest Dan.

What you should write:

In this case, Pete the police officer realized that Dan fit the description of the suspect, providing probable cause for arrest, *because* Dan was extremely tall at 6'4", was wearing a green and tan sweater with purple patches and pointy-toed alligator cowboy boots, fitting the description provided by the eyewitness to the robbery.

What not to write:

ABC Inc. engaged Dr. Jones to develop a drug that reduced hair loss. Dr. Jones worked in his own laboratory, hired and fired his own assistants and set their working hours as well as his own. He met with the President of ABC every Friday morning to discuss progress on the project and at this time, Dr. Jones submitted his timesheet for payment. The President paid Dr. Jones weekly.

What you should write:

Here, Dr. Jones can be considered an independent consultant for ABC Inc. *because* he completes all the research and development work in his own laboratory, in a separate facility from that of ABC, where he has direct control over the employees *because* he hired his own assistants, setting their work hours. He also exercises direct control over his own work *because* he sets his own work hours and only meets with ABC once a week. Further, *since* he only meets with the President of ABC on a weekly basis to discuss progress on development of the hair loss product, the President does not supervise Dr. Jones on a daily basis as to the work which goes on in the laboratory.

■ *Address the ambiguities*

A hallmark of a solid analysis is one that identifies and addresses the ambiguities in the facts. That's the essence of analysis – seeing the possible ways to interpret a fact scenario and then explaining the consequences which flow from each interpretation. What this means is that your job is to look closely at the facts and to look at them from all possible angles. Typically, there is more than one way to look at anything – and you can be certain of that on a law school exam.

For example, suppose the facts on your Criminal Law final indicate the following:

> *"It was 5:00 p.m. when Dylan smashed a window and entered the house, using a flashlight to find the light switch in the dark."*

you need to address whether this was a nighttime event. It was only 5:00 pm but because you are told Dylan needed a flashlight to find the light switch in the dark, you may have a basis to infer that it was already "night."

■ *Articulate the arguments*

A thorough analysis requires that you present and evaluate counter-arguments – which is usually referred to as "arguing both sides." The ability to see the ambiguities in the facts is critical for seeing both sides of an argument. And that's just what you must do in this part of your essay – set forth the arguments. There are a couple of ways to do this and the choice is yours. In each case, you'll achieve the same result but the approach will be different.

When we talk about learning to see both sides of an argument, we're talking about the very essence of legal analysis. So it's important – actually, it's essential – that you develop and communicate this skill. It's not easy learning to see and argue both sides, but there are steps you can follow to help you find all the arguments you're supposed to find, both on the exam and in practice. *You can train yourself to see the possibilities in the facts.*

HOW TO FIND THE COUNTER-ARGUMENTS:

The first step is to focus your thinking. The next step is to decide what to focus on. You can work with either the rules or the parties as your organizing principle.

Let's work with the following problem dealing with the contract principle of frustration of purpose as our example.

George made an agreement with Oscar Mayer for $5000 to dress up like a hot dog and ride a scooter in Macy's Thanksgiving Day Parade on Thursday, November 20. He signed a contract to buy a scooter for $8000 from Brands Inc. for delivery on or about November 19. George explained that while he had always wanted a scooter so he could go riding in Central Park in the spring, he needed the scooter by November 19 because he had a contract to ride in the Thanksgiving Day Parade on November 20. George waited all day on November 19 and at 5:00 p.m. Brands called to say that the delivery would be made on November 21. As a result, George could not ride in the parade and was paid nothing by Oscar Mayer, which hired a replacement. George refused delivery on the 21st, claiming that his performance as a hot dog had been frustrated and he had no need for the scooter. Brands sued and George counterclaimed. What result?

Assume that you've identified the issue,

"Whether George's principal purpose in purchasing the scooter was frustrated when delivery was not in time for the parade"

and that you've identified the controlling rule,

"Where the bargained for performance is still possible, but the purpose or value of the contract has been totally destroyed by some supervening event, such frustration of purpose will discharge the contract. The pur-

pose that is frustrated must have been a principal purpose in making the contract. The object must be so completely the basis of the contract that without it, the transaction would make little sense."

FOCUSING ON THE RULES

Using the rules to focus your thinking allows you to consider the facts of your problem objectively. Instead of taking sides in the dispute by looking at the facts from the point of view of a particular party, you're holding them up to the light of the rule and asking whether the requirements of the rule have been satisfied or not. In short, you're working with the same set of facts but looking at them from completely opposite points of view.

Here's how it works:

(1)   Select one element, factor, or component of the rule that you've identified and explained.

(2)   Examine the facts in light of that element *(and only that element)*. Ask yourself why the requirements of that element have been satisfied by the facts. Account for each fact and consider all the possible ways of looking at how that element might have been met. *These are the "pro" arguments.*

Using our example with George and the scooter, let's consider the rule's requirement that the supervening act totally or nearly totally destroy the purpose of the contract in order to find frustration of purpose. *Our focus is to identify all the arguments why the principal purpose of the contract was to ride in the Thanksgiving Day Parade.*

Arguments why the parade was the principal purpose:

■ George purchased the scooter only after making the deal with Oscar Mayer which indicates that the deal prompted the purchase.

■ He could have bought a scooter at any time but did so only after agreeing to ride in the parade.

■ George was to earn $5000 by riding in the parade and this represented more than half the purchase price of $8000 for the scooter. Without the contract to ride in the parade, George might not have had the money or incentive to purchase the scooter.

(3)   Now consider all the possible arguments why the requirements of the element have not been satisfied. In this case, we'll consider all

the arguments why the parade was not the principal purpose for the contract. *These are the "con" arguments.*

■ Because George can still ride the scooter in Central Park in the spring, a claim he made at the time of purchase from Brands, it's very likely that riding in the parade was not his only purpose for purchasing the scooter.

■ It is arguable whether the sole purpose of the scooter was to ride in the parade since George was to earn only $5000 for dressing up like a hot dog and the scooter cost $8000. Because it cost $3000 more than he was to earn from the parade contract, it is very possible that George's purpose in purchasing the scooter was for more than just riding in the parade.

FOCUSING ON THE PARTIES

Using the parties to focus your thinking can be just as effective as the rules in helping you find the arguments. Some students prefer this style of argument, finding it easier and more like the "real thing." The point of view is from that of the party and your task is to present their theory of the case.

Just be sure to guard against the following:

■ Writing a ping-pong prose of "he said, she said" where you get lost in the volley. When you go back and forth between the parties, you run the risk of confusing yourself and the reader. You can avoid this situation by focusing on one party at a time – consider all of plaintiff's arguments before moving on to consider all of defendant's.

■ Becoming so heavily invested in one party that you fail to see the other side's point of view. It's easy enough to see only one side of the argument – especially when you're dealing with a sympathetic party. Still, you can't allow yourself to take sides because it obscures your judgment and prevents you from being objective and seeing "all sides."

CONSIDERATIONS OF PUBLIC POLICY

No discussion of legal analysis would be complete without consideration of public policy concerns. It's often appropriate to include in your discussion why a particular rule was enacted, the underlying policy, how that intent would or would not be met by its application in the particular case, its impact on the affected parties, and the larger society. You'll want to be prepared to evaluate a problem in light of such concerns.

There are no hard and fast "rules" about when to include public policy discussions, but the following guidelines should help:

(1)   *The question you are asked requires a consideration of public policy.* Sometimes an exam question will ask you to evaluate competing policy interests, recommend whether a jurisdiction should adopt a particular rule, or consider how implementation of a particular rule will affect a given population. To be responsive to the question, you must raise and address policy issues.

(2)   *Your professor has raised public policy questions in the course of class discussions.* There's no better guide to knowing what to do on an exam than following the lead of your professor. Just think about your class discussions – here your class notes should be very helpful – and note whether she emphasized any of the following when analyzing case holdings:

- The consequences which would flow if the court adopted one position over the other.

- The impact of a particular rule's adoption on a particular segment of society.

- The court's consideration of fairness or justice in reaching a particular outcome.

- The need for adherence to principles of *stare decisis* for purposes of stability and consistency in the law.

- The need for flexibility and adaptability in the law to adjust for changes in society and societal expectations.

(4)   Drawing a logical conclusion

You should offer a conclusion with respect to each issue. The conclusion need only be suggestive of a possible outcome – rarely, if ever, definitive. After all, the factfinder makes the ultimate decision, not you. But for purposes of completing your discussion of the topic, you should venture some assessment of the strengths of the arguments you've just put forth and offer a resolution.

For example, with respect to the question of whether George's principal purpose in purchasing the scooter was frustrated when delivery was not in time for the parade, you should complete your analysis of the arguments both pro and con with something like,

> *"Therefore, it is not likely that George's principal purpose in purchasing the scooter was frustrated because he had indicated another significant use for it."*

(5)   *Moving on to the next issue*

Once you've completed your analysis of one issue, you're ready to move on to the next. And it's as simple as that – begin with a new paragraph and write,

> *"The next question is whether Jerry's offer was accepted when Ben said he'd take two cartons."*

Some students find it difficult to make these transitions but it's not really difficult. You follow the structure of the rule – in the above example, the first issue was a discussion of whether an offer was made so the next logical question was whether the offer was accepted, and so forth through the formation of the contract.

In general, your analysis will follow the requirements of the rule followed by its limitations, exceptions, or defenses, according to the facts of your problem.

F.   THE SHORT ANSWER QUESTION

The short answer question is a single issue question, requiring brevity and specificity in the response. Sometimes, the professor will go so far as to limit the length of your response to a couple of sentences. While the short answer question is something of "a horse of a different color," the difference is not so much in the question as it is in the student's response to it. Herein lies the challenge, especially for students used to following a "kitchen sink" approach to exam writing. Not only is it inappropriate to "kitchen sink" this type of question, but it can and often leads to lost points – not to mention lost time.

Generally, short answer questions appear in one of two formats: the stand-alone and the sequential. The stand-alone is probably the most common and what you're most likely to encounter. It consists of a brief fact scenario followed by a narrow and specific query:

- "Did Sam commit a battery?"

- "Was the assertion of jurisdiction by the Superior Court of State X over Jones, a non-resident defendant, proper?"

- "Was the court correct in denying the defendant's motion to suppress the in-court identification?"

- "Will Dylan, a minority shareholder, be successful in a suit to force the dissolution of ABC Corporation?"

The second format is where you're presented with a series of questions based on a single, long fact scenario which can vary in length from one to two pages, or even three. Typically, the questions alter the facts of the main hypothetical and ask you to consider additional or different facts.

Whether faced with a stand-alone or sequential-type question, the approach is pretty much the same and requires the same careful attention to the call of the question.

1. ANSWERING A DIRECT QUESTION WITH A DIRECT ANSWER

The common denominator with either format is that you're asked a direct question which requires a direct answer. These questions require that you adopt a position. You can't equivocate and dance around an answer with evasive responses which rely on "what if" scenarios. Short answer questions are written to support a particular outcome and without the factual ambiguity which would otherwise make a definitive answer impossible.

A suggested approach:

a. Read the call of the question.

b. Read the fact pattern.

c. Re-read the call of the question.

d. Identify exactly what you've been asked to answer. For example, if you've been asked whether the defendant's testimony is admissible, then respond with either a "yes" or a "no" and follow it with a reasoned explanation in support.

2. BLENDING RULE AND FACT

Since the short answer question frames the "issue" by identifying the precise question to be addressed, you move immediately upon answering the question to incorporate the rule into your analysis of the facts. Essentially, your answer follows a "C,R/A" format.

Consider the example where you're asked whether the defendant's motion to suppress a handgun should be granted. After reading the problem, you decide that it should be granted because it was the result of an illegal search. Your response, depending on the precise situation raised by the facts in the hypothetical, might read something like this:

Yes, the defendant's motion should be granted. The gun was seized in violation of defendant's Fourth Amendment rights and therefore should be suppressed under the Exclusionary Rule. The police search of the locked glove compartment was conducted after the defendant had been removed from the car and handcuffed. Since the defendant had been safely removed from the vehicle, posed no danger to the officer, and the glove compartment was not within the defendant's "wingspan," the officer was required by the Fourth Amendment to obtain a search warrant signed by a neutral, detached magistrate specifying the place to be searched and the items to be seized. Since the search violated defendant's rights, the fruits of the illegal search are inadmissible.

As you can see, this answer responds directly to the question presented and follows it with a reasoned explanation, weaving together rule and fact. While blending rule and fact together is the most effective use of your time in writing exam answers for any kind of exam question, it's essential with the short answer question. Often, it's the only way to comply with space and time limitations. I would strongly suggest that you practice writing exam answers in this format until it becomes second nature.

3.   KNOWING WHEN TO STOP

Once you've answered the question, move on. Don't be tempted to add more to your answer simply because you think your answer is too short. If you've answered the question, provided legal authority, and related the law to the facts, then anything else is superfluous. It won't add points to your grade, might well result in lost points, and certainly uses up valuable time.

G. ADDITIONAL ESSAY WRITING SUGGESTIONS

1.   WRITE ON ONLY ONE SIDE OF THE PAPER.

Consider writing on only one side of the paper even if your professor has not requested that you do so. It makes for a much neater and easier exam to read. If you write on only one side of the paper in the booklet, the left side is available to add explanatory notes. Hopefully, your use of an outline will avoid the need to direct the reader to additional notes but should it become necessary, this is the least disruptive method of doing so.

2.   WRITE IN PARAGRAPH FORM.

You would be surprised how many students forget basic paragraph formation and write in a "stream of consciousness" style worthy of William Faulkner. When your essay appears as one solid mass to your professor who has upwards of 70 papers or more to read, imagine the result. Instead, make your paper easy on the eyes. Use paragraphs to show your progression of thought and the sequence of your analysis. Indent and skip a line between paragraphs. Whatever you do to make your grader's job easier, makes you the grateful beneficiary.

3. DO NOT OVERLY RELY ON UNDERLINING, CAPITALIZING, ETC.

If you emphasize everything you write, the effect is lost. You can underline "buzz words" but if you are writing in the language of the law, all you write is worthy of your professor's attention.

H. EMERGENCY MEASURES OR "WHAT TO DO IF"

1. YOU FREEZE AND BEGIN TO PANIC.

Exams make people anxious. Hopefully, you've taken every precaution outlined earlier, but for some reason you find that when you read the question, your mind goes blank. Stop whatever you're doing and breathe deeply. You want to regain your sense of control and composure immediately. Implement the following step-by-step approach:

(a) *Review the question.*

(b) *Start with what you know: identify the specific area of law and see if it provides insight.*

(c) *Focus on the basics. See if you can provide definitions. Remember, rules are really just definitions. The next step is to see if you can build on these definitions to write your paragraph of law.*

(d) *Finally, call on your inner resources and what you've been learning about the legal profession. Lawyers act; they do not react. Think deliberately and respond accordingly.*

2. YOU DON'T KNOW THE RULE OF LAW.

This is everyone's greatest fear, law student and lawyer alike. What you must do is rely on your training and instinct. Force yourself to go through the following steps:

First, ask

"What is the issue?" You can formulate this from the question you are directed to answer. Even if you're not sure of the rule, you can figure out what it is that your professor wants you to consider. Focusing on identifying the issue will allow you to regain your composure and lead you back to the structure of thinking like a lawyer.

Write the issue, whether or not you "know" the rule you need to apply. Formulating the issue will get you some points because it shows that you can identify the legal problem from the facts.

Second, ask

"What principle of law is implicated by this issue?" Now you're thinking like a lawyer.

This will either lead you to the rule from the recesses of your memory or you'll have to improvise. When you improvise, rely on your knowledge of general legal principles and standards to guide you. Use what you know about the law in general to build a specific rule for your problem.

In such cases, begin by identifying the general legal concept implicated in the problem. As appropriate, some possible questions to ask to prompt your thinking include,

- Can the court assert jurisdiction over the non-resident defendant?

- Did the homeowner owe a duty to his guest?

- Has there been a violation of a fiduciary obligation?

- Are the standards of due process /equal protection implicated?

- Has the requirement of good faith been breached?

- Are the "best interests of the child" at stake?

These questions become your starting point. As you study, you'll find more basic questions that you can rely upon to trigger your thought process. Think of them as your mental checklist.

For example, if you're asked about recoverable "damages" in a particular case, rely on what you know about "damages" in particular areas of the law and proceed from there.

- If it's a contracts problem, you know every breach of contract entitles the aggrieved party to sue for damages. The general theory of damages in contract actions is that the injured party should be placed in the same position as if the contract had been properly performed, at least so far as money can do this. Compensatory damages are designed to give the plaintiff the "benefit of his bargain."

- On the other hand, if it's a torts problem, you know that the overall goal is to compensate plaintiff for unreasonable harm which he or she has sustained and also to punish the tortfeasor.

And finally, even if you can't find the issue or principle of law, you can break down the problem into the elements common to every case and proceed from there:

- Identify the parties and the nature of their relationship. Is it that of employer/employee, landlord/tenant, buyer/seller, parent/ child, husband/wife ?

- Identify the place(s) where the facts arose. Did the events occur in a public area, a private home, a school, a waterway, a farm?

- Identify whether objects or things were involved. Was there a transaction involving the sale of goods? Is the ownership of land or chattel in dispute?

- Identify the acts or omissions which form the basis of the action. Was there a robbery, an assault, an act of discrimination?

- Determine whether there is a defense to the action.

- Is there a basis for self-defense, justification, privilege?

- Characterize the relief sought. Are the parties seeking damages? Are they monetary or equitable damages, or both?

These questions allow you to gain access to the problem when your initial read is fruitless. From any one of these topics, it's a short step to finding the principle of law implicated in the question. It might be a very good idea to memorize these topics and have them readily available to "jump-start" your thought process.

I. SOME FINAL CONSIDERATIONS

1. DEALING WITH NOT SO INNOCENT "OPINION" QUESTIONS

This topic doesn't fit neatly into any particular category because it's not so much about the structure of the essay but its substance. I'm referring to the type of question where your professor asks you to reflect on a case or topic covered in the course. What's often overlooked is that even though you're asked for an "opinion," it's necessary to ground that opinion in legal principle.

For example, suppose you're asked to comment on a criminal law question where the defendant faces the death penalty. The question could be phrased in any number of ways but your task is most likely to evaluate the legality of the death penalty and not just the situation raised by the particular facts. Of course you must read the question carefully and address only what is asked of you, but you can be certain that your professor is looking for an answer that incorporates a solid understanding of the constitutional issues raised by a death penalty sentence.

Finally, there is no one-size-fits-all approach to opinion questions. Your best approach is to read the question carefully and seek to identify the underlying issues. Then you can provide a thorough explication of the policy considerations in support of your "opinion."

2. THE MOST COMMON MISTAKES

No chapter on exam writing would be complete without some advice on "what not to do." However, since the chapters on An Exam Make-Over and Forensic IRAC provide extensive coverage of these topics, I suggest that you turn to these chapters for advice on avoiding typical exam-writing mistakes. I've included the common errors such as stating the rule without applying it, repeating the facts without using them, making conclusory statements, and failing to identify and consider competing arguments, among others. Each topic is complete with examples (many student-written) so it's well worth reading these chapters before taking exams and not waiting until after.

J. OPEN-BOOK EXAMS

The open-book exam is something of a mixed blessing: the need for pure memorization is eliminated because you can bring materials into the exam but you can lose valuable time searching through them if you're not well organized. Your best bet is to learn the law as if you were taking a closed-book exam. Then you can think of the materials you bring into the exam as a security blanket and not a life preserver.

In taking the exam, proceed exactly as we've outlined earlier but consider the following as well:

- Cite to specific statutory provisions in your rule analysis if you're allowed to use your statute book. Your professor will set a heightened standard when you have the materials readily available to you and will expect to see specific references.

- Include case references to support your arguments if appropriate. Case names are an effective short hand for conveying your knowledge when on point.

- Get the rules right. If you're allowed to bring your outline or statutes or casebook in with you to the exam, then you'd better make sure that all statements of the rule are complete and correct.

- Do not copy long passages of text from the casebook or statutes into your exam booklet.

K. TAKE-HOME EXAMS

The take-home exam elicits mixed reviews from students. There are valid arguments on both sides. However, since your professor decides whether you'll have one or not, there's no point in debating the issue. Instead, concentrate on the following when you take one:

1. TIME CONSIDERATIONS

Although the clock isn't ticking in quite the same way with a take-home exam, you still have time restraints and must work efficiently and productively. After allocating your time as suggested in the previous chapter, follow the guidelines in this chapter for reading the questions, outlining your answer, and writing your response. They represent the most effective use of your time, no matter what the test environment.

Don't procrastinate and leave the exam until the last minute, thinking that if it's a take-home, it will be easier. That's not true and as the next section explains, professor expectations are typically higher with a take-home exam. You'll need all the time that's been allocated to do a thorough job.

Finally, save your files as your work and do not leave printing out your exam until the last minute. If something can go wrong with a printer, it will. Also, do not switch computers and printers between home and school. Settings are different and you're likely to give yourself formatting problems. When you've completed your work, back it up, print out two copies, and turn it in.

2. MEET PROFESSOR EXPECTATIONS

With a take-home exam, it's only natural for your professor to have heightened performance expectations. There's no excuse for turning in a disorganized and carelessly written exam. Generally, professors give take-home exams to provide you with the opportunity for a more thoughtful and thorough analysis and therefore the burden on you is greater to provide one.

Expectations run higher in other areas as well so make sure you account for the following:

- Write an organized exam. While your professor is willing to overlook the usual forms of disorganization that occur in the heat of the typical exam, there's a lot less forgiveness with a take-home exam. Here you're expected to turn in a polished and organized response.

- Adhere to page limits and formats. There's no better way to "turn off" your reader than by exceeding the page limit or handing in a handwritten paper when typing is required.

■ Proofread for spelling, punctuation, and grammatical errors. Since you're given the extra time, the extra effort required to check your work is expected. Don't skip this vital step because it shows a sloppiness and carelessness that will be reflected in your grade.

3. COMMON ERRORS

(a) Copying rules verbatim

One common mistake students make on take-home as well as open-book exams is to copy rules right out of statute books, restatements, or cases, directly into their exam books. Nothing could be a greater waste of time or effort – especially on these kinds of exams where it's a given that you'll get the rule right. The emphasis is on your analysis and insightful probe of the facts, not your ability to copy.

(b) Overwriting

The other well-known danger with a take-home exam is the propensity to overwrite. There's never a need to make a point more than once and there's certainly no need to do it here just because you have more time. Fight the tendency toward wordiness and repetitiveness by editing your work carefully and adhering to the exam's page limits. Your task is not to write a treatise but to answer the question that is asked of you. While this is true of all exams, you need to keep it in focus at all times when answering a take-home exam because there's more time for your mind to stray.

L. ESSAY WRITING CHECKLIST

I. ALLOCATING YOUR TIME

1. Do you have your watch in plain view?

2. Did you set up a timetable on your scrap paper after allocating the time for each question based on point value?

II. READING THE QUESTION

1. Did you begin by reading the call-of-the question?

2. Did you determine whether it's a general or specific style essay?

3. Did you skim through to get a sense of the problem?

4. On your second read, did you read "actively"?

    a) Have you identified the area of law and the legal relationship between the parties?

    b) Have you circled amounts of money, dates, locations, quantities, and ages?

CHAPTER 7 | TAKING THE EXAM

    c)   Have you noted the words "oral" and "written"?

    d)   Are you perfectly clear about who is doing what to whom?

III. OUTLINING YOUR ANSWER

1.   Have you set up a mini-outline by identifying the rules you need to discuss based on the issues raised in the problem?

2.   Have you compiled the building blocks for the rule of law by considering,

    a)   elements?

    b)   definitions?

    c)   exceptions to the general rule?

    d)   distinctions ?

3.   Have you followed a hierarchy of concepts by,

    a)   moving from the general to the specific?

    b)   defining each legal term of art?

IV. WRITING THE ESSAY

1.   Does your statement of each issue include the word *"when"* to ensure that you include the relevant facts?

2.   Does your statement of the rule identify the controlling law: common law, federal rule, state-specific statute, etc.?

3.   Did you use *"Here"* or *"In this case"* to introduce your application?

4.   Did you use *"because"* to make the connection between rule and fact?

5.   Did you match a "fact" with each "element" or "definition" in your rule of law?

6.   Did you address the ambiguities in the facts?

7.   Did you articulate the arguments and counter-arguments?

8.   Did you consider questions of public policy?

9.   Have you answered the question you were asked?

10.   Did you draw a logical conclusion before moving on to the next issue?

M. MULTIPLE-CHOICE QUESTIONS

1. ABOUT MULTIPLE-CHOICE EXAMS

By the time you get to law school, you're pretty familiar with the structure of multiple choice questions: there's a short story or fact pattern, a question, and a set of answer choices. A common variation is when several questions are based on one story but each question adds a few new facts. In general, you've seen multiple choice questions like this throughout your educational career and certainly when you sat for the LSAT.

Having said all this, you can forget most of what you know because the legal version is different from what you've experienced in the past. The questions may look the same, but that's pretty much where they part company. Law school multiple choice questions test your knowledge of the substantive law, your reading comprehension skills, and your legal reasoning skills. Even where the professor writes questions which tend to be more "subjective" than "objective," they tend to test your analytical skills and not simply the ability to memorize.

The good part, however, is that taking a multiple choice exam shouldn't be very different from one of your regular practice sessions – assuming, of course, that you've prepared according to the approach outlined in this book. In this case, you'll just allocate your time and get to work.

2. READING THE QUESTIONS

Just as we discussed the importance of "active" reading for essay fact patterns, you'll do the same for multiple choice questions. Because of time constraints, it's likely you'll have time for only one reading of the fact pattern so you'll want to make it count.

(a) Read "actively"
Active reading for multiple choice questions is pretty similar to active reading for essay questions. You'll focus on the same information and circle the appropriate words or numbers so that you can find them again easily.

- Identify legal relationships because they indicate legal obligations: landlord/tenant, employer/employee, buyer/seller.

- Amounts of money, dates, quantities, and ages.

- Words such as "oral" and "written," "reasonable" and "unreasonable."

- Words that indicate the actor's state of mind such as "intended," "decided," "mistakenly thought," and "deliberately." These are critical in criminal and torts questions.

(b)   Never assume facts

Your professor has carefully crafted the problem to contain all the facts you need to answer the question. While you're often required to draw reasonable inferences from the facts, you can't create your own. The ability to read carefully and rely only with the facts presented and the reasonable inferences which can be drawn from them is a critical legal skill and one your professor seeks to test.

In addition to keeping to the facts in the problem, resist the tendency to go off on tangents. When you read a fact pattern, you may see any number of possible causes of action. However, you must refrain from moving forward on your own and formulating responses based on what you "think" might be asked. This is one of the very reasons you read the question stem before you read the fact pattern – to keep you from going astray.

(c)   Identify the issue

In most cases, a law school multiple choice question is a mini-IRAC and works the same way: you must frame the issue to answer the question. If you fail to identify the issue, then all the facts in the problem seem relevant and you have no means by which to identify the correct answer choice.

(d)   Pay attention to your professor's particular use of language

The typical law school multiple choice question is written by your professor. This means that however "objective" your professor tries to be in writing the question, it's certain to reflect her voice and how she presented the material in class. This is an important consideration when reading the question and choosing between answer choices. Once again, it shows how important it is to attend class, listen carefully to every word, and take accurate notes. I cannot tell you how often these words find their way back to you in the form of an exam question.

3.   APPROACHES FOR ANALYZING THE QUESTIONS

(a)   When it's **not** an IRAC-based question

Not every multiple choice question is of the analytical variety. Sometimes the question is pretty straightforward and you either know the answer or you don't. If you have one of these questions, you'll eliminate the issue-formation steps. Here what counts are your reading comprehension skills, your substantive knowledge base, and what was discussed in class. Consider the following example (reprinted with permission from Professor Rodger Citron):

Which of the following statements about *Mullane v. Central Hanover Bank & Trust Co.* is not correct?

(A) The Supreme Court permitted notice by publication with respect to the beneficiaries whose interests or addresses could not be determined.

(B) The property at issue was a common trust fund.

(C) The Supreme Court required personal service via hand delivery to in-state residents with known addresses.

(D) Whether notice was sufficient raised a constitutional question of due process.

The correct answer choice is (C). You either read the case and knew the answer or you didn't. There's no "reasoning" your way through this one.

(b)   When it is an IRAC-based question

The following are the four basic steps for answering these questions. You will:

- Read actively from the call-of-the-question or "stem" and then to the fact pattern

- Find the issue in the fact pattern

- Move from the issue to articulation of your own answer

- Translate your "answer" to fit an available "answer choice"

(1)   Read from the "bottom up"

Begin by reading the call-of-the-question. Reading the question stem first lets you narrow your focus when you read the fact pattern. For example, if you know you're task is to "identify Dan's best defense" or "decide whether Vic is guilty of manslaughter," then you will read the fact pattern with an eye toward this goal.

(2)   Find the issue

Your ability to identify the main issue in each question is crucial to selecting the correct answer choice. Most questions are organized around a central issue in the fact pattern and individual issues in each of the responses. The only way to distinguish between the answer choices is to identify the legal question raised in the fact pattern.

The process is the same you use to spot issues in essay questions. After you read the call-of-the-question ask, *"What is the legal theory behind this question?* As soon as you've identified the legal theory, you're in a position to articulate the rule of law that addresses that issue.

Consider the following Multi-state Bar Exam ("MBE") question. It's one of the questions released by the National Conference of Bar Examiners (2006 Information Booklet question 25). Some professors like to create questions similar to these because they require a high level of analysis and thoughtful application of the rule.

> *Pedestrian sued Driver for personal injuries sustained when Driver's car hit Pedestrian. Immediately after the accident, Driver got out of his car, raced over to Pedestrian, and said, "Don't worry, I'll pay your hospital bill."*

Pedestrian's testimony concerning Driver's statement is

(A) admissible, because it is an admission of liability by a party-opponent.

(B) admissible, because it is within the excited utterance exception to the hearsay rule.

(C) inadmissible to prove liability, because it is an offer to pay medical expenses.

(D) inadmissible, provided that Driver kept his promise to pay Pedestrian's medical expenses.

In this question, once you've identified the issue in the fact pattern, the correct answer will practically pick you. But you must be very specific and narrow in your articulation of the issue in order to differentiate between the answer choices. Here the issue is whether an offer to pay medical expenses is admissible. Once you articulate this issue, and summon the rule – under the Federal Rules of Evidence, evidence of offering to pay medical or hospital expenses is not admissible to prove liability for the injury – it's a quick move to the correct answer choice, which is Choice (C).

(3) *Move from the issue to articulation of the answer*

After you've identified the issue raised in the facts, apply the rule of law to the facts, and reach a conclusion – all without so much as a peek at the answer choices. By determining the appropriate outcome before looking at the answer choices, you're in control and not at the mercy of the professor's distractors.

However, this approach is not practical when you have the type of question where the answer choices provide additional information which must be individually evaluated. This happens where you're asked a question such as

"Which of the following questions will NOT present a substantial issue in Plaintiff's claim for damages"

as opposed to

"Will Dan prevail?"

In the first example, you must consider the merits of each individual answer choice before you can make a decision.

(4)   Fill the gap from "answer" to "answer choice"
After you've decided what the answer should be, you're ready to look at the answer choices. Don't expect the answer to be phrased in the words you're looking for – they won't be there. Instead, you'll have to "fill the gap" between your words and the words chosen to express the answer. Sometimes it's a matter of determining which of the answer choices leads to the same result.

4.   APPROACHES FOR ANALYZING THE ANSWERS

(a)   Identify the issue in each answer choice
Frequently, there's an issue or legal theory operating in each of the answer choices as well as the fact pattern. In this case, you must figure out each theory or you won't be able to distinguish between the answer choices. Only the issue that addresses and answers the one presented in the fact patten can be the correct answer choice.

(b)   If necessary, use "the process of elimination"
Sometimes, despite all your best efforts to work through a question, you find that the only way to arrive at an answer choice is through the process of elimination. In these cases, examine each of the answer choices and eliminate those that can't possibly be correct. Consider the following approaches for eliminating incorrect answer choices.

(1)   When an answer choice is not completely correct, it's incorrect.
The most basic rule for eliminating incorrect answer choices is that an answer choice must be entirely correct or it's wrong. For example, suppose an answer choice recites a correct statement of the rule of law but its application to the facts in the problem is flawed. Or vice versa: perhaps the answer choice is factually correct but cites an inapplicable rule. In each case, the answer choice is incorrect and can be eliminated. Don't allow yourself to be misled simply because the statement is partially correct.

(2)   When it misstates or misapplies a rule of law.
Here's where solid preparation on learning the black letter law is essen-

tial. You need to know the law to distinguish between answer choices that misstate or misapply the law.

Some common examples include the following:

- Answer choices that improperly identify the requisite elements of a crime or tort by either overstating or understating the necessary elements.

- Answer choices that rely on inapplicable principles of law.

For example, if you're working with a problem dealing with the sale of goods, then you must apply Article 2 of the Uniform Commercial Code. If you apply the common law, it's likely you'll be led astray and choose the incorrect answer choice. You can be sure one of the answer choices will present the common law approach.

This is by no means limited to contracts. Look for similar situations to arise. Evidence questions are another good example. Here the potential conflict is between the Federal Rules of Evidence, the common law, and the rules of your particular jurisdiction. This means that you must be alert, read carefully, and apply the appropriate rule to arrive at the correct answer choice.

- Answer choices that rely on the minority rule instead of the majority rule.

Generally, the rule to be applied is the majority rule. Unless the directions or your professor has indicated otherwise, you should apply the majority and not the minority rule.

(3)   *When the answer choice mischaracterizes the facts.*
Once again, active reading skills will go far in detecting this type of error. Look for contradictions between the facts in the story and the facts as characterized in the answer choice. Such an answer choice cannot be correct. Nor can an answer choice that requires you to make assumptions that go beyond the facts in the fact pattern. While it's often necessary to make reasonable inferences, you should never have to add facts to arrive at the correct answer choice. If your professor wants you to consider additional or different facts, they'll be provided.

(c)   Watch out for "because," "if," and "unless"
You have no idea how a single word can so muddy the waters. You'd think it would be enough to have four or sometimes five answer choices to test your

ability to work through a problem without resorting to further modification of the text of each alternative. But some professors are experts at getting the most out of a question. With a single, well-placed word such as "because," "if," or "unless," they're able to transform the entire meaning of a sentence.

While doable, dealing with "because," "if," and "unless" takes a bit of practice. It also takes active and careful reading. A "modifier" – whether it's "because," "if," "unless," or some equivalent – is used in the answer choice to connect the "conclusion" (the outcome to the interrogatory) with the "reasoning" in support of that conclusion. For example, an answer choice might state,

> *"Yes, because Dan was a third-party beneficiary of the original Smith-Jones agreement."*

Here, "yes" is the "conclusion" or direct answer to the question asked; "Dan was a third-party beneficiary" is the reason that supports the conclusion; and "because" is the link between the two.

(1) Working with "because"

The following is a typical "because" answer choice:

> *"Succeed, because Ben had promised her that the offer would remain open until May 15."*

Such "because" statements are relatively straightforward. Simply ensure that the reasoning supports the conclusion both on a factual and legal basis. If either is incorrect, then the entire answer choice is incorrect and can be eliminated.

In addition to "because," remember to look for words that act like "because" in answer choices such as "since" and "as." These words are synonyms and serve the same function as 'because." Your analysis will be the same.

(2) Working with "if"

Unlike "because," when "if" is the answer choice modifier, you need determine only whether the reasoning could support the conclusion. It need not always be true, but only possible under the facts in the hypothetical. Be alert to possible "if" synonyms: "as long as" and "so long as." Remember, "if" is a conditional word and words of condition will be the trigger in such instances.

(3) Working with "unless"

In its own way, "unless" is as restrictive as "because." For an "unless" answer choice to be correct, it must present the only circumstance under which the conclusion cannot happen. If you can conceive of even one other way the result could occur, then the answer choice cannot be correct.

(d)   If you must guess, do so with a strategy

While it sounds like an oxymoron to "guess with a strategy," it's true nonetheless. Even if you can narrow the odds only slightly, you've got a decent shot at making a correct selection.

(1)   Eliminate all the obviously incorrect answer choices.

Usually you can safely eliminate one or even two responses as incorrect. Now that you've narrowed the field a bit, even if it's a little bit, you're ready to make the most of some informed guesses.

(2)   Find your compass – the issue.

When in doubt anywhere on the exam, remember that the legal issue is your guide. It allows you to distinguish between relevant and irrelevant rules and facts, thus providing the single most effective answer choice eliminator.

Reread the question and focus solely on finding the issue in the fact pattern. Then identify the issue addressed in each of the answer choices. One should address the issue in the fact pattern.

(3)   Be skeptical of words which speak in absolutes.

Assuming that the issue is disguised or that it's not an IRAC-based question, you still need to distinguish between answer choices. In this case, consider statements that include such words as "always," "never," and "must." No doubt you've learned as a law student that there are few if any certainties in the law. For practically every rule, there is an exception – if not two or three. Use this knowledge wisely and be wary of answer choices which include words of certainty. If you can think of just one instance where it wouldn't be true, then the statement can't possibly be your best choice and you can safely eliminate it.

(4)   Finally, after you've given it your best shot, move on.

With only limited time per question, there's only so much time to allow for doubt. No matter how well you've prepared, there are bound to be questions that present difficulty. Just don't dwell on them or you'll squander precious time that could be spent on questions you can answer.

CHAPTER 8:
AN EXAM MAKE-OVER

A. GETTING A DISAPPOINTING EXAM GRADE

It's hard to be on the receiving end of a poor grade and there's nothing more frustrating than trying to figure out what went wrong. It's hard to understand and even harder to explain how hundreds of hours spent in attending classes, reading required materials, diligently writing case briefs, and preparing a course outline could possibly result in a grade of C or lower. But it can and it does, leaving you feeling bewildered, disheartened, and somewhat betrayed. So I'm not about to minimize your disappointment if you received a low grade – it really hurts – but what matters now is what you learn from the experience. It's okay to take a couple of days off (I'd prefer if it were only a couple of hours!) to console yourself but absolutely no more. We must get back to work. Only now, we work differently.

What we're going to do next won't be easy but it's essential if we're going to improve your grades. You see, it's not enough to go through the exercise of looking over the exam with your professor or comparing what you've written to a sample answer – you need to know why what you wrote on your exam didn't earn the grade you think it deserved. To do this, we need to get inside your head to see where what you were thinking departed from what you should have been thinking.

This is the course we need to follow for a couple of reasons. First, and most important, it's because when you answered the exam question, you thought you were reading and thinking about the problem correctly. Since you genuinely tried to do your best on the exam, when your grade indicates otherwise (a grade is the professor's evaluation of your thought process regarding the problem as you communicated it in writing), we need to step back inside your head to see the problem the way that you did – how you approached it, why you chose that approach, how you read the facts, and what they meant to you. It's like what you do when you realize that you've been traveling down the wrong road: you go back to where you made the wrong turn and proceed again. It's the going back and finding where the wrong turn was taken that's our job. And since what we see on paper is pretty much a "mirror image" of what's going on in your head, we can use what you've written to figure out where and why you took the wrong fork in the road.

Second, it's critical that we examine exactly what you've written to make sure that what you intended to say, and what you thought you said, is really what you wrote. Sadly, I've learned from too many of my students that there is often a disconnect between thinking and writing – between what you meant to say and what you actually wrote. Quite often, what you think you've written is either not what you wrote or it failed to convey to your reader the meaning you had in mind. What may be perfectly clear to you in your head is not always clearly expressed in what you've written. This can happen for a number of reasons but until we figure out why it happens to you, the risk remains that you'll do it again.

I'll show you how to look at what you've written with an objective eye – very much the way athletes view tapes of their performance. Coaches insist that players watch these tapes for precisely the same reasons that we'll be reviewing what you've written: to see exactly what you've done right and where you've gone wrong.

1. FINDING OUT WHAT HAPPENED ON THE EXAM

For the most part, students who come to see me can identify the problems they need to address. Very often, they provide their own "diagnosis" and are looking to me for the "cure." For example, they readily confess:

"My professor said I was sketchy on the law."

"My analysis is conclusory."

"My writing is disorganized."

"I just need to put in a little more application."

"I didn't follow the format the teacher wanted."

"I knew the law but I didn't write it right to satisfy my professor."

I can practically hear you thinking, *"okay, that's exactly what my professor said to me when I met with her to go over my exam. You're not telling me anything new."* Of course, you're right. I'm not really telling you anything different from what your professor already told you – remember, I'm a professor too and I'm pretty familiar with the kinds of errors students make in their work and how we describe them.

What I can tell you that's different is how we're going to use these comments to make changes in your thinking and your writing, and ultimately, your grades. What I can do is give you a personal "exam make-over." Everyone loves a make-over. Why not an exam make-over?

2. MEETING WITH PROFESSORS

What I am about to share with you is based on my work with students, much of it spent in meeting with them after they've met with their substantive course professors to review exams. We go over the exams again. In doing so, I've learned a lot, and not just about the types of exams that other professors like to give.

For example, I've learned that

- You believe that there's a magic formula for writing the right answer, one that works for every question and pleases every professor. You're sure that if only someone would tell you what that formula was, you'd get an "A" on every exam.

- Some of you are reluctant to let your professors know that you still don't understand where you went wrong, even after talking about it for an hour or more.

- Even after the professor has discussed the exam with you, you don't see why what you've written doesn't say what the professor said she was looking for and, in fact, you're pretty convinced that you wrote exactly what she wanted.

- Until you can see the difference between what you wrote and what you think you said when you wrote it, we won't make any progress.

Although it may sound as if I'm suggesting that you forgo meetings with your professors because you might not get all the answers you're looking for, believe me I'm not: these one-on-one opportunities are so essential to your development that I've included some guidelines for making the most of this time in Chapter 5. I strongly recommend that you review this section to prepare properly before meeting with your professor.

Reviewing your exam with your professor is essential to developing your written communication skills. If you think about it, your primary interaction with your professor thus far has been primarily oral – either you were called upon in class or you met outside of class to talk about the material. What you'll learn from your written exam will probably surprise you. For example, you might learn that you "knew the law' but failed to receive credit because your answer wasn't responsive to the professor's question. Or you might discover that your reading of the problem was so flawed that you added your own facts or misconstrued them, either of which could have led to disappointing results. Only by meeting with your teacher to go over the exam will you get a sense of how your thinking and response to the questions differed from what your professor had in mind.

So now we're pretty much back to where we started this section – you've met with your professor and you're left with criticisms of your work that you're not quite sure how to correct. Here's where this chapter can help. I can show you how to translate the seemingly general statements professors write in your blue book into specific changes in your work – the kind of changes guaranteed to improve your performance.

B. LEARNING TO ASSESS YOUR OWN WORK

It is absolutely essential to learn how to help yourself. Not only are you in the best position to assess your own learning issues, but you are the only one who knows what you know and what you don't. While it's helpful to listen to questions asked by other students both in and out of class, it's not always the question you need answered.

Sometimes, however, you may find difficulty in framing the very question you need to ask. You think, *"how can I get help when I don't even know what to ask? How can my teacher or study group partners help me when I don't know where to begin?"* It seems like a vicious cycle.

This is a very common problem, especially when you're new to the enterprise. After all, articulating a question presupposes that you have a solid enough understanding of the material to identify the part you don't understand. In short, you need to understand what it is you don't know before you can get the help you need. Unfortunately, quite a few students get stuck here and don't know how to identify problem areas with some degree of specificity. Instead, they approach the professor with such general questions as,

"I just don't get remedies."

or

"I'm okay with the act part of criminal liability but I have a problem with intent."

You can rightly imagine that you won't be getting the help you seek when you ask for an explanation of an entire subject area. More likely, you'll get a quizzical look and a response like, "what about remedies?" So once again, the ball is back in your court and you have to come up with a question that can be answered.

First, let me assure you that it's possible to get sufficient insight into what you don't understand to allow you to articulate the questions you need to ask. This requires some work on your part, but work that is well worth the effort because it puts you in control. As opposed to other places in the learning process, here we happen to be in pretty good shape because we have something concrete to work with – what you wrote on your exam and your professor's responses to it. Now you just need a way to get it to work for you by interpreting what it means.

Once again I can hear you thinking, how can she interpret what my teacher said about my work when

she hasn't read the exam question
or, better yet, *she hasn't even read what I've written!*

Of course these are legitimate concerns but need not trouble us for a couple of reasons. First, as I've already explained, students tend to make the same kinds of errors in their work so it's a pretty safe bet that I'm familiar with whatever particular mistakes you've made and can anticipate them; and second, since this is a collaborative effort, you're going to be filling in the gap between the examples and explanations I provide and your own work. You'll recognize yourself in my examples because I'm going to use actual students' work whenever possible, not my own. Here, the novice will be far more helpful than the expert because it will be easier for you to identify with what's written.

Let's get started by taking a look at a hypothetical you might have encountered on your Contracts exam. For our purposes, I've edited the problem to a single issue so that we can examine the response in detail. In contrast to the way we worked through sample exam questions in the earlier chapter on Taking the Exam, here we'll be looking back and analyzing what the writer did rather than planning ahead for what might be done on exam day. As you'll see, this involves a very different way of thinking and looking at the material.

1.   SAMPLE EXAM QUESTION ONE

Ben, a 21 year old college student, had formed his own band and wanted to become a famous rock artist. In September, while Ben's band was playing at a local club, Elaine, a well-known music agent, approached Ben and invited him to have dinner with her to discuss his career. At dinner, Elaine told Ben that he could be the next Mick Jagger, a hugely popular music and video artist. She offered to be Ben's agent and handed him a closely-written, 20 page typewritten contract. When Ben asked Elaine if he could have some time to review the contract, Elaine said that this was Ben's "golden opportunity" and that if he didn't sign the contract then and there, it would be withdrawn. Ben signed the contract immediately.

The next day, when Ben was reviewing the contract with his mother, they realized that it gave Elaine the exclusive right to represent Ben for the next ten years, as well as 60% of all of Ben's gross income from employment in the music field during that period. Shortly thereafter, Ben learned that the standard percentage for a music agent is 20% and the usual term of such a contract is three years. Ben then promptly advised Elaine that he would not comply with the terms of their contract.

Will Elaine be successful in a suit to enforce her contract with Ben?

2.   SAMPLE ANSWER ONE

No, because there was unequal bargaining power. I don't feel that a court would validate the contract due to unconscionability. Elaine knew more about such contracts than Ben did. Elaine did not let Ben properly review the contract, and it would seem he had no choice but to sign the contract then and there, since she told him that if he did not sign it, he would miss his chance. Ben could show that Elaine had the stronger bargaining position and that she used that to her advantage in dealing with a lesser party.

Clearly, Ben was the oppressed party and there was surprise in the terms. Ben was surprised upon his review of the contract the next day to find that the terms were such as they were. The terms of the contract were very one-sided, clearly favoring the agent over the musician. I feel the court will hold that unjust contract provisions are unenforceable. Unenforceable provisions are contrary to public policy and what we feel is an unfair advantage on the part of the stronger party attempting to usurp all of the benefits for themselves at the expense of the weaker party.

Elaine can argue that Ben is an adult in the eyes of the law and therefore free to contract. She can also show that Mike had legal capacity to contract and could not hold himself out to be an incompetent. Ben was a college student. I think the court will reject Elaine's arguments and deem the contract void based on aspects of unconscionability found in the contract.

3. ANALYSIS

This answer vividly illustrates the most common mistakes students tend to make in writing exams. In reading it through yourself, you might have noticed that the answer is missing any discussion of the law, relies on conclusory statements, lacks IRAC form, and strays from the relevant issue. Now let's take a close look at each of these mistakes individually.

(a) Where there's no rule of law

Like a lot of law students, this one ended up writing an exam answer without any discussion of the controlling rule of law. Now it's true that professors don't want students to provide lengthy quotes from cases or an endless regurgitation of the rules, but it's also true that they intend for you to show that you've acquired a working knowledge of the law. In this case, that means that you should have included a general statement regarding unconscionability as a basis for non-enforcement of the contract, a working definition of what it is, and then a further discussion of the two types of unconscionability – procedural and substantive. Why are both necessary, you may ask? Because the facts in the hypothetical implicate them both. Let's see what I'm talking about.

Facts for procedural unconscionability:
The following "facts" in the hypothetical indicate a need for you to discuss whether the *manner of negotiations* and the *circumstances of the parties* at the time of the agreement were so one-sided as to find a basis for procedural unconscionability.

- Elaine was a well-known music agent and Ben was a 21 year old college student.

- Ben asked to review the contract but Elaine told him it was his "golden opportunity" and he had to sign then and there.

- The contract was "20 pages" long and featured "closely-written" text.

Facts for substantive unconscionability:
Here, the following facts signal a need for you to discuss whether the terms of the agreement so favored one party as to "shock the conscience."

- Elaine had an *exclusive right* to represent Ben for *10 years* and was to receive *60%* of Ben's gross income.

as opposed to

- The *industry standard* for a music agent is *20%* for *three years.*

The "general rule" to follow when writing the "rule" is to include a sufficient discussion of the law to provide an adequate context for your analysis of the facts.

In this sample answer, there are "clues" that the student had a rule in mind – the doctrine of unconscionability – but there was no definition or explanation of what the rule required or how it would operate in this case to prevent enforcement of the parties' agreement.

How do I know that the student knew which rule was involved?
It was the student's choice of vocabulary that gave it away: the writer impliedly relied on the doctrine of procedural unconscionability by mentioning "unequal bargaining power" in the first sentence and by referring to Ben as an "oppressed party" in a subsequent sentence. But without first defining the rule of unconscionability to provide a context, these characterizations lack legal significance. Further, the writer subsequently relied on the principle of substantive unconscionability in describing the contract terms as one-sided. But once again, the writer's argument for non-enforcement fails for lack of a legal foundation.

From reading this example, you might have figured out that a major consequence of omitting the "rule" in an exam answer is a response that's long on conclusion and short on analysis. This also means that there's nothing more for us to consider under this heading: since the student neglected to discuss the rule, it's time to move on to see what happens when the "R" in IRAC is missing. Now we can see exactly what makes for conclusory statements.

(b)   Where the answer is conclusory

Typically, if your work suffers from a conclusory-style analysis, you'll just see the comment "conclusory" on your paper. But there are really two types of "conclusory" statements and both are at work in this sample answer. It's important for us to distinguish between them because each presents a different problem for the student and requires a different response.

The first kind of conclusory statement is one that states a legal conclusion. This occurs when there's an insufficient legal foundation to provide authority to support the statement. The second kind states a factual conclusion. This appears as either a restatement of the facts in the hypothetical or a judgment about what the facts mean without explaining the basis for the judgment. Typically, however, the lines between the two blur and the sentence is conclusory for one or both reasons. It doesn't really matter whether it's one or the other except to recognize why it's conclusory and to fix it.

I'm sure you're thinking that this sounds real good but what you'd really like is to see what each of these looks like. The following sentence is a good place to start

No, because there was unequal bargaining power.

First, notice that the answer begins with an emphatic "no" to the fact pattern's interrogatory. If you hadn't already figured out, it's not the conclusion you reach, but the way you get there that's of interest to your professor. It's a pretty safe bet your professor isn't looking for a "yes" or "no" response unless you're answering a short answer question. Even assuming this problem called for a direct answer, it would be unlikely you'd begin with one. Instead, you'd have to work your way through an analysis of the facts in light of the relevant rule before you could even suggest a possible outcome. But that's not what happened here. Here the student simply declared that there was "unequal bargaining power" without providing a factual basis to explain why there was an imbalance in bargaining strength between Elaine and Ben or why this would be legally relevant.

I can almost hear the student say, *"professor, if you would only read on a bit, I explained why there was no bargaining power when I wrote,"*

Elaine knew more about such contracts than Ben did.

Yes, the professor would most likely respond, it's true you said that but you didn't tell me why she had more bargaining power (translation: you should have written "Elaine knew more about such contracts than Ben did because she was a well-known music agent and Ben was only an inexperienced college student who started his own band"). Nor did you tell me why it should matter whether one party holds an upper hand in negotiations (translation: you should have included something like "a contract will be found unenforceable as unconscionable when there has been an absence of meaningful choice because of a great imbalance in the parties' relative bargaining power").

If you're beginning to get the hang of this, you'll see why the following sentence, although somewhat improved, is still conclusory

> *Elaine did not let Ben properly review the contract, and as it would seem he had no choice but to sign the contract then and there, since she told him that if he did not sign it, he would miss his chance.*

Here the problem is twofold: first, without the definition of procedural unconscionability to provide a context, there's no legal basis to conclude that Elaine denied Ben a right when she refused to allow him to review the contract and insisted that he sign immediately. And second, without using the facts to show how Elaine prevented Ben from reviewing the contract, all you have is an assertion that Elaine's behavior was improper. Using facts instead of merely reciting them can be easily remedied by writing something like this

> *Elaine did not allow Ben to review the contract properly because she insisted that he sign the 20 page document then and there at the dinner table or his "golden opportunity" would be withdrawn, even though he asked for additional time to review the lengthy document.*

Now look at the following sentence which seems a bit different because it uses legally significant language – "oppressed" and "surprised" – but it's still conclusory.

> *Clearly, Ben was the oppressed party and there was surprise in the terms.*

I could tell that the student relied upon legally relevant facts in the hypothetical to write this sentence but that doesn't change its conclusory nature. The sentence is legally conclusory because without the "rule" to tell us the significance of oppression in the contracting process and connecting that with the "facts" to show us how Ben was oppressed, we're just left with a declarative statement. There's no legal significance in describing Ben as an "oppressed" party who suffered "surprise" unless we know that procedural unconscionability concerns the manner of negotiations and the circumstances of the parties at the time of the agreement. Only then does it become relevant that denying Ben time to review the contract could be construed as an "oppressive" act by a party in a superior bargaining position. This also assumes that at some point the writer had explained how there was an imbalance in the parties' bargaining positions.

And lest I forget, it's rarely a good idea to begin a sentence with such words as word "clearly" or "obviously." Typically, the facts in your exams are so purposely ambiguous that nothing is ever "clear." Chances are if you're finding clarity, you're missing the real issue!

Now take a look at the following sentence

> *Further the terms of the contract are very one-sided, clearly favoring the agent over the musician.*

Once again, we have a conclusory sentence which is both legally and factually conclusory. First, there's no legal significance to this statement unless we know that substantive unconscionability refers to the situation where the terms of the agreement are so one-sided that they "shock the conscience." Second, this sentence is factually conclusory because we're not told how the writer came to decide that the contract terms were one-sided. We're simply told that they were. In order to reach this conclusion, the student must have compared the terms Elaine offered in the contract to those we're told were the standard in the industry. Only after finding a significant discrepancy between the two – an agent fee of 40% more than the standard for seven years longer than the usual contract period – could the contract terms be construed as "one-sided." Unfortunately, while the student must have been thinking about all of this, it wasn't articulated in the exam answer. And unless it's written for the professor to read, the poor student can't get any credit.

(c)   Recognizing the gap between what you meant and what you said

The frustrating part about this situation is that since the student apparently engaged in the right thought process, she believes that it should be apparent to the professor. This is what I referred to earlier as the gap between what you wrote and what you think you said when you wrote it. Here's a case where the student was perfectly clear in her own head what she meant when she wrote that the terms were one-sided but without expressing the basis for that statement, the reader can't possibly know for sure that this is the meaning the writer had in mind. Contrary to what you may think, professors are not mind readers.

So how should this have been written?

> *Substantive unconscionability arises when the terms of the agreement are so one-sided they "shock the conscience." One measure of substantive unconscionability is a large disparity between the contract price and the prevailing market standard. Here, Elaine charged a fee of 40% more than the standard music agent for a period of seven years longer than the usual term in such contracts. Since the contract terms were so one-sided in favor of Elaine, they could be construed as unconscionable, and therefore, unenforceable.*

I think you're beginning to see how this works. I hope you noticed that I couldn't write all that needed to be written in one sentence. It took a bit more to explain everything. All too often, students confuse being concise with being cryptic. You don't want to be overly wordy in your responses but you can't afford to leave out pertinent information either. It's a balance between the two, and as you've now seen, if you leave out the legal and factual explanations, all you have are conclusions.

(d)   Where IRAC isn't followed

Actually, I could have started our analysis of this answer with the student's basic mistake in not following the familiar "Issue, Rule, Application, Conclusion" structure of legal analysis. While using IRAC doesn't guarantee an "A" from the professor, it's extremely useful in organizing an answer. And even though it's not the only way to structure an answer, it helps to make sure that all the bases are covered. Perhaps if the student had followed IRAC, discussion of the rule of law might not have been omitted. And there's also the strong likelihood that the answer wouldn't have strayed from the relevant issue.

As I explained in an earlier chapter, IRAC is an organizing principle. It helps to organize your thinking and writing. Very often, it can lead you through the steps of a legal analysis, albeit in a mechanical way, but until the process becomes automatic for you, there's nothing wrong with having some support.

In this example, if the student had been using IRAC, the first sentence would very probably have been something like this,

> Whether Elaine can enforce the contract depends on whether it was unconscionable at the time of its making.

Now here's a direction in which to proceed. By having identified the issue of the contract's enforceability as turning on the question of whether it was unconscionable, the logical next step is to talk about that principle. This is how the rule follows the issue and makes for a logical, orderly discussion. For each issue you identify, you go through the IRAC process.

In addition to omitting discussion of the relevant rule, this student's answer digressed to a non-issue in the problem. Would careful adherence to IRAC have prevented such a departure? While I can't guarantee that you won't make mistakes in your analysis even if you follow an IRAC format, chances are you'll minimize the risk.

For example, in this question, if the student had identified the issue as one of contract unconscionability and articulated the legal standard, then we wouldn't find these sentences in the answer

> Elaine can argue that Ben is an adult in the eyes of the law and therefore free to contract. She can also show that Mike had legal capacity to contract and could not hold himself out to be an incompetent.

You might be thinking there's nothing wrong here – this is simply a counter-argument to the question of contract formation. In one sense, you'd be right. This is a counter-argument but it's based on the concept of incapacity and there are no facts to support it. If the student had been working with an issue-based analysis, then Elaine's argument in support of enforcement would have focused on why the contract terms were fair and properly presented and not that Ben was "an adult in the eyes of the law." For example, the student might have written

> Elaine might argue that her fee was not excessive in light of her knowledge and reputation in the industry even though it was 40% above the average. She might also argue that the 10 year duration of the contract was necessary for her to achieve a return on her investment in a young, inexperienced talent.

This counter-argument flows from the issue of whether the contract was unconscionable as opposed to the student's argument which suddenly introduces a new theory of incapacity. If the student had followed through with a factual analysis of the unconscionability issue, then it's unlikely an argument for incapacity would ever have been made. It just wouldn't come up while you're mulling over reasons why the terms might be considered acceptable to a court. You should be beginning to see how IRAC serves to keep you focused and organized in dealing with exam questions.

(e)   Some additional comments on "I think" and "I feel"

While we've covered the major mistakes in this student answer pretty thoroughly, I would be remiss if I didn't spend a moment or two commenting on the student's frequent use of the phrases "I think" and "I feel." Unless your professor specifically asks for your opinion on a subject, your thoughts and feelings are not appropriate on a law school essay. Nor are they appropriate in a classroom discussion. When you're called upon to respond to a question, your professor is looking for a legal response, not an emotional one.

Still, this is such a common student mistake that we shouldn't dismiss it too lightly. There must be a reason so many students make it. I would suggest that the explanation is rather simple. I bet these students are thinking, hey, I'm just a law student. What do I know about the great legal issues of the day? I'd better preface what I say with something to the effect that it's only my opinion.

Well, the extraordinary and exciting thing about law school is that it's all about your opinion – your legal opinion, that is, and from the very first day of law school we treat you like your opinion is as valuable and important as the ones you're reading in your case books. We treat you like this because it's true: as a lawyer, you'll be hired for your opinion on the law. A client will come to you and explain her situation. In turn, she'll want your legal opinion on the matter. Since that's what you're going to be doing, we commence your legal education by treating you like a lawyer from the very beginning. And we expect you to respond like one.

If you think about this for a minute, it will begin to make sense. Now you just need to know how to correct the problem. It will be easier to do in writing than in speaking. The only advice I can give you to help eliminate these words from your speech is to take your time to respond when you're called on in class. I know that it feels like an eternity when all eyes are upon you, but it's not. It's okay to take a minute to collect your thoughts, take a deep breath, and then speak. If you do, chances are very good that you'll have sufficient control to leave out the offending words.

On the other hand, when you write, you'll simply go back and edit the irrelevant language. You'll be surprised to see how nicely the words stand on their own and make a far more compelling legal statement without reliance on either "I think" or "I feel." For example, let's look at the following sentences from the sample answer

> *I don't feel that a court would validate the contract due to unconscionability.*

> *I feel the court will hold that unjust contract provisions are unenforceable.*

> *I think the court will reject Elaine's arguments and deem the contract void based on aspects of unconscionability found in the contract.*

In each case, we can easily eliminate the inappropriate words and in the process strengthen the statement

> *A court would not enforce the contract due to unconscionability.*

> *The court will hold that unjust contract provisions are unenforceable.*

> *The court will reject Elaine's arguments and deem the contract void based on aspects of unconscionability found in the contract.*

Although our editing results in a conclusion, this is acceptable if it appears in the proper place in the analysis. After all, that's the "C" in IRAC.

4.   SAMPLE EXAM QUESTION TWO

Let's consider another example. This one is quite a bit longer, involves three active parties, and multiple issues. Consequently, it presents a whole new set of challenges and a whole other set of mistakes to avoid.

Ben and Jerry were riding in Jerry's new convertible when Ben noticed some cornfields. Suddenly, he had to have fresh corn on the cob for dinner. He told Jerry to stop so he could pick some corn. Jerry said, "Look at that scarecrow. The owner of that field doesn't want the crows to get his corn and I bet he doesn't want you to get any either." Ben insisted that no one could possibly miss a few ears of corn. Jerry reluctantly parked the car on the side of the road. Ben got out of the car and entered the cornfield.

Jerry was sitting in the car when a gust of wind blew his cap off his head and into the cornfield. Jerry ran into the cornfield to retrieve his cap only to find that it had decapitated the scarecrow. Apparently, his cap had triggered a spring-gun. Thinking that it was not a good idea to hang around, Jerry turned to leave when he realized he was lost. The stalks were so tall he couldn't see where he was. Fortunately, he had a machete with him and he started hacking a path through the cornfield, knocking down the corn stalks in his way. He soon found Ben, contentedly picking up stalks of corn which had fallen to the ground. Jerry said it was time to go and the two started back to the car. Suddenly a voice rang out from behind, "Stop or I will shoot!" Ben and Jerry stopped and turned to find a farmer pointing a shotgun at them. The farmer said, "This is my property. What are you doing with my corn?" When neither Ben nor Jerry responded, the farmer shot his gun into the air. Ben dropped the corn and ran with Jerry close behind him.

Farmer Dell has sought your advice as to whether he has grounds for an action against Ben or Jerry or both. Discuss fully.

---

5. SAMPLE ANSWER TWO

The issue in this case is whether Farmer Dell has an action against Ben or Jerry or both. Trespass to chattels requires an intent to intermeddle with chattel and actual intermeddling to occur causing (a) harm to chattel or (b) dispossession for a significant period of time.

Ben told Jerry to stop the car. Ben then got out of the car, entered the cornfield and started to pick corn. Ben has the requisite intent to intermeddle with the chattel, the farmer's corn. When Ben started picking the corn, actual intermeddling occurred. Since the corn cannot then be put back on the stalk, harm to the corn occurred. Therefore, Farmer Dell can recover the cost of harm to the chattel.

Jerry did not have the requisite intent to intermeddle with the corn. Jerry was sitting in the car when a gust of wind blew his cap off his head and into the cornfield. Jerry went into the cornfield to retrieve his hat. Since he did not in fact pick any corn, Jerry did not commit a trespass to chattels. Farmer Dell has no action against Jerry for trespass to chattels but may have one for trespass to land. He'd have one against Ben too because both Ben and Jerry entered Farmer Dell's land. This is true even though Jerry only entered the cornfield to retrieve his hat and Ben entered to pick corn. Here Ben could argue that even if he had trespassed, Farmer Dell didn't have a right to use deadly force. Farmer Dell would argue that he only used reasonable force because he didn't shoot anybody but only threatened to do so. He would also argue he was defending his land and he shouted at them to stop before he shot his gun into the air. If the court finds that Jerry was privileged to enter the cornfield to get back his hat, then he would have a viable defense.

6. ANALYSIS

This sample answer allows us to examine some common mistakes we didn't get to address in the first exam question and to revisit others in a new setting. You might have noticed that this type of multi-issue, multi-party problem presents the following specific challenges:

- A test of your organizational skills

- A possibility of missed issues when there are multiple actors and actions

- A method of addressing arguments and counter-arguments without relying on "he said, she said"

It also presents some of the errors we examined in the first example and a few new ones as well:

- Careless reading of the facts

- Incomplete statements of the law

- Conclusory statements

- Reciting facts instead of analyzing them

(a)   *Where the answer is disorganized*

A lack of organization is probably a law professor's most frequent criticism of student exams. It may also be the most overused, but since it covers a multitude of sins, it's a very common comment. One problem with getting your blue book back with the comment "lacks organization" is that these words fail to provide the very specificity you need to make the necessary changes. For one thing, what does "disorganized" mean? Most likely you're also thinking, where was I disorganized? How was I disorganized? Unfortunately for you, an exam answer which lacks organization may be easy for the professor to spot but difficult to explain exactly what makes it disorganized because each paper tends to be disorganized in its own way.

Since it's a catch-all phrase for a variety of errors, it can refer to any of the following:

- Moving back and forth between issues

- Identifying one issue and then discussing the rule of law for another

- Listing all the issues in the problem in the first paragraph and then listing all the rules in the second

- Jumping between parties or causes of action without completing a discussion of one before moving on to discuss the other

(b)   *What "disorganized" really means*

Whatever form it assumes, the bottom line is that a disorganized essay is one which fails to follow the logical structure of legal analysis. Let's face it, when you're disorganized, you're all over the place! While it might not seem too terrible to you because if you've managed to cover the issues, why should it matter what order they're in? Well, for one thing, even if the correct issues are raised, you stand to lose your reader, and possibly points, if it's a struggle to follow what you're saying. Another problem with disorganization, and the one which is far more dangerous to your grade, is the genuine likelihood that you'll miss some of the relevant issues and fail to discuss them at all. But even more important to your professor, a disorganized essay reflects a disorganized mind and a well-trained legal mind is anything but disorganized.

(c)   Sources of disorganization

Now that we've identified the problem, we should take a moment to consider where it comes from before we identify some ways to correct it. Despite the varied forms disorganization may take, it flows from one source. Whether you're willing to admit this or not, disorganized writing comes from disorganized thinking. You simply cannot and do not write clearly when you're not thinking clearly.

There are any number of reasons why you may not be thinking clearly about a subject. It may be because you've just started to research an unfamiliar area of the law or because it's the beginning of the semester and you're not yet that deep into the subject matter. But this isn't true with a final exam when you're supposed to know the material inside and out. As I've said before, there's no substitute for a solid grasp of the material. It's essential for the clear thinking that leads to concise and careful analysis. If, after reviewing the exam with your professor or through the procedures I'm outlining here, you realize that you didn't really understand the subject matter or recited the rule inaccurately, then you need to go back in your study process to see where you went wrong. There had to be some point in your studying where you made a wrong turn – most likely in the preparation of your outline because this is where and how you learned the material. If necessary, return to the chapter on outlining for guidance.

But suppose that you've done all the necessary prep work, followed the strategies outlined for learning the material found in earlier chapters of this book, and you've still come away with the dreaded "disorganized" comment on your test booklet. In this case, it wasn't so much a question of knowing the material, but rather how you handled the presentation. So let's take a look at the manifestations of disorganization in the sample answer and see how we can impose some order.

(d)   Some causes and cures for disorganization

Even though this is a relatively short hypothetical, it contains just enough issues and parties to make it complicated so that proper organization is essential for an effective and complete discussion. Instead, what we have are so many starts and stops that the reader could get whiplash. And probably did.

As we examine the causes and cures for disorganization in this student essay, we'll consider the following strategies:

- Working from an outline

- Using a blueprint paragraph and sub-headings

- Avoiding "commingling"

- Avoiding "he said, she said"

- Using IRAC for a writing make-over

(1)   *Working from an outline*

In all likelihood, this student failed to take a few minutes to outline before writing. Even though it's appropriate to jump right into the analysis once you start writing, it's never a good idea to jump right into the writing without a plan. As we discussed in the chapter on exam writing, this means that you must spend some time outlining your answer before writing it. You need a few minutes after reading the problem to outline the issues and come up with an approach for handling them. Here, it's obvious that the student had not spent the time necessary to construct a working outline. It's obvious from all that's missing in the answer.

Let's see how this works. Since an outline is a list of the rules we've identified from the main issues in the problem, it should look something like this:

---

1. Dell v. Ben

   a. Trespass to land

   b. Trespass and conversion to chattel

   c. Privilege to defend

2. Ben v. Dell for assault

3. Dell v. Jerry

   a. Trespass to land

   b. Trespass and conversion to chattel

   c. Necessity defense

4. Jerry v. Dell for assault

Outline for Exam Question 2

---

(2)   *Using a blueprint paragraph and sub-headings*

Your presentation on paper, as in person, goes a long way in making a first impression. Of course there is no substituting style for substance, but sometimes a little style goes a long way in setting the stage for substance. On exams, your opening paragraph provides a general framework for what is to come – providing a much needed roadmap for both you and your reader to follow. You might then follow this introductory paragraph with sub-headings to identify parties or causes of action, depending on the particular presentation best suited to your analysis.

Let's consider the student's choice for an opening sentence:

> *The issue in this case is whether Farmer Dell has an action against Ben or Jerry or both.*

This is a good example of *how not to begin your answer* to a multi-party, multi-issue problem. All it does is repeat the call of the question. It adds nothing to respond to the question and provides no path to follow for the writer or reader. Further, it combines the parties, *against Ben or Jerry or both*, which leads the writer down the dangerous path of commingling – a topic we'll address shortly. The problem is that Farmer Dell has the same causes of action against both Ben and Jerry but the analysis for each is entirely different. The student's answer neglects to discuss several key issues for both of them – most likely the result of this initial failure to treat each party separately.

The easiest way to avoid such a situation is to set up a blueprint for your answer in the opening sentences. This question begs for the writer to begin with a paragraph that clearly lets the reader know where you're going.

The student would have done well to begin with something like:

> *Farmer Dell has several possible causes of action based in intentional tort against Ben and Jerry. This essay will consider each action separately.*

Farmer Dell v. Ben

> *In an action by Farmer Dell against Ben, Dell can assert the following causes of action: trespass to land, trespass to chattel, and conversion.*

Trespass to land

> *Dell has a solid claim for trespass to land based on Ben's deliberate entry onto his cornfield. One who intentionally, with purpose or knowledge, enters upon the land of another is liable for trespass. Here, Ben ....*

The reader and the writer now have a clear path to follow. The use of subheadings to identify first the parties and then the causes of action leads the writer quite naturally through a separate and complete treatment of each topic. It also follows the structure of the outline.

Please note, however, that there is no such thing as a "one-size-fits-all" organizational plan. In each case, you must adopt the one most suitable to your problem. The scheme I've chosen is not the only way to have structured this answer.

A key purpose of organization is to create structure by maintaining focus. In this case, the mental focus is created by setting up actual physical signposts, i.e., the subheadings. They keep your thoughts in line and act like blinders to everything else. The point is that if you're thinking only about Ben and trespass to land, you're not likely to stray and think about something else. And by thinking *only about Ben*, you're more likely to see all there is to see in the facts about Ben. By keeping your concentration narrow, it increases the likelihood that the right associations will come to you – and in the logical order.

Still, you don't want to "over-organize" by breaking your answer into so many subheadings that you sacrifice continuity and lose the inherent logic in a legal discussion. For example, while it's entirely appropriate to organize this essay around the parties and then look at each cause of action individually, the right time and place to discuss any defenses Ben might have to trespass would be after evaluating his liability. In turn, this would link naturally to a discussion of Farmer Dell's actions with respect to Ben, i.e., the privilege to defend his property. Here it makes sense that working through an analysis of Ben's trespass to Farmer Dell's land would lead the writer to consider whether Farmer Dell was privileged to defend his property and, if in doing so, whether he acted appropriately. The fact pattern is heavily loaded with facts regarding Farmer Dell's actions and they are relatively ignored in this student's answer. Once again, using appropriate subheadings to keep focused is a surefire way to avoid missing key issues.

(3)   Avoiding "commingling"

Another way to increase the likelihood of spotting key issues is to avoid "commingling." Let's re-visit the student's choice for an opening sentence but now with a focus on the commingling:

> *The issue in this case is whether Farmer Dell has an action against Ben or Jerry or both.*

As I mentioned earlier, by addressing both of the parties at once, this student is headed down the road to exam disaster. Never, ever, commingle your parties or your issues. Each deserves and demands separate treatment. Also, it's a sure bet your professor included multiple parties to test multiple areas of the law. You're just missing the point (in more ways than one!) if you overlook this frequently used test strategy.

Another reason you should avoid commingling is the possibility for error. Even if you're aware that the parties and issues must be addressed individually, and fully intend to do so, the likelihood is that during the pressure of the exam, something will be overlooked. In this case, the student overlooked quite a bit – consider just some of the missing pieces:

- Jerry's use of a machete to cut a path through the cornfield

- The presence of a mechanical spring-gun in the cornfield

- The conversion issue

- Farmer Dell's liability for assault

(4)   Avoiding "he said, she said"
Another advantage to using headings is to avoid the pitfalls of the "he said, she said" style of argument. While effective in the pens of experts, the ping-pong patter of "he will argue, then she will argue" can be disastrous for inexperienced law students. The going back and forth between parties inevitably leads to problems since the writer has to juggle as well as engage in legal analysis.

Let's consider a section of the third paragraph in the sample answer to see exactly what happens when the writer has "commingled" the parties and relied on a "he said, she said" approach:

Farmer Dell has no action against Jerry for trespass to chattels but may have one for trespass to land. He'd have one against Ben too because both Ben and Jerry entered Farmer Dell's land. This is true even though Jerry only entered the cornfield to retrieve his hat and Ben entered to pick corn. Here Ben could argue that even if he had trespassed, Farmer Dell didn't have a right to use deadly force. Farmer Dell would argue that he only used reasonable force because he didn't shoot anybody but only threatened to do so. He would also argue he was defending his land and he shouted at them to stop before he shot his gun into the air. If the court finds that Jerry was privileged to enter the cornfield to get back his hat, then he would have a viable defense.

In the first sentence, the writer introduces the question of trespass to land with respect to Jerry but immediately abandons Jerry in favor of Ben. This is significant because the reader expects a discussion of Jerry to follow. Instead, that expectation is disappointed when the writer turns back to Ben and the next two sentences weave back and forth between Ben and Jerry. Specifically, the commingling occurs in the two sentences where Ben and Jerry's activities are considered jointly:

He'd have one [action in trespass] against Ben too because both Ben and Jerry entered Farmer Dell's land. This is true even though Jerry only entered the cornfield to retrieve his hat and Ben entered to pick corn.

Also, you should note that this is as far as the writer develops the discussion of trespass to Farmer Dell's cornfield. While we'll examine the problems of the missing rule and lack of analysis in another section, I mention it here because it's very likely a consequence of commingling. In trying to juggle Ben and Jerry and the action for trespass at the same time, it's no surprise that the writer dropped the ball.

This problem could have been avoided if the subheadings suggested above had been used. Subheadings would have encouraged separate discussions of each party with respect to the question of trespass to land. Instead, the writer completely skips this necessary liability analysis and jumps into a "he said, she said" dialogue concerning possible defenses:

Here Ben could argue that even if he had trespassed, Farmer Dell didn't have a right to use deadly force. Farmer Dell would argue that he only used reasonable force because he didn't shoot anybody but only threatened to do so. He would also argue he was defending his land and he shouted at them to stop before he shot his gun into the air.

Once again, the reader's sense of what to expect is frustrated by a discussion of Farmer Dell's right to defend his property. By moving so abruptly between parties and theories, the reader is disoriented. And justifiably so. The logical, orderly sequence of discussing liability with respect to the cause of action on behalf of one party, followed by any possible defenses, and then moving to discuss the next party, has been violated. The result is that the writer has failed to meet the reader's expectations and the dialogue necessary between the two for successful communication is lost.

A disconnect between writer and reader poses a number of serious problems. The most obvious is that you've lost your reader along the way. A reader who can't follow your discussion will most likely give up the struggle. And remember, professors have dozens of blue books to read. Your goal is to make it as easy as possible for the professor to follow what you've written, not give up on the effort!

Another and more serious problem with the "he said, she said," style of argument is the danger it poses for you. Not only can it be confusing for the reader to follow, but it can disrupt your train of thought. It's far too easy to get diverted and miss important issues and the connection between issues when moving back and forth between differing points of view. Here, it's likely that the entire conversion question – *with respect to both Ben and Jerry* – was missed for this reason. Of course it's always possible that the student just didn't know the rule of law, but it's far more probable that the back and forth between Ben and Jerry prevented the writer from connecting with the facts and seeing the links between them. This is one explanation for how the student possibly could write

When Ben started picking the corn, actual intermeddling occurred. Since the corn cannot then be put back on the stalk, harm to the corn occurred

and not realize that because the corn could not be put back on the stalk, Ben's actions raised the question of an actual conversion, not just a trespass.

Similarly, how could the student have missed Jerry's possible conversion when the problem tells us that Jerry used a machete to hack a path through the cornfield? All the student writes is that

Since he did not in fact pick any corn, Jerry did not commit a trespass to chattels.

These associations should not have been missed because the student probably knew the rule regarding conversion but overlooked it in the facts. It's also pretty safe to assume that you're thinking to yourself right now, *"that's my problem – I know the rules, even my professor says that, but I just don't think of the right things at the right time, and even when I do, I don't write it right. How can you change all that for me?"*

While I cannot promise that every association will come to you during an exam, you'll certainly increase the possibilities if you narrow your attention to one perspective at a time. This forces you to take a close, narrow look at what's in front of you and this in turn increases the likelihood that you'll see the subtleties and inferences in the facts (although how hacking your way through a cornfield with a machete possibly could be seen as subtle is beyond me). It also follows that your writing will be more organized and hence you'll be more likely to write it right.

Let's be realistic for a minute – learning to analyze legal problems is neither a gift you're born with nor a hit-or-miss operation. To a very large extent, it's a skill you develop through practicing from old exams, knowing the rules with specificity, and finally, laying the groundwork to guide you through the thought process. This means using every tool in your arsenal, including subheadings and the rules.

(5) *Using the rules to stay organized*

This leads to my recommendation that you forget the "he said, she said" style of analysis until you've really mastered the art. Instead, focus on one point of view at a time and rely on the rule of law to organize your answer. As we discussed in the chapter on exam writing, using the rules as an organizational tool leads to a more focused and complete analysis.

For example, let's take a look at how using the law to organize the discussion regarding Farmer Dell's right to defend his property would read.

Instead of:

> *... Farmer Dell didn't have a right to use deadly force. Farmer Dell would argue that he only used reasonable force because he didn't shoot anybody but only threatened to do so. He would also argue he was defending his land and he shouted at them to stop before he shot his gun into the air.*

We'd have something like:

> *Farmer Dell may claim that he was privileged to defend his property – both his land and his corn – on essentially the same basis as he would have to defend himself. A property owner is permitted to use reasonable force in defense of his property. But first there is a duty to use words – the landowner must make a verbal demand that the intruder stop before using force unless it reasonably appears that violence or other harm will occur immediately so that the request to stop will be useless. Still, the landowner can never use more force than reasonably appears necessary and he does not have a general right to use deadly force even when the intrusion can only be prevented this way.*

> *Here, Farmer Dell shouted out a warning to "Stop or I will shoot" which would satisfy the requirement that a verbal request to stop be given. However, Dell*

accompanied these words with a shotgun pointed directly at Ben and Jerry, which in itself signifies the potential use of deadly force. Further, Dell then shot the gun when Ben and Jerry remained silent, making it the actual use of deadly force. Even though Dell shot the gun into the air and not directly at Ben and Jerry, this might nevertheless be seen as an improper use of deadly force to protect chattel – some stalks of corn – and would not be privileged. Even if Dell argued that he was a landowner protecting his land, shooting a gun would likely be seen as using more force than reasonably necessary to protect the property against the likes of Ben and Jerry. This assumes, however, that Jerry is not still holding the machete, which might give some basis for Dell to believe he was in imminent danger of death or bodily harm because a machete is a dangerous weapon. But the facts don't indicate whether Jerry was holding the machete at this time or whether Dell had even seen it. We do know that when Dell shouted the warning, Ben and Jerry both stopped in their tracks. Simply because they did not respond to his question did not permit Dell to shoot a gun when there did not seem any basis to believe that Ben and Jerry posed an immediate threat of harm to Dell.

It's possible that Farmer Dell's act of pointing a shotgun at Ben and Jerry can be considered an assault. Dell intended to cause apprehension of a harmful or offensive contact because he shouted, "stop or I will shoot." One doesn't threaten to shoot another with a gun unless the intent to is cause apprehension. Arguably Ben and Jerry could not feel apprehension because their backs were turned to Dell and therefore couldn't see whether the gun was pointed at them, but they were threatened with being shot which could reasonably cause apprehension. Still, words alone are insufficient to constitute an assault. There must be some overt act, a physical act or gesture, before an assault can be claimed. Here, when Ben and Jerry turned around, they saw a shotgun pointed at them. This would seem to constitute the overt act necessary to constitute assault.

It's also questionable whether Dell is privileged to defend his land against intruders with the spring-gun loaded scarecrow. A property owner is privileged to use mechanical devices only if he would be privileged to use a similar degree of force if he were present and acting himself. As we've just discussed, Dell was not privileged to use a shotgun to protect his property and therefore the use of the spring gun would similarly not be permitted as being an unreasonable use of deadly force.

In contrast, the student answer neglected to differentiate between these individual acts and failed to discuss the spring-gun on the scarecrow altogether. If I had an opportunity to discuss this answer with the student, I'd probably hear something like:

"I can see that I left stuff out but the real problem is my writing. I just don't write like you do. I do well on multiple choice exams, but when it comes to writing essays, I mess up. I know the law but once again, my problem is how I write it."

C. IS THE PROBLEM THE WAY YOU WRITE?

The answer to this question is very likely "no." The problem is not your writing, or what you really mean, your style of writing. Still, my experience in working with students is that you tend to think it is.

For example, let's consider what this student had to say on her own behalf. What strikes me, and should strike you, is that she minimized the importance of leaving "stuff" out of her answer in favor of finding fault with her writing. Of course, the "stuff" we're referring to is the law and legal analysis – the essence of any answer.

Instead, the student identifies writing as the weakness and dismisses the real problems with conclusory statements and insufficient and incomplete statements of the law. While to the novice this seems to be a writing problem, it's not. It's a legal analysis problem and an overall failure to engage in an IRAC-based analysis. But before we target these specific deficiencies, let's discuss the rather widely-held belief that *"the problem is my writing."*

There's good news and there's bad news when it comes to the writing issue. The good news is that most of you don't have a problem with basic writing skills. Consequently, when a professor makes the comment on your exam that "you have a problem with writing," it's not likely to be referring to matters of subject-verb agreement, displaced modifiers, or too many commas (while grammar problems are definitely something you need to work on and improve, in general these are not the problems which seriously detract from your grade), but rather, it concerns the substance of what you're saying and the structure in which you are saying it.

Therefore, the comment

"The problem is your writing"

more likely translates to

"Your analysis is disorganized"

or possibly

> *"Your discussion lacks substance"*

or maybe even

> *"Your argument lacks focus"*

As you can see, these comments go well beyond the mechanics of writing to the structure and content of what you've written. And here's the bad news – this is far more serious than grammar problems and requires a great deal more work. But first it requires that you give it the recognition it deserves.

Back to the good news – you can correct these deficiencies once you realize that they can't be dismissed as "writing problems." I have no doubt that you'd much rather have learned that the problem was simply a matter of punctuation – of knowing where to put the commas and such – but it's not. Rather, it's a matter of how you're thinking about the problem and how you're putting it down on paper. All of which pretty much brings us full circle to where we began our analysis of the second hypothetical – where your answer is disorganized. Frequently, organizational problems masquerade as writing problems and are easily mis-diagnosed.

Once again, consider what happens when your answer is disorganized. As we've seen, there may be any one or a mix of the following: identifying one issue but discussing the rules for another, lumping all the issues in the problem together in one paragraph and then moving on to listing all the rules in the next, and jumping between parties or causes of action without completing a discussion of one before moving on to discuss the other.

The common thread found throughout these organizational problems is the general failure to conform to the basic structure of legal writing. As we discussed in earlier chapters, IRAC is an organizational tool for both your thinking and your writing and when it's followed, you avoid many of the problems which lead to the dreaded "problems with your writing" comment.

D. A WRITING MAKE-OVER USING IRAC

Until you achieve the level of mental and written fluency where you can weave together rule and fact in a seamless web and transition between thoughts without loss of either substance or reader, I strongly recommend that you rely on some form of IRAC to keep focused. While IRAC will never cover for a lack of knowledge nor substitute for a lack of analysis, you can use it as tool for organizing your thinking and your writing. Think of it as a supporting scaffold (or training wheels) to ensure that the necessary steps are followed. Once the process becomes instinctive, then the props can be discarded. But until then, you have something you can rely on to guide you through the process.

1. WHERE THE ISSUE IS MISSING

One consequence of failing to follow an IRAC-based analysis can be a lack of focus. Typically, this flows from a tendency to begin writing without first articulating the relevant issue. A failure to properly identify the issue(s) in your exam question results in a "scattershot" approach in the rest of your answer and solicits such comments as "too general," "sketchy," and "incomplete analysis." The following are the types of writing problems associated with failure to begin with identification of the issue:

- The rule discussion is so general and open-ended that it misses the precise rule implicated by the facts.

- The discussion rambles and roams, moving without any logical transition from topic to topic.

- There is no connection between the call-of-the-question and the application section of your answer.

The principal means of avoiding these problems in your exam answer is by starting from a place of specificity. If you begin writing by identifying the legal issue, you're more likely to follow it with a sharply written analysis of the relevant rules and facts. You might want to consider reading the section, When You Have Trouble Finding the "Issue" in the chapter on forensic IRAC before proceeding. Not only will you find details on the specific problems associated with failing to start from the issue, but you'll see examples of how it results in the type of "disorganized" writing we're describing.

Now we're ready to take a look at some specific examples in the student answer and see how a make-over using IRAC would work.

MAKE-OVER #1: WORKING FROM THE ISSUE

- *What not to write:*

  The issue in this case is whether Farmer Dell has an action against Ben or Jerry or both.

Here's a case where the student seems to have written a statement of the issue, but she really hasn't done anything more than restate the interrogatory. Even though we examined this sentence quite carefully in our earlier treatment of commingling and the blueprint paragraph, now let's see what an IRAC make-over will do for it.

Assuming that we followed the suggestion for beginning with a blueprint paragraph for this type of multi-issue, multi-party problem, now we'd be ready to address one party and one of the issues. Let's consider Jerry and a cause of action for trespass to land.

- *Make-over using "whether, when":*
  The issue is **whether** Jerry committed a trespass to land **when** he entered Farmer Dell's cornfield to retrieve his hat.

By using the "whether, when" language to guide construction of the issue, we have a clear statement of the legal problem. This is critical language to use when trying to frame the issue and was discussed thoroughly in Chapter 7. You might want to review the appropriate section in that chapter before proceeding.

The revised issue statement now provides a clear path for the writer to follow. The essay should proceed to define the requirements of trespass and deal with the question of whether Jerry committed a trespass when all he wanted to do was retrieve his hat. Instead, our student merely concluded

> Farmer Dell has no action against Jerry for trespass to chattels but may have one for trespass to land.

Discussion of the rule is entirely absent as is consideration of whether the intent element was satisfied if Jerry only went onto the property to get his hat when it blew off his head (if you were wondering, the answer is yes, liability for trespass to land occurred the moment Jerry stepped onto Farmer Dell's land because he fully intended to do so. The intent requirement is simply that the party intentionally, with purpose or knowledge, enter the land of another. It doesn't matter that he just wanted to get his hat back.)

We can consider the student's sentence under a number of headings – "conclusory statement" – is one that comes readily to mind, but it's important to consider it in this particular context: the initial failure to write a specific issue most likely led to the scattered, disjointed, and rambling narrative that followed. Still, there is nothing technically wrong with the writing; the problem is with what's written.

Now let's consider another issue statement, or rather the lack of one.

- *What not to write:*
  Ben could argue that even if he had trespassed, Farmer Dell didn't have a right to use deadly force.

- *Make-over using "whether, when":*
  Here the question is **whether** Farmer Dell is privileged to defend his property with a shotgun **when** Ben entered Dell's cornfield to pick some corn.

The make-over sentence identifies the issue in terms of the rule (the privilege to defend property) and the facts which bring that rule into controversy (using a gun to defend that property). While it is not required that you write this kind of detailed issue statement on an exam, I suggest that you strive to do so for your own good. Taking the time to analyze and articulate the precise legal question will keep your thinking and hence your writing on point as you work through the analysis.

On the other hand, the student answer is problematic for two reasons: not only is essential analysis omitted, but what is discussed is handled poorly, exhibiting most of the weaknesses we've seen earlier – conclusory statements and rambling between topics and parties. When combined as they are here, the professor will simply write "disorganized" and sometimes, when meeting with the student, say something like, "you seem to have a writing problem."

2. WHERE THE RULE IS MISSING

A common result of failing to include an adequate discussion of the relevant rule of law are the troubling comments "your discussion lacks substance" and "sketchy on the law." Basically, there are two types of problems which show up in the "rule" portion of your exam: first, where there is a genuine ignorance of the law; and second, where there's a demonstration of substantive knowledge, but it's sketchy and incomplete. Here there's not "enough" rule to provide an adequate context for analyzing the facts. It's primarily the second type of problem we find in our student answer.

This answer manages to write quite a bit while avoiding any meaningful legal discussion. As we've already seen, there were at least three causes of action – trespass to land, trespass to chattel, and conversion, as well as the defense of privilege and the issue of assault. Except for one sentence which offers a rudimentary definition of trespass to chattel, we're left with little more than oblique references to the controlling rules by way of some relevant phrases. While this is not necessarily an incorrect approach, it fails here because it's not backed up with a thoughtful, complete analysis which tackles the ambiguous aspects of the rule.

MAKE-OVER #2: WORKING FROM THE RULE

Trespass to chattel

Let's look at one rule at a time and see exactly what I'm talking about. For example, with respect to the trespass to chattel cause of action, this student wrote:

Trespass to chattels requires an intent to intermeddle with chattel and actual intermeddling to occur causing (a) harm to chattel or (b) dispossession for a significant period of time.

After reading this sentence, you're probably thinking, "what's wrong with this? I see legal terms and there are elements. It looks fine to me." I can understand why you might think this is fine and most likely for the same reasons the student wrote it. But now you need to understand why it's incomplete and fails to do its job.

First, let's consider, "an intent to intermeddle" and "actual intermeddling occurs." While this is most certainly the legal language used with respect to a trespass to chattel, is it sufficient? Does it tell you what "intermeddle" means? From this statement, would you know a case of intermeddling if you saw it? How would you recognize it? While these might seem like silly questions to you, they are intended to make you realize that it's not enough to simply toss out a legal term without fully defining it. By itself, "intermeddle" doesn't tell me much. In this case, it would have been possible to compensate for the missing definition if the writer had proceeded to provide a more sophisticated factual analysis, one which would have woven the rule into the discussion so that the reader would know what it meant for intermeddling to occur. (It's getting so that I wish I'd never heard this word, but we're not done with it yet.) But that didn't happen here. All we have is:

- *What not to write:*
  Ben...entered the cornfield and started to pick corn. Ben has the requisite intent to intermeddle with the chattel, the farmer's corn. When Ben started picking the corn, actual intermeddling occurred. Since the corn cannot then be put back on the stalk, harm to the corn occurred.

When reading this answer, the professor would be expected to do quite a bit of filling in the blanks. First, there's the need to connect "entering the cornfield" with satisfying the "requisite intent to intermeddle." When reading this sentence, the professor is left asking, "how does simply entering the cornfield manifest the requisite intent to intermeddle with the corn?" Why did the act of picking the corn cause intermeddling?" The student could have filled in the missing connections with something like:

- *Make-over by bridging the gap:*
  *Ben had the requisite intent to deprive Farmer Dell of his corn **because** Ben told Jerry he wanted to have fresh corn from Dell's cornfield for dinner. Further, he asked Jerry to stop the car so he could get out and pick the corn. **Here, when Ben picked up the corn stalks which had fallen to the ground, he interfered with Dell's property just by touching the corn.***

Now look carefully at the sentence in boldface: it combines rule and fact to explain what is meant by commingling and how it occurred in this instance. This short, single sentence is all that's needed to define the act of intermeddling because it's done in such a way as to make its meaning clear. Also, this sentence doesn't rely on the word which needs to be defined for its own definition – if we want to understand what intermeddling is, we can't use the word to define itself as the student did with, when Ben started picking the corn, actual intermeddling occurred. Instead, I used "interfered with" to give needed meaning to intermeddling.

3. WORKING WITH THE RULE FORCES CLOSE READING OF THE FACTS

If the student had read the facts carefully when evaluating whether intermingling had occurred, she would have noted that Ben never actually picked any corn off the stalks, but took those which had already fallen to the ground. It takes a careful reading of the facts and a clear understanding of the rule to detect the significance in this subtle difference. And that significance is the difference between trespass and conversion. But even realizing this, it's difficult to determine the legal meaning of the difference, if any, unless we examine the facts closely in light of the rule.

This is what I mean by using the rule to organize and drive the analysis. Here, if we begin by looking at the rule, we see that conversion is an intentional interference with the plaintiff's possession or ownership of property that is *so substantial*, the defendant should be required to pay the property's full value. Further, in distinguishing between trespass and conversion, courts consider several factors in determining whether D's interference with P's possessory rights is severe enough to be conversion or simply a trespass to chattels. These factors include:

- The duration of the defendant's *dominion* over the property

- The defendant's *good or bad faith*

- The *harm* done to the property

- The *inconvenience* caused to the plaintiff

Now the question is how to use this rule to structure the exam answer. Knowing the parameters of the rule gives us the direction in which to proceed. First, we need to consider whether Ben's interference with Dell's corn was substantial. If it was, then the act may have been a conversion and not a trespass and the consequence is that the damages are different. We can write this in a couple of ways. Let's pick up where we left off.

One way would be to first state the rule and then apply the facts, which would be a clear "RA" construction:

[We left off with... Here, when Ben picked up the corn stalks which had fallen to the ground he interfered with Dell's property just by touching the corn.] The next question is whether Ben's picking up the corn up moved beyond a trespass to a conversion. A conversion requires an intentional interference with the property that is so substantial as to destroy the goods or fundamentally alter them. In this case, the defendant would be liable for the full value of the chattel. Here, Ben merely picked up corn which had already fallen to the ground. Because he did not sever the corn from the stalks, it's possible that all he was holding were defective stalks, of little or no value to Farmer Dell. In this case there was no harm done to the property because it's not likely Dell could have sold defective stalks. If he could have sold them at all, it would likely have been at a reduced value and hence Ben could be liable only for the limited value. However, a conversion may have occurred if the defendant causes harm to the property, acts in bad faith, causes inconvenience to the owner, or exercises dominion over the property for a significant duration. [I would continue with an analysis of the facts with respect to each of these factors but it's not necessary to do so now. You get the idea.]

Another way would be to weave rule and fact together:

*The next question is whether Ben's act of **actually picking up** the corn up moved beyond a **trespass to a conversion**. It's possible that Ben did not substantially interfere with the stalks at all because he **did not sever** the corn from the stalks. He **merely picked up** what had fallen to the ground by itself. Still, Ben intended to take Dell's corn and eat it for dinner which would be a **fundamental alteration** of Dell's property – it would become Ben's dinner! But this had not happened yet, and all Ben did was pick up loose corn stalks. Further, when Dell shot off his gun, Ben dropped the corn, thereby **relinquishing control** over it altogether. Dell got his corn back and the most he could seek from Ben would be any reduction in the corn's value because of Ben's touching it.*

By combining rule and fact, I've written a more condensed analysis while still covering the relevant rule and facts. I've indicated the factors of conversion in bold so you can see how I've integrated the rule right into the analysis without resorting to the clear separation I relied on in the first example.

To be honest with you, the second approach is more sophisticated and generally looked upon with greater favor by those who discourage an over-reliance on an IRAC construction. But it doesn't necessarily mean more points with the grader if you cover all the same bases with the "RA" construction. In both instances, you've worked with the rule to give structure to your writing and meaning to the facts. The benefit to the second approach is that it takes less time to write it, but if you haven't achieved this level of fluency yet, don't panic. There's no real downside to following the first approach and there's a possible benefit: you won't overlook anything because it forces you to consider each element or factor against each fact.

There's still one point we need to address before we move on. It's an important one and while we discussed it in the earlier chapter on IRAC, we need to consider it here as well. *It's **understanding that the process of legal analysis works by an unfolding of issues within issues.*** You may have heard your professor refer to is as the need to identify "the issues and the sub-issues" or the "issue and the way it breaks down." There are numerous ways to describe it but what it means is that a legal problem is typically multi-faceted and that a thorough analysis will identify and consider all the links. An examination of each link becomes, in effect, its own mini-IRAC. This is why it's critical that you don't confuse using IRAC as an aid to structuring your thinking and writing with an inflexible, one-size-fits-all formula.

This brings us to the precise fear some have about IRAC – that students will use it improperly to narrow and restrict their legal analysis by limiting themselves to looking for only one issue, to be followed by only one rule because the acronym "IRAC" is itself singular. Ironically, this argument is as limited as what it seeks to prevent. Fortunately, you've had the benefit of reading this book and won't misuse IRAC or allow it to confine your thinking to one issue or one rule. You'll know that while IRAC works for every occasion, it works only to organize and structure an analysis. Each problem is different and the analysis will proceed from a different issue based on the question that is posed in the facts.

My concern and a problem for many students is how to handle the transitions involved in the multi-issue analysis. For example, we began with the question of a trespass to chattel and in the analysis of the trespass, we came to see the interrelated issue of whether there was a conversion to chattel. I know what I'm about to say will sound corny, but this represents the natural unfolding of the issues from the facts as they are held up to the light of the rule. You don't want to stop these associations from happening; rather, you want to encourage them. IRAC does not limit you to one issue; it lets you use the equation on issue after issue. The question now is how do you make these transitions in the course of an exam? How do we use IRAC to advance from issue to issue?

Now if you go back and re-read the examples we've just covered, you'll see that when I moved the discussion from trespass to conversion, I simply identified the issue I was going to consider, "*The next question is whether Ben's picking up the·corn up moved beyond a trespass to a conversion.*" I then followed with the analysis of the rule and the facts. The secret with IRAC is that it allows you to link your statements of the issue as you proceed through your analysis. Once you complete one IRAC cycle, you move on to the next.

Now we're ready to consider the next cause of action.

Trespass to land

It's time we looked at what this student wrote for the trespass to land cause of action. While we commented on this particular passage in connection with the commingling problem, we never considered it with respect to the rule of law.

> *Farmer Dell has no action against Jerry for trespass to chattels but may have one for trespass to land. He'd have one against Ben too because both Ben and Jerry entered Farmer Dell's land. This is true even though Jerry only entered the cornfield to retrieve his hat and Ben entered to pick corn.*

Do you know what requirements must be met to determine whether a party has committed a trespass to another's property from reading these sentences? I don't. It's true that trespass is really one of the less complicated of the intentional torts, and it doesn't require more than to intend to enter the land and being on the land, but your professor expects you to sound like a lawyer when you write about it. It need not be complicated, but it must use the appropriate legal language so you sound like the lawyer in training that you are.

Your professor is looking for something like this:

> *The required action in trespass is simply being on another's property and the intent is just to be where you are. Consequently, it doesn't matter that Jerry's hat blew off his head quite accidentally onto Dell's property and Jerry was just going onto the property to retrieve it. What matters is that Jerry intended to enter the property of another and he did. That's sufficient for trespass to land.*

Now you don't have to write these exact sentences but you should make it clear that a trespass to land involves entering the land of another with the express purpose of doing so. Precisely what you write should be dictated by the facts. The student answer is not really so deficient but it doesn't quite emphasize the intent element sufficiently to convey why Jerry would be liable in trespass for just getting his hat. My example conveys a thorough understanding of this principle in the context of the relevant facts. In contrast, the student's version leaves it unsure whether this basic concept was understood. And when your professor can't be sure, you can't get credit.

Finally, we're ready to consider Farmer Dell's third cause of action.

The defense of privilege

Here's what the student wrote with respect to privilege,

> *Ben could argue that even if he had trespassed, Farmer Dell didn't have a right to use deadly force. Farmer Dell would argue that he only used reasonable force because he didn't shoot anybody but only threatened to do so. He would*

also argue he was defending his land and he shouted at them to stop before he shot his gun into the air. If the court finds that Jerry was privileged to enter the cornfield to get back his hat, then he would have a viable defense.

If you recall (and hopefully you do), we've already examined and rewritten this excerpt when we discussed how to use the rule of law to organize your analysis. Plainly we don't need to revisit the material for that purpose, but we need to take a closer look at the specific weaknesses which would most likely elicit such comments from the professor as "sketchy on the law" and "lacking substance."

It's a distinct possibility that the student would conclude from these comments that she has a writing problem. But she doesn't. She writes well enough. She just doesn't write enough. Enough law that is. And enough explanation of why that particular law and why so in this particular case. Your professor reads your exam answer like a newspaper article – looking for answers to the what, why, and how to the legal questions posed in the exam.

For example, it's insufficient to write

Farmer Dell didn't have a right to use deadly force.

without following it up with an explanation of the privilege to defend property against trespassers. I know that the writer is thinking privilege because the word "right" is used, but your professor expects the appropriate legal vocabulary. Also, there's a reference to the types of force that might be involved by the use of the phrase "deadly force" but once again, it's too cryptic to let your professor know whether *you* really know the applicable law.

Now consider this,

MAKE-OVER WITH SUBSTANCE:

Farmer Dell may claim that he was privileged to defend his property – both his land and his corn – on essentially the same basis as he would have to defend himself. A landowner is permitted to use reasonable force in defense of his property but can never use more force than reasonably appears necessary and he does not have a general right to use deadly force even when the intrusion can only be prevented this way.

You should be able to see how these sentences pick up where the student's sentence left off and fill in the blanks with respect to the concepts of "right" and "deadly force." It provides the level of specificity necessary to provide for a meaningful discussion of the facts – which is the next step in the analysis.

4. WHERE THE ANALYSIS IS MISSING

If I had to guess what most students would consider their weakest exam writing area, it would have to be the application portion of their essays. I recall listening to one of my classmates describe a meeting she had with our Torts professor to go over her final exam. She said that the professor said (note the double hearsay) that she "seemed to know the law" but she was "weak with the analysis." My friend translated this into meaning that she was doing well but "needed some more application in her essays." Even as a second semester law student, I realized my classmate had missed the point the professor was trying to make. You can't fix a deficient analysis by adding "more application" as if it were a beef stew needing a pinch more salt.

As we discussed in earlier chapters, the application portion of the essay is the heart of your legal discussion. It's where you explain the meaning to be given the specific facts in your problem in light of the controlling rule. It's also the part of the exam your professor is most interested in reading because it shows whether you've grasped the legal significance of the facts and understand why and how they are significant. Your professor can tell whether you have a solid understanding of the rule through your analysis. So if you leave this part out, what's your professor to make of your ability to reason your way through a set of facts?

The most common mistake students make in writing this section is the tendency to restate the facts from the hypothetical rather than analyze them. Repetition is not the same as analysis and even though you may very well be repeating the relevant facts from the hypothetical, without some additional work on your part to explain why and how they are meaningful, all your professor has are the very facts she provided to you. See the problem?

Let's consider the following sentences from our student's answer:

MAKE-OVER #3: APPLICATION

Sometimes it's necessary to repeat a few of the relevant facts before you discuss them but it's never a substitute for analyzing them. Some relevant facts are stated here, but that's just it – they're stated and not used.

■ *What not to write:*
Ben told Jerry to stop the car. Ben then got out of the car, entered the cornfield and started to pick corn. Ben has the requisite intent to intermeddle with the chattel, the farmer's corn.

It's possible to work with these sentences but we've got to fill in some gaps. The student tried, but didn't quite make it. She selected the relevant facts that speak to the intent element required for liability in a trespass action, but she failed to make a case why they should add up to intent. She needed to add something (could it be her own thinking?) to make the connections instead of just repeating the facts from the fact pattern.

We'll take what she wrote and fix it.

MAKE-OVER USING "BECAUSE":

We can replace

> *Ben told Jerry to stop the car. Ben then got out of the car, entered the cornfield and started to pick corn. Ben has the requisite intent to intermeddle with the chattel, the farmer's corn.*

with

> *Ben had the requisite intent to deprive Farmer Dell of his corn **because** Ben told Jerry he wanted to have fresh corn from Dell's cornfield for dinner. Ben then asked Jerry to stop the car **so** he could get out and pick the corn.*

If ever there were "magic words" for the task of learning and writing in the language of the law, they are the words "because," "since," and "so." This is so because they guide you in writing an analysis of the facts and not simply a recitation of the facts. This is because every time you use one of these words – just like I'm doing here – you are forced to give a reason. Consider them "helping words" and use them to help you build your analysis.

Now see how "because" and "so" helped in this instance. First, in using the word "because," I've linked together the legal conclusion (intent to pick corn) with the factual basis for reaching this conclusion (Ben told Jerry he wanted corn for dinner). Second, by using the word "so" in the next sentence, I've connected Ben asking Jerry to stop the car (facts) with the reason he wanted to get out – to pick the corn (intent).

In contrast, the student answer leaves it to the reader to find intent from a restatement of the facts in the hypothetical

> *Ben told Jerry to stop the car. Ben then got out of the car, entered the cornfield and started to pick corn.*

While it's true that much isn't needed to turn what the student wrote into what I wrote, it nonetheless makes all the difference between merely repeating the facts as they're given to you and analyzing them in light of the applicable law.

I'd like to provide some more examples of make-overs using "because" and "since" but that's not possible with this particular student answer. There's just not enough for us to redo because the answer is so short on application. I think it's safe to say that we've exhausted what we can do with this sample answer. We've taken it about as far as we can go. If you're interested in further work on developing the analysis section of your essays, then turn to the chapter on forensic IRAC.

E. MORE MAKE-OVERS

Since make-overs can be so helpful in showing how to correct common errors with a few choice words, I thought I'd include some additional examples to reinforce the concept.

1. AN ISSUE MAKE-OVER

- *What not to write:*
  The issue is whether the motion to dismiss was properly granted.

- *What you should write:*
  The issue is whether the prosecutor presented sufficient evidence to the grand jury to indict Jones for criminal possession of stolen property.

Note how the rewrite translates a general question (and most likely the very question asked in the exam problem) into one that identifies the legal question needing to be resolved. Now it's clear what the student is to write next: the elements required for a *prima facie* case of criminal possession of stolen property.

2. A RULE MAKE-OVER

- *What not to write:*
  A party will be excused from performance by the principle of frustration of purpose when a party's purpose in entering into the contract is destroyed by supervening events.

- *What you should write:*
  Where the bargained for performance is still possible, but the principal purpose or value of the contract has been substantially destroyed by some supervening event, such frustration of purpose will discharge party's remaining obligations. The object must be so completely the basis of the contract such that without it, the transaction would make little sense. The frustration must have resulted without the fault of the party seeking to be excused and that party must not have assumed a greater obligation than the law imposes.

Note how the rewrite includes so much more information regarding the rule. It defines it completely and with specificity, including all the factors necessary to consider in evaluating a claim for seeking discharge of a contractual obligation based on frustration of purpose.

3. AN APPLICATION MAKE-OVER

- *What not to write:*
  Sam is the sole shareholder in the corporation and should not be held personally liable for the debts of the corporation even though he used corporate funds to purchase personal items.

- *What you should write:*
  Although he is the sole shareholder in the corporation, it's possible to "pierce the corporate veil" and hold Sam liable for its debts because he used the corporation as his "alter ego" when he used his personal bank account to pay for both personal and corporate debts, used corporate income to buy a summer home, and charged airline tickets to the corporation when he visited his son at college.

F. IT'S NEVER TOO LATE

While this chapter might have seemed a bit like shutting the barn door after the cow escaped, I hope you've learned that there's still a great deal which you can do to affect the final outcome. I know it's not easy to get your energy and enthusiasm back after a disappointing grade but you must. In your case, the cow hasn't escaped – it's only wandered around a bit. By following the suggestions and approaches we've covered here, you'll be able to make the changes necessary in your studying, your thinking, and your writing to achieve the success your hard work deserves. The key is that you go forward doing things differently than you did before. That's the real point of what we've been doing – learning how to do things differently so you'll achieve a different result.

CHAPTER 9:
FORENSIC IRAC

A. INTRODUCING FORENSIC IRAC

I'm sure you discovered from even the two examples in the previous chapter how carefully you must review your exams to really learn from the experience. And I'm also sure you realized that two problems won't be enough to provide all the guidance you need. Of course, working with your professors and the academic support personnel at your school will be extremely helpful, but you can't always count on someone else to critique your work and tell you what you've done right and where you've gone wrong. You'll be writing out lots of exam answers and practicing many multiple choice questions when you study. You need to be able to rely on yourself.

The good news is that you can develop the ability to do this kind of assessment for yourself. All you need are the right tools and you can become your own guide. By learning to apply what I've termed "forensic IRAC" to your own essays and multiple choice answers, you'll be able to identify the flaws in your work and correct them.

Just as the previous chapter was an "exam think aloud" where we stepped inside a student's head and learned what she was thinking from what she wrote in her exam answers, now we'll go inside your head and figure out what you were thinking when you wrote your essays and selected multiple choice answers.

1. HOW IT WORKS WITH ESSAYS

As you've been told repeatedly in law school and throughout this book, an effective essay follows the IRAC structure. As a result, your essays should be organized around an "issue," a "rule," an "application," and a "conclusion" for each and every issue and sub-issue you identify on an exam question. Once you've written an essay, therefore, you have all the evidence you need to use our forensic principles. By examining what you've written through the legal lens of IRAC, you'll be able to evaluate your own work. Your exams speak to your professor as to what you know and don't know: our goal is to have them speak to you too.

Forensic IRAC works by examining each sentence you've written in terms of its place in the IRAC structure of legal analysis. Now don't laugh or think I've been watching too many television crime dramas (even though I have!), but I've called the process forensic IRAC because the techniques we're going to use are similar to those employed by crime scene investigators, accountants, medical examiners, and any of the forensic experts who go back over the trail of evidence to determine how that evidence led to a particular result. While such experts rely on fingerprints, ledger books, and DNA, we use IRAC.

As I've said, we need to step inside your head to see the way you thought about the exam problem – how you approached it, how you read the facts, and what they meant to you. What you've written leaves an identifiable trail – something like your DNA but instead of identifying your biologic self, it identifies your cognitive self. You should think of forensic IRAC as deciphering a code, where each sentence you've written is a clue to piecing together how you approached a problem. It works because when you write, you take the inherently private and internal process called "thought" and make it public – and provide just the way into your head that we need.

2. APPLYING THE TECHNIQUE

The first step is to have written an essay with which we can work. It can be one of your final exam questions or an essay you've written in a study session. *If it's one that you've just written, I'm going to insist that you put it away for now.* You're not ready to be objective about something you've just completed. You're too close to see what you've really written as opposed to what you think you've written. The mind's eye is funny that way: you can read something you've written over and over again and never see the errors because your eye will correct them based on what your mind intended. The only way to avoid this is to distance yourself from your work. I strongly recommend that you write an essay one day and review it the next.

Now you're ready to take out the question and your essay. Re-read the question and then your answer. Now you're ready for a step-by-step guide to performing a self-diagnostic on your essay.

B. PERFORMING A SELF-DIAGNOSTIC FOR ESSAYS: EXPLANATIONS AND APPROACHES

As you read your essay, consider each sentence with respect to its function within the IRAC structure and then examine it against the outlined criteria. Remember, each sentence you write should serve some identifiable function: stating the issue, articulating the relevant rule of law, or developing the analysis of the facts. Then, by identifying each sentence with the role it plays in your answer, you can evaluate what you've written with a critical eye and identify its strengths and weaknesses.

What follows is something like a troubleshooting section in a technical manual where system faults are identified and applicable solutions are provided. This type of neutral classification of common performance errors will help you examine your own work objectively. You'll find explanations to guide you through evaluating your statements of the issue, articulation of the rules, and development of the analysis. For example, if you're seeking assistance in dealing with a tendency to "miss the issue," be "sketchy on the law," or write "conclusory" statements, you'll find a description of how this particular fault is manifested followed by suggestions on how to correct it.

1. WHEN YOU HAVE TROUBLE FINDING THE "ISSUE"

A failure to properly identify the issue(s) in your exam question results in a "scattershot" approach in the rest of your answer –a real "hit or miss" situation when it comes to racking up exam points. You may even have written an opening "The issue is whether" statement, but it merely restates the interrogatory without articulating the legal question underlying it. As a result, you're misled into thinking you've identified the issue when in fact you've missed it altogether.

Generally, you can tell that you've had difficulty in "spotting the issue" by what you've written in either the rule or the application portion of your essay, or both.

(a) **How you can tell when it shows up in your statement of the rule**
When you fail to identify the legal issue, it's likely to turn up as a problem in your statement of the rule. One of the following may occur:

- You may find that the rule discussion is so general and open-ended that it completely overlooks the precise rule implicated by the facts.

- Your analysis glosses ("sketchy") over the rule so lightly that the professor can't be sure whether you knew the relevant rule or merely happened to mention it.

- You've stated the wrong rule altogether.

Look for examples of the following in the rule section of your essay:

■ Lengthy, treatise-like discussions of general legal topics.
This is a pretty common situation where you've provided lots of "law" but it's too general to address the particular problem implicated by the facts. Typically, what you've managed to do is dance around the topic without engaging it.

■ Long, quoted passages from cases, statutes, or restatements.
If it's an open book or take home exam, chances are that you've been tempted to copy the rules. Very rarely, if ever, should you see quotation marks in your exam answer with the following exception: brief quotes of legally significant phrases. For example, if you're discussing bases for personal jurisdiction, then the phrase "minimum contacts" should appear in your discussion. Similarly, such phrases as "genuine issue of material fact," "bargained-for exchange," "mirror-image rule," and "the act speaks for itself," among others, operate as "legal shorthand" and your use of this language in the appropriate place indicates your working knowledge of the material.

■ Hornbook-like discussions of general legal topics.
Here, you've decided to show your professor how much time you've spent studying the subject so you display that knowledge by writing everything you know. What happens is that you provide far more information than is necessary, often miss the relevant point, and take up valuable exam time without adding to your grade.

For example, suppose your problem concerns whether Ben and Dylan entered into an agreement for Dylan to purchase Ben's house and the problem presented in the facts was whether the acceptance was "timely." If you were to include a lengthy discussion of the Uniform Commercial Code and why it doesn't apply to the sale of a home, you are way off base. There is rarely a need to discuss non-applicable law. I hate to say "never" because there might be a time when you may need to make a comparison or analogy, but a good general rule to follow is not to discuss non-applicable rules. There's hardly enough time to discuss the applicable law.

Similarly, if you were to include a detailed discourse on the mechanics of the mailbox rule when no one has mailed anything or questioned the method of acceptance, then you are also off point. Yes, it's contracts law, and yes, it's about the formation of contracts, but just because there may be a question regarding the validity of an acceptance, doesn't mean that you discuss everything you know about the topic. Rather, it means that you tailor the range of your answer to the scope of the facts. In this case, since the issue deals with the timeliness of the acceptance, then that's what you need to discuss —not all the possible methods of acceptance.

■ A discussion of the "wrong" rule.

There are a couple of reasons why you might have written the wrong rule on an exam answer (see also the next section on *When you have trouble writing the "Rule"*), but one very likely reason is that you didn't begin with a proper identification of the issue. It's relatively simple: if you don't define the legal problem, how do you know which rule to apply?

This may be hard for you to believe but it's not your job on an exam to recite all the law you've managed to memorize over the course of the semester. I can understand that if you think this way, there's no such thing as a "wrong rule" and the more you write, the better off you'll be. But sorry, it doesn't work like this. As we'll discuss in the next section, writing about a rule, even if it's correctly stated, is "wrong" if it's not the rule implicated by the facts.

(b)   ***How you can tell when it shows up in your application***

In these cases, your discussion may ramble and roam, moving without any logical transition from topic to topic. Or it may simply repeat the facts from the hypothetical. What's interesting, however, is that a knowledge of substantive law may be indicated by the choice of vocabulary as we saw in the first sample answer in the previous chapter, but since what's written doesn't connect with what's asked in the question, the points gained are very few, if any.

Look for examples of the following in the application portion of your essay:

■ No connection between the call-of-the-question and the application section of your answer.

When you're asked a specific question in a problem, then your analysis must be tailored to that question. For example, if your hypothetical asks, *"Was the court correct in admitting testimony of the parties' prior oral agreement then?"* What your professor is probably looking for is an analysis of the parol evidence rule with respect to the facts. If, on the other hand, all you wrote about was the duty of parties to act in good faith in the performance of the contract, then you've completely ignored the question you were asked to consider.

■ Facts in the hypothetical are repeated instead of analyzed.

One very good reason for restating facts instead of analyzing them is failure to work from the legal question. The issue provides focus and direction: it's the "problem" you solve with your "analysis." Without identifying a problem, you have nothing to answer, so you flounder and fall back on narrative.

■ A contradiction or discrepancy between what the rule requires and how the facts are analyzed.

Often your professor discovers whether you really understand the rule by what you write about the facts. This is probably best illustrated by an example. Consider the following:

> *Sam the Farmer agrees to supply Murray Inc. at the end of the growing season in August of this calendar year with all the Spud potatoes that Murray Inc. might require at a price of $100 per ton, delivery included.*

You are also told that no specific quantity is stated in the contract but Sam estimates that Murray would need approximately 30 tons based on what other manufacturers in the area and industry require with similar needs. Because Murray is getting such a good price for potatoes from Sam, it decides to expand operations and launch a new product, thereby increasing its demand for potatoes by one-third.

After correctly identifying the issue as one involving a requirements contract and stating the relevant UCC provision, the student proceeds to discuss a "mutual mistake" in the parties' understanding of how many potatoes would be required. The student writes that a mistake was made at to the number of potatoes involved since *"Murray assumed at the time of contract that he would need 40 tons of potatoes but decided after the contract to make a new type of potato chip and would need an additional 20 tons while Sam estimated Murray would need 30 tons."*

This answer is incorrect on several levels. First, it is incorrect with respect to the rule at issue because the discussion should focus on whether Murray Inc.'s increased demand was made in "good faith" and whether it was "unreasonably disproportionate" to a stated estimate or comparable requirements; second, it is incorrect with regard to a claim for mutual mistake since the actual number of potatoes could not be a mistake since no number is defined in a requirements contract; and finally, even if it were a mutual mistake, the mistaken belief would have to be held at the time of the contract's formation, not subsequently. Here the student discusses Murray's initial assumption about the quantity and then a subsequent increased need. This is not a legal mistake but an erroneous prediction about the future.

The problem is that the analysis does not follow the requirements of the rule. Instead, there is a serious disconnect between rule and fact, indicating a genuine lack of understanding.

(c) Suggested remedies

The following is a suggested strategy for identifying the legal issue raised by a hypothetical factual situation.

SUMMARY OF STEPS:

1. Begin your analysis by identifying the call-of-the-question.

2. Articulate the issue based on the interrogatory.

3. Develop an outline of what you need to discuss according to the issue.

Learn to think of the issue as your "legal compass" or, if you prefer a sports analogy, think of it as keeping your "eye on the ball." Either way, what happens when you focus on the issue is that you write strong, effective exam answers by discussing the right rule and appropriate facts.

Strive to articulate the issue by formulating the legal question presented by the facts. Ask yourself: "what is the theory" or "what is in controversy" in these facts. That is the issue. Even in questions that ask such general open-ended interrogatories as "analyze fully," you must strive to identify the issues and sub-issues as completely as possible in terms of the relevant rules and which facts bring those rules into controversy. This is the only way to ensure that you'll be on the right path in your analysis.

Now let's see how you might do this.

(1) Begin your analysis by identifying the call-of-the-question.

Does it ask a *specific question* like one of the following:

- Was the court correct in granting the motion for summary judgment?

- Can the defendant successfully assert the defense of justification?

- Were the numbered rulings correct?

- Does Farmer Dell have a cause of action in trespass

or does it present a *general, open-ended* question like one of these:

- Discuss the rights and liabilities of all parties.

- Discuss all causes of action.

- Analyze fully.

(2) Articulate the issue based on the interrogatory.

(a) When working with a specific question:
Identify the legal controversy behind the ruling/defense/question by asking yourself:

"What is the theory behind this position?"

Let's look at some examples. Suppose the call-of-the-question is something like this:

> Was Ben's decision not to publish John's book exercised in good faith?

Do not write as your statement of the issue:

> The issue is whether Ben's decision was made in good faith.

This is merely a restatement of the interrogatory.

Instead, you need to review the facts to determine what is in controversy about Ben's decision, i.e., what he did or didn't do in reaching his decision. After carefully reviewing the facts, you'll probably find that the legal "controversy" is:

> The issue is whether Ben exercised good faith in deciding not to publish John's book when he refused to read the revised manuscript and relied only on a preliminary draft.

Let's look at another example. Suppose you're asked the following:

> Did Ben and Dylan have an enforceable agreement?

Once again, your task is not restate the question, but to look closely at the facts to see what is in dispute between the parties regarding the agreement and come up with something like this

> The issue is whether Dylan's acceptance of Ben's offer after 10 days constitutes a valid acceptance when Ben's offer stated that the acceptance must be soon.

By identifying the legal issue as one concerning the timeliness of the acceptance, your subsequent discussion of the rule and the facts will focus on the requirements for a valid acceptance, and specifically, on the duration of the power of acceptance.

(b)   When working with a general-style question:
Identify the nature of our task by determining whether you need to identity causes of action, possible defenses, remedies, etc.

Let's return to our Farmer Dell example where you were presented with the following:

> Farmer Dell has sought your advice as to whether he has grounds for an action against Ben or Jerry or both. Discuss fully.

As we saw when we worked through this example, a problem like this takes a bit of mental organization before you write and your answer will likely break down into separate actors and/or causes of action. But you still need a starting point and it can be something like this

Whether Farmer Dell has a cause of action depends on whether Ben and/or Jerry were trespassing when they entered his cornfield.

Now at least you have a launching pad from which to discuss the various acts and defenses of the individual parties. You should notice that when you have a general-style question, you can't possibly put all the relevant facts into your issue but you want to begin with something that connects to the primary question you need to consider. In this case, it's trespass.

(3) Develop an outline of what you need to discuss according to the issue.

Once you've identified your issue, stay with it and let it guide you through your analysis. By keeping the issue in sight at all times, you'll avoid getting side-tracked and going off on tangents.

(a) When working with a specific question

- Each issue forms the basis for a separate IRAC analysis. Still, you must remember that there are usually issues within issues. Each main issue is very likely to break down into sub-issues and each sub-issue gets its own IRAC treatment.

  For example, in our Ben and Dylan problem regarding the question of Dylan's acceptance, a sub-issue might be whether the offer was revoked before it was accepted. Of course, all of this would have to be determined from the facts you're given.

- Outline the rule. List any elements or factors. Note only the exceptions or limitations relevant to your facts. The same is true with defenses. Note only the defenses to be raised based on your facts.

For example, suppose you have a problem which asks

Will a New York court be able to assert personal jurisdiction over Jill based on its long arm statute?

and you've identified your issue as turning on whether Jill has sufficient minimum contacts with New York. In this case, there's no need to discuss any of the "traditional" bases of jurisdiction but to work solely with the long arm statute.

- As you write your analysis, work only from your articultion of the rule to guide your application of the facts. Here your statement of the rule provides a blueprint to follow for your discussion of the facts. You simply match up each element/factor you've identified in the rule with a fact, using the word "because" to make the connection between rule and fact.

While this will be explored further in the section on writing the application portion of your essay, it's still helpful to have an example to see how nicely the task unfolds when you let the issue drive your analysis.

Suppose you've outlined the factors to consider for satisfying the "minimum contacts" test. Now you're ready to match up each factor with a fact from your hypothetical. This process looks something like this,

> *Factor:* substantial and continuous contacts
>
> *Fact:* one visit in 20 years; $500 donation to alumni fund
>
> *Factor:* benefit from the forum state
>
> *Fact:* one visit to attend a class reunion
>
> *Factor:* connection between the contact and the cause of action
>
> *Fact:* visit occurred a year earlier and cause of action is based on employment activity in Los Angeles

which translates to

> *Here, Jill did not have substantial and continuous contacts with New York because she only visited once in 20 years and made a single donation of $500 to her Law School's alumni fund. She did not receive a benefit from New York simply because of one overnight visit to attend a class reunion. Further, there's no connection between this contact and the cause of action because the visit occurred a year earlier and is wholly unconnected with the action which arose from Jill's employment as a fashion stylist in Los Angeles.*

(b)   *When working with a general-style question*

With this type of interrogatory, you've got more work to do but it's not any more of a challenge if you consider the following:

■ Use subheadings to organize your response

Sub-headings are a great way to keep answers organized. They are as useful for the writer as for the reader. Sub-headings promote organization – both of thought and expression. Your choice of sub-headings should be simple and direct. In the case of our problem with Farmer Dell, you could organize your discussion around the parties or the causes of action.

> "Farmer Dell v. Ben"
> "Farmer Dell v. Jerry"
> "Trespass to Chattel"
> "Trespass to Land"

■ Structure discussions around the issues/sub-issues and defenses. If you're working with a fact pattern that's long on issues but short on characters, sometimes it's useful to organize around the causes of action.

This might come up in a criminal law problem where you're dealing with one actor who has committed a series of possible crimes. Here, you might consider organizing your IRACs around each crime as a way to avoid jumping from one act to another. This will ensure that you focus on one crime and its attendant elements at a time. You'll want to discuss whether each element is satisfied and whether there are any defenses before moving on to consider another crime.

A similar situation arises in torts where one set of facts may indicate more than one tort but you still need to focus on each one individually.

Once you get in the habit of organizing your thinking around (directing your thinking from) the issue, you'll find your writing becomes organized as well.

2. WHEN YOU HAVE TROUBLE WRITING THE "RULE"

There are two separate and distinct problems which can show up in the rule portion of your exam analysis. The first, and by far the most troublesome is where there's a genuine ignorance of the law. You may state the wrong rule for the issue in controversy or refer to the right rule, but state it incorrectly, either in whole or in part. The second problem occurs where there's a demonstration of substantive knowledge, but it's sketchy and incomplete. Here you don't state "enough" rule to provide an adequate context for analyzing the facts.

No doubt these are both very serious problems because your professor accepts it as a given that you can recite the relevant rule, completely and correctly. However, while your professor may treat both problems alike with respect to the amount of points lost on your exam and the comment in your blue book – problem with the rule – we need to do better to figure out which problem is yours. It makes a difference in how we go about fixing it.

(a)   When you don't really know the applicable rule

We've repeated this so many times by now that it should come as no surprise to read once again that if you don't really know the rule – by which I mean understand it thoroughly, its elements, its consequences, and how it operates – then you can't answer the question correctly. There's no way to fake your way through an exam answer because the language of the law is precise and your explication of the rule must be clear to allow for a meaningful analysis.

Your professor knows when you don't know what you're talking about. The question is do you? *Can you tell when what you've written shows you don't really know the applicable law?*

First, let's consider an overview of how this problem "presents" and some general "remedies." Then we'll discuss each one in detail to understand how the problem occurs, what it looks like, and consider some specific remedies.

THE OVERVIEW:

- *How you can tell*

  Look for examples of the following in the "rule" section:

  - Substituting your words for legally significant language.
  - Using imprecise language and meaningless phrases.
  - Relying on buzz-words.
  - Failing to use legal terminology, thus sounding as if written by a non-lawyer.
  - Misstating the law.
  - Writing illogical, disjointed statements of the rule.

  Look for examples of the following in the "application" section:

  - Repeating the facts without stating their legal significance.
  - Writing logically inconsistent statements.
  - Failing to distinguish between relevant and irrelevant facts.

■ *How you can remedy*

As you well know, there are a number of reasons why you don't know something. The most obvious reason is that you simply didn't spend enough time studying and memorizing the black letter law. On the other hand, a lack of knowledge can result from an inability to integrate and learn legal principles. Sometimes, you may spend adequate time in study but the time spent is ineffective because you're not focused on the right stuff.

In addition to reviewing your notes and memorizing black letter law, you are going to integrate the following tasks into your study plan:

- Re-write the rules of law in your own words while conserving the legal "terms of art."

- Put the parts/elements of rules together in a way that forms a logical whole. Memorize them.

- Having memorized the rules, make sure you understand how to apply them to new fact situations. Write out answers to hypotheticals and practice answering objective, multiple choice questions in that area of the law.

- Practice turning rules into issues and questions. Don't stop at memorizing the definition of a "merchant." Learn to ask yourself, "what's the *consequence* of finding that the party was a merchant with respect to the transaction in dispute?"

THE SPECIFICS:

Now we're ready to get to work. The best way to tell that you really don't know the rule is by checking what you've written for *imprecise or incorrect use of legal language*. When you don't really understand the rule, it "presents" through a failure to use precise legal terminology, incorrect paraphrasing, or the substitution of legal buzz-words for legal analysis. Another way a lack of true understanding "presents" is a failure to use legal vocabulary where it would be appropriate and expected. You want to incorporate the basic vocabulary of each subject into how you think and what you write.

As we work through the following examples and explanations, remember that one of your primary tasks on an exam is to communicate in the language of the law, thus demonstrating your mastery of the material.

(1) *Substituting your words for legally significant language*

The language of the law is precise: change the word and you change the meaning. Not only will you change the meaning, but you'll show your professor in a word (sometimes a single word will betray you) that you've totally disregarded the case law and failed to appreciate the special meaning of key language. While it's often necessary to paraphrase the rule, it's essential that you maintain the integrity of the rule by preserving the legally significant language.

Consider the example of a student who consistently substituted the word "entities" for "unities" on her property exam. The question required that she analyze the four unities required for the creation of a joint tenacy. She claimed she "knew the rule" and believed she should have received full credit for her answer. I said that if she really "knew the rule," she would not have used the wrong word. She didn't understand how one word could make the answer incorrect. To her, the words were the same. But they aren't and it was critical that she understand why and how she made this mistake.

First, we checked her class notes. Then we looked at the cases in her casebook. Finally we reviewed a hornbook on the subject. In each case, the word "unities" was used to discuss this common law principle. The only place the word "entities" appeared was in her outline. She wrote "entities" on her exam because that's what she studied from her outline. At some point in her studying she thought it was okay to replace legal language with her own because she didn't see that "unities" was "legal language."

SUGGESTED REMEDIES

- Make sure you understand what you read by being able to express it in your own words.

- Look up all words and terms you don't understand (legal and non-legal) and add them to your vocabulary notebook; writing it down reinforces it in your memory.

- Pay careful attention to the court's use of language, especially when words or phrases are repeated.

- Strive to incorporate legal terminology into all you write, beginning with your case briefs.

- Make sure you fully understand what you're reading – whether a court decision, a hornbook, or a statute – before you attempt to paraphrase. This way you'll preserve the language of the law by not altering essential vocabulary when you paraphrase the rules. Even ordinary sounding words may have a special legal meaning: you must take care to recognize and preserve this meaning. Often the problem occurs when you're not quite sure you understand what you're reading.

(2)   Absence of legal vocabulary

Like every other profession, the legal profession has its own specialized language and your job upon entering the field is to speak it fluently. Developing that fluency begins with your very first reading assignment. From that moment on, you should strive to absorb the language of the law by immersing yourself in it. The next step is for the language to find its way into your oral and then your written vocabulary. The following examples show how minor modifications effect major transformations.

- *What not to write:*

    These damages are the difference between the cost to the buyer and what the buyer would have purchased the goods for if the seller had not repudiated the sale.

- *What you should write:*

    The buyer may recover from the seller as cover damages the difference between the cost of the substitute goods and the original contract price, plus any incidental or consequential damages but less expenses saved as a result of seller's breach.

- *What not to write:*

    In determining how to divide the spouses' property, the court will consider what each spouse had prior to the marriage and acquired during the marriage.

- *What you should write:*

    In determining an equitable distribution of marital assets, the court will consider a spouse's separate property as well as the marital property.

- *What not to write:*

    Citizenship depends on the state of the parties' permanent homes.

- *What you should write:*

    Citizenship for the purposes of federal court jurisdiction is determined by a party's domicile, not mere residence in the state.

- *What not to write:*

    A motion for summary judgment is used when there is a cause of action but there is no genuine issue of material fact to be tried.

- *What you should write:*

    The court will grant a motion for summary judgment if the moving party can show that there is no genuine issue of material fact in the lawsuit and that he is entitled to judgment as a matter of law.

    or

A party will make a motion for summary judgment when it can show that there is no genuine issue of material fact in the lawsuit and that he is entitled to judgment as a matter of law.

I included two re-writes of the last example because the student's meaning wasn't clear from what she wrote. When you fail to use the *proper legal vocabulary properly* you obscure the meaning as well – which is a nice transition to our next topic.

(3)   *Imprecision in language*

Like a toddler reciting the pledge of allegiance as "one nation, under god, *invisible*, with liberty and justice for all," this is the case where a gap in knowledge is filled in with an artful substitution. It may sound the same, but it's not.

Consider the following substitution of *"deferential"* for *"differential"* in part of an equal protection analysis. The student wrote,

"the Supreme Court gives differential consideration to acts of Congress"

and that's pretty much all she wrote with reference to the concept of judicial review of legislative acts. While it's easy enough to make a spelling error on an exam, this case wouldn't qualify. In addition to using the wrong word, there's too much missing. The problem is two-fold: first, the legal reference is too cryptic to demonstrate any real understanding of the principle; and second, it's questionable whether the right principle has been identified. The reader doesn't know whether the student is referring to the principle of judicial deference to the legislative branch when it acts with respect to social and economic regulations, a separation of powers concern. Unless the student uses the precise language or explains the concept more fully, the presumption is that she doesn't know something that is clearly fundamental to the subject matter.

SUGGESTED REMEDIES

- Learn the language of the law by memorizing basic vocabulary.

- Make it a priority to memorize basic definitions and the elements of rules because you need to know the law to write the law.

- Learn the language in the appropriate context to ensure proper usage.

The language of the law is precise. Your must learn that language and use it carefully to convey precisely what you mean. To do this, you have to memorize vocabulary. If necessary, make lists and flash cards, but learn the language. While the process may begin with rote memorization, the end result is knowledge of the material – for the exam and for practice.

Further, you must learn to use legal language in its proper context. This is especially true for words-of-art because failure to use such language appropriately indicates either a true lack of understanding or carelessness, neither of which is acceptable. For example, a party "makes a motion" (hence "a moving party") while a court either "grants" or "denies" a motion. While the language is not interchangeable, I've often come across student papers where courts are "making" motions.

A far more serious problem arises when language particular to an area of law is twisted beyond recognition. For example, I recently came across this sentence:

- Example: *"The occurrence of a condition triggers the duty to perform a promise."*

This sentence is incorrect for a number of reasons, but what concerns us here is the phrase, *"the occurrence of a condition."* The problem is that a condition doesn't occur. An event which has been made the condition of performance occurs. Whether the event occurs then determines whether the promisor's duty to perform will arise. This is a major difference and anyone who knows the differences between conditions and promises would never write this sentence.

(4)   Meaningless phrases and misuse of language

These are phrases that consist of relevant legal terms but the way the words are put together make them meaningless. Or at least meaningless to the professor. For example, what does the following phrase mean?

- Example: *"A condition switches on a promise."*

I'll save you a lot of time: this sentence doesn't mean anything. At least I can't find any meaning in it. It appeared in a student's answer to an exam question where the question required the student to discuss the difference between words of condition and words of promise.

- Example: *"If the promise was material..."*

Here's an example of how using legal language, even the appropriate language for that specialized area of the law, can still go wrong. The individual words may be correct, but the way they are used together lets the teacher know that the student is ignorant of that area of the law. "Promises" are not material – "breaches" are. The statement should have been, "if the breach of the promise was material."

■ Example: *"His work was innocent and unintentional."*

This phrase appeared in an exam answer where the student was asked to determine, given the facts in the hypothetical, whether the contractor's failure to install the flooring specified in the contract was a material breach. One factor in determining whether a breach was material would be whether the breaching party's non-performance was wilful or the result of purely innocent behavior.

Apparently, the student mixed it together and came up with this statement. But it's not quite right. The problem for the professor is determining whether the student knows the rule. The contractor's work was not innocent and unintentional – the flooring he installed was the wrong type which was a breach of the party's agreement. The relevant inquiry then becomes whether the breach, i.e., failing to install the correct flooring, was done intentionally or whether it was an innocent oversight. Now it might seem as if the student is saying the same thing, but she's not. It's not clear what's being said when two separate and distinct questions are combined. The only thing that is clear is that the student doesn't know the difference.

SUGGESTED REMEDIES

■ Memorize with meaning: aim for complete understanding when learning the rules.

■ Practice multiple choice questions to place rules in the context of facts.

■ Practice each rule in terms of a hypothetical to make sure that you understand as well as memorize the rules. Play around with the facts of the hypothetical – ask yourself whether the change affects the outcome.

You can avoid meaningless phrases by learning legal vocabulary and using it correctly. If you do this, you won't end up with an exam paper full of colorful, yet incorrect, language. But more essential to curing this problem is to truly understand the rules: if you know what the rule means, you won't write legally meaningless sentences.

To make sure you understand a rule, you need to practice it. Here's where it helps to work through objective-style questions and hypotheticals. By applying the rule in a factual situation, you'll gain much needed context. For example, if you're studying criminal law, ask yourself whether it's a burglary when the entering of the apartment occurred at 3:00 pm? At 8:30 pm but it was still light outside? Apply different rules to the same fact scenario. What result if you apply the common law to this set of facts? What result if you apply the rule in your jurisdiction? Simply memorizing a rule without understanding how it works is insufficient. This type of practice provides the context you need for understanding as well as memorizing the rules of law.

(5) *Dependence on "buzz-words" without back-up*

Now that I've told you to use precise legal language, I'm going to add a caveat: don't substitute legal vocabulary for legal analysis – even when it's the right legal vocabulary. While the right word will carry you far, it won't get you there by itself. When used properly, "buzz-words" are an appropriate shorthand for conveying information, but that must be followed with solid analysis where required – which turns out to be most of the time.

Frequently, students rely on buzz-words instead of explanations – when speaking in class and when writing exam answers. Let's take a closer look at what I mean.

■ Example:
Probably one of the best examples of this phenomenon is "promissory estoppel," the all-around favorite of first year law students. It seems that hardly a question I ask in a Contracts class cannot be answered by this handy-dandy legal principle.

Whether I ask –

Is this contract enforceable?

or

What is the measure of plaintiff's recovery?

I get the same answer: "promissory estoppel." It doesn't matter whether we're discussing contract formation or contract remedies, students love to find promissory estoppel. And often they're correct. It's quite likely to be the right answer. But it's not the whole answer: what the student sees as the end of the answer, the teacher sees as its beginning. All the student has done is identify a possible legal principle to be used to consider the problem. I'm waiting to hear (or to read) what comes next. Law professors are not interested in the bottom line. We're interested in how you got there. So instead of "promissory estoppel" as an answer to my questions, I was looking for more, beginning with full sentences.

So, if my question was,

Is this contract enforceable?

I'm looking for some variation of,

*It's not likely that this contract is enforceable because it lacks **consideration**, but the defendant's **promise induced** the plaintiff to **rely** to his **detriment**, something the defendant should **reasonably have foreseen**, and therefore **promissory estoppel** would allow for a recovery.*

Whether you're speaking in class or writing out an exam answer, the first step is to respond in full and complete sentences. Certainly, you want to incorporate key language, but you cannot rely on one or two words to do the job. If you consider the words that appear in bold, I've used six legal terms associated with "promissory estoppel" to answer the question. And this is just the beginning. If this conversation occurred in the classroom, the professor would follow up with additional questions, leading the student through a discussion of each of these concepts with respect to the particular facts of the problem. If this were an exam essay, you would have more to write as well.

The point is that this response demonstrates an understanding of the principle. It incorporates the basis elements of the doctrine – promise, inducement, reliance, foreseeability, and detriment. They are used to convey the student's understanding of the rule and how it applies in this case. The professor can be pretty sure that the student understands the doctrine of promissory estoppel. If you can turn a buzz-word into a complete explanation, then you understand it too. But if you can't, you're in trouble. It's a pretty good indication that you don't really know the rule.

Similarly, if we look at my question,

What is the measure of plaintiff's recovery?

I'm looking for,

While plaintiff can't recover his full expectation interest because the contract lacked consideration and was therefore unenforceable, it's possible to seek reliance damages based on plaintiff's reliance on defendant's promise to his detriment of $10,000 when....

I'm sure you get the point by now. We're ready to look at another example.

■ Example:
Let's consider another law student favorite: "substantial certain-

ty." These two words figure prominently in any first year Torts class because they're central to the study of intentional torts and specifically, to the meaning of "intent." For our purposes, we'll narrow our discussion to the intent required to commit a battery.

Students learn that the intent element for commission of a battery is satisfied not only when the actor intends harmful or wrongful behavior, but if she acts with purpose or knowledge to a "substantial certainty." Unfortunately, students often limit their discussion of intent to just these two words. However, it's necessary to explain what it means to act with "substantial certainty." A more complete response would read something like,

> If the defendant knows with substantial certainty that a **particular effect** will occur as a **result of her action**, she is found to have intended that result. The defendant need not have understood her act to be "wrongful" to have formed the requisite intent: she need only know what would be the **likely consequence** of that act.

Certainly, some credit would be given for using the appropriate buzz-words, but a solid analysis of the relevant facts requires more of an explanation of the rule than can be conveyed by two words. It needs the foundation of the meaning that comes from the words I've highlighted: particular effect, result of her action, and likely consequence.

SUGGESTED REMEDIES

- Develop the practice of thinking, speaking, and writing in complete sentences.

- Make sure you can define each buzz-word.

The tendency to rely on catch-words in place of complete sentences is a pretty good indication that you lack a solid understanding of the rule. Unless you can fully articulate what the buzz-words mean, you probably don't understand them adequately.

The cure for relying on buzz-words is to cultivate and reinforce the habit of thinking, speaking, and writing in complete sentences. A good place to begin is by taking your class notes in complete sentences. If you can't write fast enough to keep up with class discussions, then type (but only if your typing is fast and accurate) or tape the classes. Since your notes are a key source of information, you want to make sure that you capture what's important in sufficient detail so that you'll understand what you've written when reading your notes after class. Nothing is more frustrating than no longer knowing what you meant by what you wrote.

Similarly, make sure your outlines explain the rule adequately and, once again, write in sentences, not phrases. In this way, you'll cultivate the habit of thinking in complete sentences and consequently, you'll write your exams in complete sentences too. This might be a good time to review the chapter on outlining – specifically the section that explains what you need to include about a rule to make sure you learn it fully.

(b)   *When your statement of the rule is incomplete or unorganized*

A majority of students who receive disappointing grades fall into this category. That's the bad news. Here's the good news: it's a relatively easy situation to correct because the problem isn't that you've identified the wrong rule or don't know the rule, but you haven't written enough of it in your analysis. Not only may there not be enough law, but it may not be expressed in a logical and coherent manner.

First and foremost, your professor expects your exam answer to demonstrate a firm grasp of "black letter law." Quite aside from a sound mastery of legal principles and basic knowledge of core substance, a firm "grasp" of the law means that you know exactly how much detail is necessary to provide for a meaningful factual discussion.

Once again, let's begin with an overview of how this problem "presents" and some suggested "remedies." Then we'll follow up with detailed explanations.

THE OVERVIEW:

- *How you can tell*

    Look for examples of the following in the "rule" section:

    - "Snippets" of law, buzz-words, and catch phrases in place of complete sentences and full explanations.

    - Lists of "elements" without definitions.

    - Identification of the relevant exception but no statement of the general rule to provide context.

    - Statements of law without a logical connection between them.

- *How you can remedy*

    Follow the building block approach to construct your rule of law

    - *Explain* the elements in your rule.

    - *Define* the legal terms.

- *Identify* the general rule that provides the context for the exception.

- Include any relevant *federal/state distinctions or common law/statutory law distinctions.*

Look for examples of the following in the "application" section:

- Solid factual discussion that appears element-based but without any explanation/identification of the element.

- Recitation of the legally-relevant facts but without reference to the supporting legal framework.

- *How you can remedy*

- Build your legal context by working backwards from what you've stated in the facts to determine the scope of the rule necessary to lay a foundation for what you've discussed.

- With respect to a fact, ask yourself *why* you found this fact sufficiently relevant to be discussed. This forces you to identify the legal basis for relevancy.

THE SPECIFICS:

The challenge for most students is deciding what to include and not writing too much or too little. The other problem is writing the rule in its logical order. We'll break this down into two steps and begin with writing enough of the rule.

(1)   Writing enough of the rule

Even after reading the Overview, I can practically hear you thinking,

- I'm still not sure what you mean about not writing enough rule.

- Isn't there such a thing as too much rule?

Happily, I can provide a "general rule" when it comes to writing the rule. We'll be working with it throughout this section and the next when we consider writing the application. The rule is relatively simple,

Write enough about the rule to provide the context in which you will analyze the facts. The rule and the facts are inextricably linked. Your analysis of the facts will not make sense unless you have first identified the rule which determines the relevance of those facts.

The question we now need to consider is *"how do you know when your statement of the rule is inadequate, incomplete, and insufficient to do the job?"* It's likely to appear as follows:

- You write "snippets" of law, relying on buzz-words and catch phrases.

- You list "elements" without explanation or definition.

- You discuss the "exception" and omit the context of the "general rule."

Look for examples of the following in the rule section of your essay:

- Buzz-words and legal phrases instead of complete fully developed statements of the law.

Your statement of the rule of law is one of the most important parts of your exam essay, second only to your analysis of the facts. First, it lets your professor know that you have identified the legal problem and second, it shows that you know the relevant law. The major problem, and where students fail to get as many points on an exam as they can and should, is that they do not write enough law to provide a solid anchor for their analysis of the facts.

Exactly what are "snippets of law"? I created this phrase to describe the smatterings of "legalese" I found myself reading in one student paper after another. The sentences were like skeletons – the frame was there, but the bones and the muscles and the connective tissue were all missing.

Consider the following sentence – which was all the student wrote concerning plaintiff's burden in seeking a preliminary injunction:

A plaintiff must balance the equities and show he would succeed.

This sentence speaks to me. First, it tells me that the student doesn't know the whole rule because critical elements are missing. Second, it tells me that it's likely the student doesn't really understand any part of the rule because the elements that are included are incompletely or incorrectly expressed.

If the student had incorporated the rule into her analysis of the facts, then this sentence would merely have served as an identification of the rule and the problem would have been solved. Somehow she needed to include the following three-part test somewhere in her discussion, either in her "rule" paragraph or developed within the factual analysis of each element – but she didn't.

To determine whether a moving party is entitled to a preliminary injunction, she must show: first, that she would suffer an irreparable injury absent the granting of the preliminary injunction; second, that a balancing of the equities between the parties favored the granting of the injunction; and third, that the plaintiff enjoys a likelihood of ultimate success on the merits of the underlying action.

Also, you should note that there's still more "rule" to be discussed in the body of the analysis. For example, the term "irreparable injury" would need to be defined to provide context for discussion of the facts to determine whether plaintiff meets this burden. What is her injury? Why is it irreparable? Further, you would need to explain what it means to "balance the equities." Each of these sub-issues would be taken up in the appropriate section of the discussion as a natural unfolding of the analytic process.

FIGURING OUT WHY THIS HAPPENS

I've often wondered why students would leave out an adequate legal discussion when they actually know the rules. It took quite a bit of thought and working closely with students to figure it out but I finally realized it has to do with how some students see their job on exams.

(a)   Not wanting to "teach the teacher"

A common explanation for failing to include sufficient explanations of the law is that the teacher already knows it. It's certainly true that the professor knows the law – and it's not likely you're going to teach her anything new. But she doesn't know whether you know the law and that's the point of the whole exam – to see what you know. If you don't write it, she won't know you know it. Think of your job on the exam as an opportunity to be a show-off. It's your recital, your moment on the stage. If you realize that your job on an exam is to convey what you've learned, and especially that you've mastered the substantive material of the course, you won't leave out the main course.

(b)   Not realizing the goal is problem-solving

Another reason for an inadequate legal discussion is that some students fail to appreciate their role as "problem solvers" and skip right to the "bottom line." They don't see exam questions as problems to be analyzed but rather as questions to be answered – and it's exactly the other way around. Typically, your professor cares little about your conclusion, unless the question asks specifically for an answer, and even then the emphasis will be on how you arrived at the answer and not the answer itself. In fact, one of my professors told us never to include a "conclusion" because as he put it, "who do you think you are – the judge or the jury?" Your "conclusion" is largely irrelevant: it serves only to provide a logical close to your argument.

> Note: *While I'm mentioning this tendency here with respect to inadequate statements of the rule, it's just as true when it comes to analyzing the facts. Maybe more so.*

(c)   Not knowing you need to "show all work"

This problem goes hand in hand with the one we just discussed: when you're focused on the bottom line result, you leave out the analysis of how you got there. On a law school exam, your job is to show all your work. It's a lot like when you took a math exam and the teacher said you needed to show all your work because you could get part credit even if you arrived at the wrong answer if she could see that you followed the right process. The same principle applies here although there's very rarely even a "right answer."

■ "Elements" without explanation

The following is an example where elements or factors are identified but not otherwise defined. Unless the student were to develop each further in the course of a factual analysis, this is far too cryptic to serve as the complete recitation of the rule.

> *There are four elements required to form an agency relationship: a. manifestation of assent; b. subject to control of the principal; c. fiduciary relationship and d. act on his behalf.*

Suppose you were given a set of facts and asked to determine whether an agency relationship existed and the only information you had to work with was this one sentence. Would you be able to make a determination? Where would you begin? As you can see, there are too many gaps in information to allow you to evaluate any facts. After all, you wouldn't know any of the following:

- Who has to "manifest assent"?
- Assent to what?
- What's a principal?
- What's a fiduciary?
- What does it mean to "act on behalf of another"?

Strangely enough, students try to analyze problems with such gaps all the time and wonder why they don't succeed. As I've said so many times, you need to know enough about the rule to find meaning in the facts. *And you must include enough of the rule or the factual arguments you make will have no legal foundation to support them.*

Therefore, when you write a sentence like this on your exam, it conveys two messages:

(1)   It tells your professor that you don't know the whole rule. Or at least not enough of it to show sufficient mastery of the material to appreciate its complexity and depth. Of course it's possible you know more than you're writing down, but your professor doesn't know that. She can only go by the words in your blue book and if they're not there, the presumption is that you

don't know.

and

(2)   It sets you up to write a very weak analysis because you have nothing on which to build.

Fortunately, the remedy is simple: include more substance by working from the foundation you've created. If you've listed elements, then define them; if you've identified factors, then explain them. You can include this in your essay either in your "rule paragraph" or by weaving the rule into your factual analysis.

■ The "exception" without the "general rule

If you've identified an exception to a general rule as the critical factor in your problem, then you must also include the general rule. A statement of the general rule provides much-needed context for understanding the exception.

A good example of working from the exception to the general rule are questions that test the Fourth Amendment's prohibition against unreasonable searches and seizures and its corollary, the exclusionary rule. Of course such questions are not limited to the Fourth Amendment. Given the nature of the law, the list is practically endless: when is there not an exception to a rule? All this means is that when your task is to analyze whether an exception applies, you want to include a statement of the general rule before you turn your attention to the specific exception brought into controversy by the facts of your problem.

Let's consider the following three examples: first, a search incident to a valid arrest; second, the dying declaration exception to the hearsay rule; and third, the seller's right to cure an otherwise non-conforming shipment.

■ Example: Fourth Amendment and warrantless searches

Don't just write...

Pursuant to a lawful arrest, the police officer can make a warrantless search of an automobile if there is reason to believe it contains contraband.

without preceding it by the general rule...

Under the Fourth Amendment, a person has the right to be free from unreasonable searches and seizures by the government. A search will normally be considered unreasonable if it is not conducted pursuant to a validly executed warrant based upon probable cause unless one of the exceptions applies. However,...

■ Example: Hearsay and the "dying declaration"

Don't just write the exception...

> *The officer's statement may be admitted as a "dying declaration." In order to be admissible, the statement must meet the following criteria.......[assume the valid criteria are identified].*

without preceding it by the general rule...

> *Under the Federal Rules of Evidence, hearsay is an out-of-court statement offered for the truth of the matter asserted. Hearsay is inadmissible unless it falls within an exception or is excluded from the definition of hearsay. One such exception is the dying declaration....*

- Example: the "perfect tender rule" and the "right to cure"

Don't just write the exception...

> *The buyer may not cancel the contract and must accept conforming goods if the seller gives notice of the intent to cure and does so by the time performance is due.*

without preceding it by the general rule...

> *The general rule for buyer's rights on receipt of non-conforming goods is that a buyer may reject the goods entirely, retain units that conform to the contract, or accept the non-conforming goods. However, there is an exception to this "perfect tender rule" when a seller ships non-conforming goods before performance is due and notifies the buyer of his intent to cure.*

Just as exceptions make for good exam questions, responses that provide the context of the general rule make for good exam answers because they make for complete answers. This, in turn, demonstrates your complete understanding of the material.

(2)   Writing the rule in its logical order

There is a structure to follow when writing a rule of law. You should strive to present your statement of the law in its logical order. This demonstrates your understanding of the material and makes it easy for the professor to follow. In the process, it helps insure that you write enough of the law by covering related concepts.

Thoughtful legal analysis requires a logical development and presentation of the applicable law. The bottom line is that you must know how a rule breaks down to write it in an organized manner; you must understand the flow of the rule and how the pieces connect. You must learn and understand not only the individual parts but the links between them.

Writing the rule according to its logical order is really just another way of saying that your writing should be organized. Using these principles will keep you organized without thinking about it – follow them and you're discussion will be naturally organized.

Consider the following hierarchy of concepts when you write the rule:

Move from the general to the specific.

Your analysis should begin with a statement of the general rule and move to the exception. Moving from the general to the specific is simply the natural order of things.

Define each legal term of art.

When your statement of the rule contains a legal term of art, your next sentence should be a definition of that term. This is one of the easiest ways to go about building a complete statement of the rule in a logical and methodical manner. The sentences flow almost effortlessly (and seamlessly) because one statement leads naturally to the next.

■ *What not to write:*

A party can acquire property by adverse possession. It must be for the entire statutory period and exclusive to the adverse possessor. It must also be open and notorious. Exclusivity means that the physical occupation was solely by the adverse possessor and not shared with the true owner. The adverse possessor must hold the property continuously for the entire statutory period. Further, the adverse possessor must act to exclude all others from the property, as would a true owner. The adverse possessor's presence on the property must be such that a reasonable owner would have notice of his presence on the property. The possession must be hostile to the interests of the true owner.

■ *Having imposed a little order, here's what you should write:*

One may acquire title to real property through adverse possession. In order to assert a claim, the adverse possessor must satisfy four requirements. The first is that the possession must be exclusive. Exclusivity means that the physical occupation was solely by the adverse possessor and not shared with the true owner. Further, the adverse possessor must act to exclude all others from the property, as would a true owner. The second is that the possession is open and notorious. This requires that the adverse possessor's presence on the property be such that a reasonable owner would have notice of his presence on the property. The third is that the possession must be hostile to the interests of the true owner, which means that the adverse possessor is there without the owner's consent. And finally, the adverse possessor must hold the property continuously for the entire statutory period.

For learning purposes, we've separated the various ways what you've written may indicate problems with your understanding of the rules. However, I hope you realize how integrated the problems tend to be. In this respect, our delineations are artificial, although they've been useful to illustrate the types of problems you're likely to encounter. Still, it's likely that you'll find combinations of these problems in your writing. Now we're ready to move on to the final piece in the forensic puzzle: the analysis.

3. WHEN YOU HAVE TROUBLE WRITING THE "APPLICATION"

This is by far one of the easiest problems to correct – that is, once you understand what it means to "analyze the facts." That's because identifying the issue and articulating the rule is the hard part; once you've done that, it should be clear sailing. So why is it such a stumbling block for so many?

THE OVERVIEW:

- *How you can tell*

    Look for examples of the following in the "application" section:

    - Mere repetition of the facts from the hypothetical.

    - Conclusory statements.

    - Reliance on such language as "obviously," "clearly," and "evidently."

    - Avoiding the question to be analyzed by using "if" and "should." For example, leaving the discussion at stating "*if* the breach was material" instead of evaluating whether or not it was. Or turning the question over to the judge – "*should* the court find that the words constituted a dying declaration" – and then not evaluating whether they were and what consequences would flow from that finding.

    - There is no mention of any of the individual facts – no use of dates, times, ages, amounts, relationships, locations – nothing that ties the analysis to the specific facts of the problem.

    - Absence of the word "because."

- *How you can remedy*

    - Match up each element/sub-element in the rule to a fact.

    - Use the word "because" to make the connection between rule and fact.

    - Make sure that every conclusion you reach is supported by an explanation of the "why" behind it.

    - Make sure you "use" every fact of consequence in your analysis.

THE SPECIFICS:

For the most part, your professors are pretty clear from the beginning what they want from you on exams: it's analysis, not answers. Your exam essay should demonstrate your ability to engage in legal thought and reasoning.

The key in writing the "application" and not simply a recitation of the facts from the hypothetical is to understand that application is analysis. It is explaining to the reader the legal significance and consequence of each fact. Generally, this is a golden opportunity to rack up exam points because once you've identified the rule, all you have to do is discuss the facts with respect to each of the identified elements. Some refer to this as a "cut and paste" between the law and the facts or a "matching up" of rule with fact. Either way, the end result is the same: a solid legal analysis.

How can you train yourself to engage in thoughtful analysis and not simply restate the facts of the problem?

- Examine the inferences/implications of each fact in light of the rule.

- Look for the ambiguities in the facts.

- Focus on explaining how these facts can be interpreted.

- Expect to show how each fact fits with the requirements of the rule and why it fits, and the opposite – why it doesn't.

- Consider the underlying policy of the rule and how it is implicated in these facts.

LET'S SEE HOW THIS WORKS

We'll begin with the most common form of application error – recitation in place of analysis. Recitation occurs when you've simply rewritten the facts that were given to you in the hypothetical. In a way, I can see why this practice is so wide-spread: until you understand what it means to interpret facts and explain why they are meaningful, it's makes sense to fall back on what you've learned in other educational settings and write "narratively" instead of "analytically." We can change all that in a word.

(a) The importance of "because"

Use the word *"because"* to draw the connection between rule and fact. "Because" is the single most important word to use when writing your application. Using the word "because" forces you to make the connection between rule and fact. You'll find that you can also make use of the words "as," "since," and "when" – they often serve the same function as "because."

There are two types of recitation: first, where a statement is "conclusory" and second, where a statement is a narration of facts. The word "because" works in both situations to transform the sentence into something meaningful.

(b)   Conclusory statements

While we've worked quite a bit with conclusory sentences in other chapters, it doesn't hurt to take another look at them in this context.

■ *What not to write:*

> The specifications in this agreement are express conditions.

■ *What you should write:*

> The specifications in this agreement can be considered express conditions **because** the contract language uses that of express condition **when** it states the hardwood floor "shall be" of a particular type.

The following two sentences are also "conclusory" with a little more to them so you might be tempted to consider them "analysis." Don't be fooled – they're not.

■ *What not to write:*

> In addition, Newman will say that the oral agreement contradicts the writing of the agreement which is not allowed under the parol evidence rule.

■ *What you should write:*

> In addition, the oral agreement contradicts the written the agreement **because** the oral conversation between Ben and Newman allowed Ben to wallpaper the kitchen any time while the written agreement specifies that wallpapering must be done after the cabinetry is completed.

■ *What not to write:*

> In this case, while Pete the police officer was giving Dan a sobriety test, he noticed that Dan fit the description of an eyewitness to the robbery, giving the police officer probable cause to arrest Dan.

■ *What you should write:*

> In this case, Pete the police officer realized that Dan fit the description of the suspect, providing probable cause for arrest, **because** Dan had bright red hair, was wearing a green and yellow sweater with purple patches and pointy-toed alligator cowboy boots, fitting the description provided by the eyewitness to the robbery.

Now let's consider some examples of straight narrative writing:

■ *What not to write:*

> ABC Inc. engaged Dr. Jones to develop a drug that reduced hair loss. Dr. Jones worked in his own laboratory, hired and fired his own assistants and set their

> *working hours as well as his own. He meets with the President of ABC every*
> *Friday morning to discuss progress on the project and at this time, Dr. Jones*
> *submits his timesheet for payment. The President pays Dr. Jones weekly.*

■ *What you should write:*

> *Here, Dr. Jones can be considered an independent consultant for ABC Inc.*
> ***because*** *he completes all the research and development work in his own labo-*
> *ratory, in a separate facility from that of ABC, where he has direct control over*
> *the employees* ***because*** *he hired his own assistants, setting their work hours.*
> *He also exercises direct control over his own work* ***because*** *he sets his own*
> *work hours and only meets with ABC once a week. Further,* ***since*** *he only*
> *meets with the President of ABC on a weekly basis to discuss progress on devel-*
> *opment of the hair loss product, the President does not supervise Dr. Jones on a*
> *daily basis as to the work which goes on in the laboratory.*

I would strongly recommend that you practice inserting the words "because," "since," and "as" to something you've already written. Do it now. It's the fastest and most dramatic change you can effect in your writing. But just as important as the change that you'll make in your writing, is the change that you'll make in your thinking if you learn to question every fact in a hypothetical with "why is this fact here and what can it mean?" Because when you do, you'll discover that the key to thinking and writing analytically is to realize that every exam question asks *"Why?"* and you're job is to answer with *"because."* It's the same with clients.

(c)   How analysis is avoided with "if"

This is the problem where the student alludes to what needs to be discussed – *if the courts finds bad faith* – and then fails to evaluate the conduct. Either the student doesn't know what it means to evaluate the facts or considers the job done by simply referencing them. In either case, it's a point-buster.

I come across this problem so frequently in reviewing student exam answers that I've tried to think of a way to explain it in a way that makes it clear. So I now tell students that writing an exam answer is like solving a math problem and you have to show all work. If you leave out the evaluation, it's like saying that to solve for X, you need to first multiply and then divide – and then not doing it!

This analogy seems to find a receptive ear with students and hopefully they won't be writing something like the following again:

> *If the court decides that The Delicious Donut failed to act in good faith when*
> *doubling its requirements for donut mix, then the court will not uphold the*
> *contract.*

C. USING FORENSICS ON MULTIPLE-CHOICE QUESTIONS

1. HOW IT WORKS WITH OBJECTIVE QUESTIONS

Our use of the forensic IRAC method operates somewhat differently when we apply it to objective, multiple choice questions. That's because in some way, short answer questions have already narrowed the field of possible errors. As we discussed in the chapter on taking multiple choice exams, there are two basic skills at work in answering multiple choice questions: your knowledge of the law and your ability to analyze the questions, which in turn relies heavily on your reading comprehension skills. An incorrect answer choice, therefore, is the result of a flaw in one of these areas.

The key to working with multiple choice questions, therefore, is learning to identify the flaw in the reasoning behind an incorrect answer choice. Just like we needed to figure out what you were thinking when you wrote an essay, we need to get inside your head and figure out what you were thinking when you selected a multiple choice answer. Since we have less to work with on multiple choice questions than we do with essays, what we do is focus on the thought process involved in reading and analyzing the question.

2. APPLYING THE TECHNIQUE

The first step is to go over the exam with your professor. This is important even though one of the approaches we'll take when working through problems – recreating your thought process – will not be possible when you meet with a professor because too much time has passed between taking the exam and reviewing the question. Still, this is a valuable opportunity to review the substantive material with your professor and should not be missed.

Now we're ready to take up the "thinking through" part. When practicing multiple choice questions, if you answer a question incorrectly, you must go back to that question and reread it to reflect on what you were thinking the first time you read the question. Specifically, your task is to recreate your thought process, retrace your steps, and compare your reasoning in the two instances to find the flaw in your analysis. This may be the only way to figure out how you made a mistake. And until you know why you select wrong answer choices, you can't make the necessary corrections. That's why it's essential – absolutely essential – that you answer only one question at a time when working with multiple choice questions. If you try to answer more than one at a time, you won't remember what you were thinking when you selected an answer choice with respect to a particular question. Self-awareness is essential to the analytical process – you need to know how you reasoned through a question.

HOW TO PROCEED:

1. Answer a question following the approach outlined in an earlier chapter on taking multiple choice exams:

   - Read actively from the stem (or call-of-the-question) and then to the fact pattern

   - Find the issue

   - Move from the issue to articulation of your own answer

   - Translate your "answer" to fit an available "answer choice"

2. Check your answer

   ### (a) If you answered correctly:

   Read the explanation for the correct answer choice if explanations are available. Even if you answered correctly, you want to make sure that you did so for the right reason. If you got the "right" answer for the "wrong" reason, proceed as if you answered incorrectly.

   ### (b) If you answered incorrectly:

   If you made an incorrect answer choice, you must go back to the question and read it again, beginning with the stem. As you read, pay close attention to what you are thinking and compare what you are thinking now to the first time you read the question.

   What's most important in this exercise is the real-time feedback. If I were sitting with you while you were reading, I would stop you every 30 seconds or so and ask you to tell me what you were thinking. This forces you to put into words exactly what's going on in your head at the moment, something you're probably not doing – at least not consciously – and you must do it. That's because the only way to identify if you've gone down a wrong path is while your thoughts are still fresh in your mind.

   You can learn to see why a thought is the wrong one to be having at the time by answering the questions I've posed for you below. Even though I'm not with you to lead you through the steps, you can do it for yourself by asking the questions I would ask:

   (1) Look at the question stem: was my first answer choice one that answered the precise question that was asked?

   (2) As I re-read the fact pattern, am I noticing facts that I overlooked the first time?

   (3) Did I confuse the parties and that's why I evaluated the problem incorrectly?

(4)   Did I overlook such legally significant words as "reasonable," "unexpectedly," or "accurately"?

(5)   Do I find my mind wandering as I read?

(6)   Am I rereading the same sentence because I have trouble remembering what I've just read?

(7)   Am I reading into the problem words and facts that are not there?

The problem addressed in question #7 is difficult to detect, but it is a primary reason for incorrect answer choices. You therefore must find out if this is something you do. This is how:

■ Start by examining your incorrect answer choice. Re-read it and ask yourself what led you to choose that answer.

■ This requires that you go back to the fact pattern and see if you can find which words or facts led you to select that particular answer choice.

■ Identify the basis for your answer. There had to be a reason – some basis you relied on for selecting that particular answer. We know it was the wrong reason, but we still need to know what your reasoning was at the time in order to step in and correct it at that point.

■ Determine whether you "read into the facts" or added your own. This alters the nature of the problem. You must never "assume" facts. Your professor has carefully constructed the question to contain all the facts you need to answer the question. You must rely solely on these facts and no others. Of course you may draw reasonable inferences but you cannot fabricate your own facts or create "what if" scenarios. Unfortunately, far too many students allow their creative side to surface when reading these questions, and they stray from the fact pattern.

■ Don't let yourself go off on tangents based on possible theories you see raised in the facts. Sometimes when you read a fact pattern, you'll see the potential for a number of possible causes of action. Let the stem for the question guide your analysis.

■ Sometimes you don't "add" facts but see implications which have no basis in the facts. This leads you astray in your analysis as well. Let the facts dictate your direction.

(8)   Am I disregarding an important exception and jumping immediately to the general rule?

(9)   Am I not connecting with the significance of the facts and that's why I can't identify the legal problem?

(10)   Does this question require application of statutory law and not the common law? Did I disregard this before?

(11)   Am I applying the minority view instead of the majority rule?

(12)   Am I misapplying the rule to the facts?

(13)   Am I "reacting" to answer choices instead of "acting" in response with an analysis of the issue presented?

(14)   Did I get emotionally involved with the problem and substitute my instincts for what I know is legally correct?

(15)   Did I become "practical" and replace the black letter law for what I thought would occur in actual practice?

3. FIGURE OUT WHAT YOUR ANSWER MEANS

If you answered "yes" to questions 1 through 7, then you most likely have a reading problem.

You therefore choose the incorrect answer choices because you've misread a fact either in the fact pattern or the answer choice. This is usually the result of sloppy reading because you're intent on reading quickly rather than carefully. A hasty reader is likely to overlook the specific use of vocabulary and the significance of modifiers in the answer choices. These types of errors and omissions go directly to your reading of the problem, not necessarily to your knowledge of the substantive law or to your analysis of the legal question. In fact, your difficulties with reading may prevent you from getting to the actual problem in controversy.

If you've been able to identify your problem as one of reading, now you have a direction in which to work. You can and must learn to read questions "actively." Because of time constraints on an exam, you may have time for only one reading of the fact pattern. However, you can't sacrifice a careful reading for a quick one. You must read carefully to spot signal words and legally significant facts. *Slow down and watch what happens.* Train yourself to look for the following as you read and if you may write in your test booklet, do not hesitate to circle the relevant language:

■ Relationships between parties that signal the area of law and legal duties: landlord/tenant, employer/employee, principal/agent, buyer/ seller.

■ Amounts of money, dates, quantities, and ages.

- Words such as "oral" and "written," "reasonable" and "unreasonable," among others; and

- Words that indicate the actor's state of mind such as "intended," "decided," "mistakenly thought," and "deliberately," among others.

If you answered "yes" to questions 8 through 15, then you may have a problem with either application or the rule.

It's often difficult to distinguish between the two problems because they are closely related in the dynamic of answering multiple choice questions. Problems with analysis are process-oriented while problems with the rule are substance-based. But they can and do overlap as evidenced in these questions.

ANALYSIS PROBLEMS

Conquering a problem with analytical skills not only involves close, accurate reading of the text, but it also requires exactness in following the structure of legal analysis in the context of multiple choice questions. This requires that as you re-read the question, you focus on answering the following:

- Did you properly analyze the question?

    1. Did you begin by reading the call-of-the-question?

    2. Did you identify the issue in the fact pattern?

    3. Did you move from finding the issue to forming your answer?

    4. Did you fill the gap from "your answer" to find one of the answer choices?

- Did you properly analyze the answer choices?

    1. Did you identify the issue in each answer choice?

    2. Did you use the process of elimination by determining when an answer choice can't be correct?

        (a) Was the answer choice completely correct?

        (b) Did the answer choice misstate or misapply a rule of law?

        (c) Did the answer choice mischaracterize the facts?

What you should do
The basic remedy for reading and application-based problems is practice – lots and lots of it. ***There's no real secret: the more questions you work your way through, the more careful and conscious a reader you become.*** In some ways, answering a multiple choice question is more a science than an art but rigor in application of the method will yield favorable results.

RULE PROBLEMS

Let's face it: if you don't know the black letter law, you can't distinguish between the answer choices. The key in analyzing the question after you've identified the issue is to articulate the rule of law that addresses that issue. If you don't know the rule, you can't get to this step. Remember, it's not enough to know bits and pieces of rules or simply be familiar with the terminology. Buzz-words will not help you here. The only thing that works is complete and thorough understanding of the rule – in its entirety.

If you answered "yes" to questions 8 through 12, consider the following:

If you cannot summon to mind the relevant rule as soon as you've articulated the issue, then you must return to your notes and review the substantive law in detail. Your problem is with knowledge of the rules and you must be comfortable with answering the following questions as soon as you read a fact pattern:

- What is the legal problem presented by the facts?

- What area of law is implicated?

- What is the specific rule of law that governs under these facts?

On the other hand, if you answered "yes" to questions 13 through 15, then something slightly different may be happening and requires a different approach. Let's look at each one individually.

If you "react" instead of "act":

When you find yourself "reacting" to answer choices instead of "acting" in response to them with a careful analysis of the issue presented, then some changes in procedure are required. This type of problem is basically one of control: Because you've lost control of your thought process in analyzing the problem, you've placed yourself at the mercy of the answer choices. Then they pick you, instead of the other way around. How do you act and not react to the answer choices? *The answer is simple: formulate your own answer to the interrogatory before you even look at the answer choices.* Practice questions this way until it becomes habit and you'll see what a difference it makes.

If you ignore the rule:

If you find yourself substituting your instincts for what you know is legally correct, you're headed for trouble. You must apply the rule of law to the facts without equivocation. You can't get afford to get emotionally involved with the parties and let your sympathies interfere with what you know is legally correct. It's not your place to find a criminal defendant not guilty when in fact her actions satisfy every element of the crime. And conversely: if an act doesn't violate the provisions of a given statute, then whatever you happen to think about the nature of the act (or actor) doesn't matter. It's not a crime if the jurisdiction doesn't make it one. Your job is to follow the law and apply it to the facts mechanically.

If you substitute "practice" for "theory":

If you find that you become practical on exams and replace the black letter law for what you think would occur in the real world, then you're going to end up with some incorrect answers. Your exam is not the time or place to become "practical" and consider what you think would happen in actual practice. Many students have defended incorrect answer choices to me by explaining "I know it couldn't happen like that in practice. That's why I didn't choose that answer." My response is that this isn't "real" life. It's a law school exam! This is not to say, however, that exam questions have nothing to do with the practice of law or the "real world." It's just that in law school, we are studying and working with the theoretical rule of law and what should be, not necessarily what is. When answering a question from your professor, apply the rule of law as you've learned it and you'll be fine.

4. DEVELOPING YOUR "THOUGHT MONITOR"

Whether we're aware of it or not – and the whole point of this chapter is learning to be conscious of what we are thinking – we engage in an internal, ongoing conversation with ourselves when we read. When I work with students on analyzing multiple choice questions, I play the part of the thought police and enter these conversations. It happens simply enough: I give the student a problem and ask her to read it. After a couple of minutes, I stop her and ask,"what are you thinking when you read this sentence?" And that's how I get inside her head.

There's no better way to learn something new than by seeing how it's done and then by doing it yourself. Thus far we've outlined part of the process of developing your thought monitor by identifying the questions you can ask to focus your thought process. Now I need to show you exactly how to engage in this kind of internal monologue.

Let's work with a real problem. An example from a past MBE will work nicely for us.

> *Peavey was walking peacefully along a public street when he encountered Dorwin, whom he had never seen before. Without provocation or warning, Dorwin picked up a rock and struck Peavey with it. It was later established that Dorwin was mentally ill and suffered recurrent hallucinations.*
>
> *If Peavey asserts a claim against Dorwin based on battery, which of the following, if supported by evidence, will be Dorwin's best defense?*
>
> > *A. Dorwin did not understand that his act was wrongful.*
> >
> > *B. Dorwin did not desire to cause harm to Peavey.*
> >
> > *C. Dorwin did not know that he was striking a person.*
> >
> > *D. Dorwin thought Peavey was about to attack him.*

Here's what I'm thinking as I read this problem, sentence by sentence (my thoughts are in italics in the parentheses):

(First I'll check the interrogatory.) If Peavey asserts a claim against Dorwin based on battery, which of the following, if supported by evidence, will be Dorwin's best defense? *(Since a person is bringing the suit and not the state, it's a civil suit and not a criminal case. I'm looking for Dorwin's best defense to battery, so I'd better keep the rule in mind as I go through this – "a battery is the intent to cause a harmful or offensive contact with the person of another." I'll be looking for something that negates an element of battery or possibly self-defense.)* Peavey was walking peacefully along a public street when he encountered Dorwin, whom he had never seen before. *(Nothing has happened yet, but it may be important that this was a "public" and not a "private" street but maybe not because the question stem tells me that Peavey brought the action against Dorwin in battery so the state is not involved and it's not a constitutional issue. Maybe "peacefully" goes to provocation and since Peavey never saw Dorwin before, there's no past history between them.)* Without provocation or warning, Dorwin picked up a rock and struck Peavey with it. *(Here's the act required for the battery and I was right about the lack of provocation. Now the issue is one of intent. The facts say that Dorwin "picked" up a rock. This sounds like he acted with purpose. The intent element is satisfied not only when the actor intends harmful or wrongful behavior, but if he acts with purpose or knowledge to a "substantial certainty." Dorwin need not have understood his act to be "wrongful" to have formed the requisite intent: he need only to know what would be the likely consequence of striking Peavey with a rock.)* It was later established that Dorwin was mentally ill and suffered recurrent hallucinations. *(What's the relevance of this? The majority view is that insane persons are liable for their intentional torts. So if Dorwin made a choice to pick up the rock and hit Peavey with it, it doesn't matter if it was an irrational or crazy choice.)*

(On to the answer choices. I'm looking for Dorwin's best defense to battery. I know the act occurred, so any defense will have to negate the intent element or provide for self-defense, which doesn't seem likely since Dorwin wasn't provoked or even knew Peavey.) CHOICE A: Dorwin did not understand that his act was wrongful. *(This one isn't right because Dorwin doesn't have to understand his act to be wrongful to commit battery; he only has to act with purpose or knowledge to a "substantial certainty." He need only know what would be the likely consequence of hitting Peavey with a rock.)* CHOICE B: Dorwin did not desire to cause harm to Peavey. *(This is just a variation of A. Even though a battery is the intentional, harmful or offensive touching of another, Dorwin need not have intended harm to be found liable in battery.)* CHOICE C: Dorwin did not know that he was striking a person. *(This sounds funny, but if Dorwin had no idea – no "knowledge" – he was striking a person, then he could not have formed the requisite intent to do the act. This one may be it but I need to read D.)* CHOICE D: Dorwin thought Peavey was about to attack him. *(This sounds like*

self-defense, which is a defense but there's nothing in the facts to lead Dorwin to believe Peavey was about to attack him but even assuming Dorwin believed he was about to be attacked and he needed to defend himself, this still admits that he committed the battery. The questions asks for the "best" defense and that's one that says he never committed the battery. I'll go with C.)

Choice C is the correct answer.

It probably seems as if it would take a long time for me to think through this problem, but it really doesn't. Just a couple of minutes. It takes much longer to write it and for you to read it than it actually takes to do it. That's because what I think as I read is so mechanical that it happens automatically. It takes practice, but the process can become automatic for you as well.

Now it's time for you to work through a problem on your own and share your thoughts with me. Here's what to do:

1. Begin by reading the interrogatory and proceed to the fact pattern. This is the sequence we just followed with our good friends Peavey and Dorwin.

2. As you read, pause after each sentence and write down exactly what you think. Don't stop to censor your thoughts; write them as you have them. To borrow an old phrase, "go with the flow."

3. After you complete your reading of the fact pattern, form your own answer in response to the call-of-the-question.

4. Read each of the answer choices and once again write down exactly what you think. Translate your "answer" to fit one of the available answer choices.

5. Now read my thoughts on the problem and compare them to what you've written. Don't expect them to be the same but your thinking should parallel mine. After all, the same problem should elicit a similar analysis. While what we've written won't be exactly the same, it should be close – what I found important, you should have found important, what I questioned, you should have questioned, and how I responded to each of the issues raised in the facts, you should have responded.

Here's another example from a past MBE. It will work nicely for us.

Bye Bye telegraphed Vendor on June 1, "At what price will you sell 100 of your QT-Model garbage-disposal units for delivery around June 10?" Thereafter, the following communications were exchanged:

1. *Telegram from Vendor received by Bye Bye on June 2: "You're in luck. We have only 100 QT's, all on clearance at 50% off usual wholesale of $120 per unit, for delivery at our shipping platform on June 12."*

2. *Letter from Bye Bye received in U.S. mail by Vendor on June 5: "I accept. Would prefer to pay in full 30 days after invoice."*

3. *Telegram from Vendor received by Bye Bye on June 6: "You must pick up at our platform and pay C.O.D."*

4. *Letter from Bye Bye received in U.S. mail by Vendor on June 9: "I don't deal with people who can't accommodate our simple requests."*

5. *Telegram from Bye Bye received by Vendor on June 10, after Vendor had sold and delivered all 100 of the QT's to another buyer earlier that day: "Okay. I'm over a barrel and will pick up the goods on your terms June 12."*

Bye Bye now sues Vendor for breach of contract. Which of the following arguments will best serve Vendor's defense?

(A) *Vendor's telegram received on June 2 was merely a price quotation, not an offer.*

(B) *Bye Bye's letter received on June 5 was not an acceptance because it varied the terms of Vendor's initial telegram.*

(C) *Bye Bye's use of the mails in response to Vendor's initial telegram was an ineffective method of acceptance.*

D) *Bye Bye's letter received on June 9 was an unequivocal refusal to perform that excused Vendor even if the parties had previously formed a contract.*

As before, here's what I'm thinking as I read through the problem, sentence by sentence, beginning with the call-of-the-question:

(Okay, what does the interrogatory ask me to do?) Bye Bye now sues Vendor for breach of contract. Which of the following arguments will best serve Vendor's defense? *(I'm looking for a defense to a breach of contract and it seems like a sales contract, why else "vendor.")* Bye Bye telegraphed Vendor on June 1, "At what price will you sell 100 of your QT-Model garbage-disposal units for delivery around June 10?" Thereafter, the following communications were exchanged: *(I was right. It's a sales problem because garbage-disposal units are goods so I have to apply the UCC. There's a lot of info here. I have dates, quantities, and writings because "telegraphs" are writings. But they are not signed. I don't know if that's important yet, so I'll have to watch it. I'm going to think about each exchange separately and see what it means. I hate series of exchanges, but there's no other way to deal with them. As to this first volley, it sounds like a preliminary inquiry because it's asking "at what price" the goods would cost.)* Telegram from Vendor received by Bye Bye on June 2: "You're in luck. We have only 100 QT's, all on clearance at 50% off usual wholesale of

$120 per unit, for delivery at our shipping platform on June 12." *(Okay. This looks like the offer. It's definite in terms of delivery terms, quantity, and price. It doesn't need a payment term because the UCC has gap fillers for this. This is something Bye Bye can accept.)* Letter from Bye Bye received in U.S. mail by Vendor on June 5: "I accept. Would prefer to pay in full 30 days after invoice." *(Now we have a letter instead of the usual telegraph. Doesn't seem to mean anything so don't read into it now. Date makes it seem timely. The words are those of acceptance. But then it adds a payment term. There was nothing mentioned about payment in the offer so this is an additional term. Does that impact the acceptance? No, not here. The common law requires a mirror-image. This looks like it might be a 2-207 problem where there's an additional term in the acceptance. There's still an acceptance but we may have to figure out what to do with the additional term. It doesn't seem like Bye Bye has made its acceptance conditional on this additional term, only that it would "prefer" – which says to me, "would like to" pay in 30 days. So under 2-207, this is still an acceptance but the additional term becomes a "propos-al" for addition to the contract unless one of the exceptions for merchants apply.)* Telegram from Vendor received by Bye Bye on June 6: "You must pick up at our platform and pay C.O.D." *(Looks like the offeror is not accepting the additional term. Certainly noted their objection quickly enough since it's the next day. Now what to do. Because the parties are merchants – the names tell me that they are, i.e., Vendor and who else buys 100 units – the additional term becomes part of the deal unless it's a material term. This would seem to qualify since there's a big difference between COD and credit for 30 days. So the payment term doesn't come in but we still have an acceptance and a deal)* Letter from Bye Bye received in U.S. mail by Vendor on June 9: "I don't deal with people who can't accommodate our simple requests." *(Bye Bye's letter is a repudiation. It's a clear, unequivocal statement that Bye Bye won't perform. So Bye Bye is in breach.)* Telegram from Bye Bye received by Vendor on June 10, after Vendor had sold and delivered all 100 of the QT's to another buyer earlier that day: "Okay. I'm over a barrel and will pick up the goods on your terms June 12." *(Looks like Bye Bye is trying to retract its repudiation. But it's too late. Vendor was right to treat Bye Bye's June 9 letter as a repudiation and could sell the goods to another. Let's see which answer choice allows for this situation.)*

(On to the answer choices.) CHOICE A. Vendor's telegram received on June 2 was merely a price quotation, not an offer. *(This was too definite to be merely a quote. It was sent in response to a pretty specific inquiry from Bye Bye which set quantity terms and a delivery date. Vendor's response was an offer so this "A" is incorrect.)* CHOICE B. Bye Bye's letter received on June 5 was not an acceptance because it varied the terms of Vendor's initial telegram. *(I've already accounted for   this. The UCC rejects the common law "mirror image" rule requiring the acceptance to be the exact match of the offer. The UCC allows for an acceptance with different or additional terms, as long as it's clear that there was an expression of acceptance. So the June 5 letter was an acceptance even though it added the term for the 30 days of credit)* CHOICE C.

Bye Bye's use of the mails in response to Vendor's initial telegram was an ineffective method of acceptance. *(Finally something about all the back and forth between letters and telegrams. But it really doesn't matter because the mail is just as valid a form of acceptance as telegram. Vendor didn't specify how the offer had to be accepted and the UCC is lenient here too and Bye Bye could use any means reasonable under the circumstances. There's nothing to indicate in the facts about the goods or the market that would indicate time to be of the essence so a letter would be fine.)* CHOICE D. Bye Bye's letter received on June 9 was an unequivocal refusal to perform that excused Vendor even if the parties had previously formed a contract. *(Okay. This is it. It accounts for Bye Bye's repudiation and this would excuse Vendor from its obligation under the contract. If Vendor is excused, then it's not in breach. And that the best defense.)*

Choice D is the correct answer.

I realize it's not practical to write down your thoughts each time you answer a multiple choice question. But now that you know what should be going on in your head as you work your way through a problem, your task is to be conscious and deliberate during each step of the process. This way you'll remember what you thought and can go back and revisit it should you arrive at an incorrect answer choice. *If you make the effort to put your thoughts into some concrete form – even if it's just articulated in your head – you will remember what you thought. Words give form to thoughts. And once there's form, there's something to remember.*

D. IRAC DIAGRAMING

Sentence diagraming is the final component in the forensic IRAC trilogy. Years ago, students were shown how to diagram the parts of a sentence to learn grammar. While this may no longer be the way grammar is taught, the principle of mapping the parts of the sentence to show how they work together is very useful for showing how the parts of a legal argument are structured.

Diagraming an essay allows you to see IRAC in action. It's insufficient to tell you to organize an answer around IRAC without showing how it's done. The process works sentence by sentence, where each one is labeled according to its role in the IRAC equation. A sentence is either issue, rule (rule can be further broken down – general statement, element, factor, definition of element/factor), fact analysis (fact can break down into argument/counter-argument), or conclusion. This works particularly well when multiple issues are tested on an exam and organizing the response in a meaningful manner is essential. Diagraming lets us see how and where issues may have been mixed together.

1. HOW IT WORKS

(a) It provides a visual display of the thought process

For example, suppose I am working with a student, Ben, and we're reviewing his exam answer to a Torts mid-term. We review each sentence he's written and identify whether that sentence is a statement of the issue, one discussing the applicable rule of law, or a sentence applying the rules to the facts of the particular case. In fact, we label each sentence with an "I," an "R," or an "A." The sentence must "fit" somewhere.

(b) It "physically" identifies organization problems

If Ben has discussed the "facts" of the particular problem before he has recited the relevant "rule," then we find "A" sentences before there are any "R" sentences.

(c) It identifies the function each sentence serves in the IRAC equation

Ben can see whether a sentence is repetitive, for which he will lose time and not gain any points, whether a statement is an analysis of facts because it connects law to relevant facts by means of such language as "because," or whether it is merely a recitation of the facts contained in the hypothetical, serving no purpose at all. By breaking down and labeling the sentences, Ben can "see" what he has written.

(d) It spots problems at the appropriate step in the thought process

Ben can see by what he has written whether he understand the rules and how to use them. And once identified, problems can be corrected.

2. APPLYING THE TECHNIQUE

As just described, the process works by labeling each sentence with either an "I," an "R," an "A," or a "C" to identify which function it serves in the essay. Issues can be numbered to accommodate problems where multiple legal questions are raised – I^1 is followed by I^2 and so forth. This numbering scheme would extend to the rule and application where all rule-related sentences with respect to the first issue would be labeled R^1 and similarly, all application-related sentences would be A^1. The same procedure would follow for the second issue (I^2)

You may find that not every sentence you read fits one of the IRAC letters. Typically, this happens with the "A." You'll find you're reading something that seems like it should be analysis, but it's nothing more than a statement of the facts you've been given. I would suggest labeling this sentence "S" for statement. It's important to recognize such sentences since writing "recitation" instead of "application" is a common mistake and must be corrected. However, some "S"s may be necessary as background leading to what will be analyzed. Still, these types of sentences should be minimal and quickly progress to the analysis. Diagraming is one way to let you see whether there's a tendency to rely on such statements. Finally, it's likely that you'll find sentences that merely repeat what's already been written. Unfortunately, there's a tendency to be repetitive, but there's no time to be wasted on exams and no points to be gained from repeating the same thing but in different words. Consequently, if you find sentences that merely repeat what was already written, you might tag such sentences with a "U" for useless. You'll be surprised by the number of "U"s you discover!

Having said all this, the most effective way to communicate the process is simply to show it to you. Consider the following essay answer. As you read, note the letters in parentheses at the end of each sentence but don't be concerned about them. After you've read through the entire essay, we'll examine each sentence separately and I'll explain the notations.

■ *Example:*

The issue is whether Jessica committed a battery when she threw her slipper out the window and hit Nick on the head (I^1). While Jessica's words that she was going to kill him would not be sufficient, by themselves, to give rise to an assault, they were combined with the physical act of throwing the slippers out the window. (A^2) An assault is the intentional causing of an apprehension of a harmful or offensive contact. (R^2/G) Here, we have an indirect contact because Jessica threw a slipper which made the actual contact with Nick. (A1) A battery is the intentional infliction of a harmful or offensive bodily contact. (R^1/G) Nick must be aware that the slippers are coming at him to feel apprehension and since we do not know if Nick saw the slipper coming at him, there is no way to know if he felt apprehension and hence no assault. (A^2/C^2) Here, it may be difficult to find knowledge to a substantial certainty because Jessica threw a fuzzy slipper and not a hard object – it was not a boot or even a shoe – out of a 5th floor window. (A^1)

On the other hand, if he saw the slipper coming at him, it could be an assault because then he would have an expectation of contact. (A^2/CA^2) The contact can be either direct or indirect where an indirect contact is one that results from a force set in motion by the defendant. (R^1/D) It is possible that throwing a high-heeled slipper to get someone to stop singing could indicate intent to make contact. (A^1) However, it is questionable whether she knew with substantial certainty she would effect a contact because of the failure to take aim and the likely distance between her room and the ground. (A^1/CA^1) The intent for battery is satisfied not only when the actor intends harmful or wrongful behavior, but if he acts with purpose or knowledge to a "substantial certainty." (R^1/D) Here it may be hard for Jessica to believe a contact of any kind would be possible, much less substantially certain, because a slipper is soft and the distance she tossed it was quite far. (A^1) Therefore, it is not likely she had the intent to commit a battery. (C^1)

■ *Analysis:*

(1) The first sentence stated a question concerning battery:

> *The issue is whether Jessica committed a battery when she threw her slipper out the window and hit Nick on the head.* (We'll tag this sentence I[1] because it's the first issue statement in the essay.)

(2) The second sentence shifted to a factual discussion of assault:

> *While Jessica's words that she was going to kill him would not be sufficient, by themselves, to give rise to an assault, they were combined with the physical act of throwing the slippers out the window.* (We'll label this sentence A[2] because it's analysis of the facts, but facts related to assault and we haven't identified an assault issue yet, only battery.)

(3) The next sentence stated a rule regarding assault:

> *An assault is the intentional causing of an apprehension of a harmful or offensive contact.* (We'll label this sentence R[2] because it's a statement of a rule, but related to the second issue. We can also consider it a general statement of the rule and refine its tag to R[2]/G. As you know, a general statement of the rule is a good starting point but not always sufficient for a complete analysis so it's important to identify the part of the rule that you find. This lets you see exactly what you've included and also what you may have omitted.)

(4) The fourth sentence was a fact application regarding the battery:

> *Here, we have an indirect contact because Jessica threw a slipper which made the actual contact with Nick.* (We'll tag this sentence A[1] because it's a fact analysis regarding the physical contact which has to do with battery).

(5) The fifth sentence stated a rule regarding battery:

> *A battery is the intentional infliction of a harmful or offensive bodily contact.* (We'll mark this sentence with R[1] because it relates back to the first issue, battery. Once again, we can be more specific and tag it R[1]/G where the G stands for "General" because it is a statement of the general rule.)

(6) The next sentence discussed the facts of the assault and offered a conclusion regarding the assault:

> *Nick must be aware the that the slippers are coming at him to feel apprehension and since we do not know if Nick saw the slipper coming at him, there is no way to know if he felt apprehension and hence*

no assault. (We'll tag this sentence with A²/C² because it is a fact analysis of the assault issue and it contains a conclusion with respect to that issue.)

(7) The next sentence returned to battery:

Here, it may be difficult to find knowledge to a substantial certainty because Jessica threw a fuzzy slipper and not a hard object – it was not a boot or even a shoe – out of a 5th floor window. (We'll label this A¹ because it's a fact analysis of the battery issue.)

(8) The eighth sentence returned to analyze the assault (which is interesting because this issue was concluded two sentences earlier):

On the other hand, if he saw the slipper coming at him, it could be an assault because then he would have an expectation of contact. (We'll tag this A²/CA² because it is a fact analysis of the assault issue and it is also the counter-argument – hence the "CA²".)

(9) The next sentence added to the rule on battery:

The contact can be either direct or indirect where an indirect contact is one that results from a force set in motion by the defendant. (We'll label this R¹ because it refers back to the rule of battery but as you can see, it adds to the rule by distinguishing between the types of contact. Once again, we can be more specific and tag it R¹/D where the D stands for "Definition." This indicates that we've gone beyond the general rule to include a more specific definition.)

(10) The following sentence analyzed the battery:

It is possible that throwing a high-heeled slipper to get someone to stop singing could indicate intent to make contact. (We'll tag this A¹.)

(11) The next sentence also analyzed the battery and added a counter-argument:

However, it is questionable whether she knew with substantial certainty she would effect a contact because of the failure to take aim and the likely distance between her room and the ground. (We'll tag this A¹/CA¹ because it analyzes the battery issue and presents a counter-argument. It also analyzes the intent element of the battery rule, but thus far there has been no mention of the rule regarding the intent required to commit a battery.)

(12) The next sentence added to the rule on battery by defining intent:

The intent for battery is satisfied not only when the actor intends harmful or wrongful behavior, but if he acts with purpose or knowledge to a "substantial certainty." (We'll label this R¹/D because it is a statement of the rule regarding battery but it adds to it by providing a definition of the intent element.)

(13) The following sentence analyzed the battery and focused on the intent component:

Here it may be hard for Jessica to believe a contact of any kind would be possible, much less substantially certain, because a slipper is soft and the distance she tossed it was quite far. (We'll label this A¹.)

(14) The last sentence stated a conclusion with respect to battery:

Therefore, it is not likely she had the intent to commit a battery. (We'll tag this C¹.)

3.   USING THE TECHNIQUE TO SEE DISORGANIZATION

Perhaps the greatest value of diagraming is that it lets you "see" disorganization. By tagging the lines in an essay, it becomes possible to identify when sentences jump between issues or where facts are analyzed before the relevant rule has been discussed (i.e., where there's no R¹ before an A¹) Disorganization becomes visible when sentences are labeled objectively.

For example, we can now see the disorganization in this essay answer. If we strip away the text and just look at the tags at the end of the sentences, we find the following:

Paragraph 1:   (I¹) (A²) (R²/G) (A¹) (R¹/G) (A²/C²) (A¹)

Paragraph 2:   (A²/CA²) (R¹/D) (A¹) (A¹/CA¹) (R¹/D) (A¹) (C¹)

To find meaning in the tags, we look to the arrangement of the letters and the sequencing of the numbers:

- First, the letter arrangement should follow IRAC and proceed from Issue to Rule to Application to Conclusion, without doubling back along the way (of course it's often appropriate to weave back and forth between "R" and "A" but it must be with respect to the same issue and rule)

- Second, the sequence for numbers within an IRAC should be consistent. Although it may not matter which issue you choose to discuss first, what matters is that you complete discussion of one issue before moving to another. In other words, all the 1s should be together, all the 2s, and so forth.

In this example, it's easy to see the disorganization in the first paragraph because the assault issue is analyzed (A^2) before there's a statement of the issue (no I^2) or even a statement of the rule regarding assault (no R^2 until after the A^2) There should never be a specific fact application before a general statement of the relevant rule. Further, you can see that a conclusion was reached in the first paragraph with respect to assault but then this issue was revived and revisited in the second paragraph for a counter-argument.

4. HOW TO DIAGRAM

To be of true value, you must be able to diagram your own essays. It's easy. Here's what to do:

   (a)   Write out your essay answer.

   (b)   Put the answer aside for a couple of hours so you can look at it with fresh eyes.

   (c)   Now read it, sentence by sentence. Label each sentence according to its IRAC function.

   (d)   When labeling, be as specific as possible, breaking down the rule of law and the analysis. You can create your own identification letters – just be consistent and use letters that have meaning for you. Be careful not to break it down too far – you don't want to get lost in the details.

   (e)   Isolate the tags at the end of each sentence.

   (f)   Find the meaning in the tags by examining the arrangement of the letters and the sequencing of the numbers. The key to organization is finding that the tags are consistent in both sequence and number.

   (g)   In addition to checking for organization, note whether you have sentences that fill no particular role (statements instead of analysis) or merely repeat something you've already written. This process is very helpful for detecting repetitive statements, a very common writing problem. These sentences simply waste valuable exam time and yield no additional points.

5. LIMITS TO DIAGRAMING

Undoubtedly, IRAC diagraming has useful applications for identifying problems with general structure and for providing a roadmap for reorganization. However, IRAC diagraming is only a map of what's written. It cannot explain why something isn't quite right, nor is it effective where the problems presented are ones regarding the more sophisticated levels of rule construction: i.e., a recognition of the hierarchical structure of the law and the various turns and twists of how a specific rule unfolds based on its particular requirements. When difficulty presents in this area, it's necessary to turn to a further exploration of your understanding of the law itself. In this case, the principles of forensic IRAC, as applied to the rule section, should be the next step.

CHAPTER 10: PRACTICE MAKES "A"

A. NOT JUST MEMORIZATION BUT APPLICATION

The key to success in any endeavor is preparation. While you prepare for class by reading and briefing the assignment, you need to prepare for exams by writing out practice essays. Familiarity with the structure of essay questions and how to respond to them will go a long way in alleviating your anxiety on exam day. The key to success on exams is to engage in this practice on a regular basis and to begin well before the final examination.

Your law professor expects an exam answer that is a well-reasoned, well-organized, articulate analysis of the relevant rules of law with respect to the facts. This demonstrates your mastery of the material covered during the course of the semester and your ability to write in the language of the law. Your professor does not expect you to do this without adequate preparation by practicing from prior exams. Consequently, many professors have copies of their old exams on file.

You should begin writing sample answers as soon as you have covered enough "law" to analyze a factual situation. This usually occurs within the first two to three weeks of class. From there, you are ready to take up a new topic every time you have covered another principle of law. Just as you continue to add to your outline as you progress through the semester, you should continue to practice what you have learned in the context of factual hypotheticals. This practice should continue throughout your law school career; it is not simply for first year law students.

B.   SOME ADVICE ON USING HYPOTHETICALS

1. Don't delay.

Begin working with practice questions as soon as you have covered a topic.

2. Start simple and build to the complex.

Begin with single issue problems and work your way to increasingly more complex problems until you have covered every principle that has been studied in your course.

3. Vary the type of essay that you answer when practicing.

Be sure to work with both short essays and long, complex fact patterns with multiple issues and parties. Each presents a different challenge in issue spotting and organization.

4. Use exam questions to let you see the relationships between concepts and how topics come together.

As you proceed through each area of doctrinal law, you'll often find it necessary to take a very narrow, focused approach because there is only so much information you can assimilate at a time. But the same tunnel-vision that lets you navigate enormous amounts of knowledge limits your consideration of other perspectives. Here's where hypotheticals can help by showing you the connections where all you've been focused on are the distinctions. Typically, these connections emerge when you study for finals but there's no need to wait until the end of the semester when it can assist your learning along the way.

5. Develop your reading skills as carefully as your writing skills.

Pay attention to the directions that accompany exams – specifically with respect to what you are asked to do in the question.

For example, if your professor identifies the following task,

"You are counsel for Plaintiff. What are the strongest arguments you can make on her behalf?"

you must know whether this means to address only plaintiff's arguments or if your evaluation must include counter-arguments (defendant's) as well. This can be a tough call. Typically, when evaluating a claim, you consider both sides as part of a full analysis. However, if your directions tell you to consider only one side, then that is what you must do. In this case, the professor wanted his students to answer the question asked and they would receive no credit for giving defendant's arguments and explaining why defendant would lose.

The only way to know exactly how your professor expects you to address a question comes from experience in reading your professor's exams and in asking what she expects in an answer.

C. HOW TO USE THESE SAMPLE QUESTIONS

The following questions were carefully selected to provide a range of content, style, and format. Several professors have allowed me to include their exam questions which allows you to experience a variety of individual styles. There are single issue problems and multi-party, fact-laden hypotheticals. There are targeted questions and general, open-ended inquiries. Each serves a different function in your course of study. As discussed in the chapter on exam preparation, you'll want to work with a single issue problem initially to develop your analytical skills and work your way to multi-issue problems to hone your organization and time management skills.

Each question is followed by either an evaluation sheet, issue checklist, or sample answer. Most questions will have an evaluation sheet or answer outline rather than a sample answer. This was a deliberate choice: since it's possible to write a solid answer in so many ways, a single "sample" answer can be misleading. Still, I have included a number of sample answers so you'll see how the IRAC elements transform into complete sentences and how to transition from one issue to another.

These problems are intended to provide opportunities for you to write and get feedback on what you've written. While each question is grounded in doctrine and the evaluation sheets identify the relevant rules, you must answer the questions according to the law as presented by your professor. Consequently, there might be differences in emphasis and approach in your answer as opposed to the provided sample or checklist. If there is a difference between the sample evaluation sheet's articulation of the controlling rule (for example, it identifies four factors for a given cause of action or principle and your professor has identified six), then use your professor's articulation of the rule. After writing an answer to a question, use the checklist to identify the points you've covered and note what you've missed. The checklists are very specific in outlining the issues, the rules, and the relevant facts to allow you to assess your own work. Then refer to Chapter 9 and use the forensic IRAC principles to identify errors and correct them.

One final point worth noting is that the questions presented here are meant to supplement and not replace those available from your professor. His or her exams remain your primary source for practice materials.

D. QUESTIONS

1. BUSINESS ORGANIZATIONS

Question topic: Agency
   Sample Answer: "The Latte"
Question topic: Partnership
   Sample Answer: "Muffing Morning"

2. CIVIL PROCEDURE

Question topic: Personal jurisdiction
   Evaluation Sheet: "Club Cornet"

Question topic: Personal jurisdiction
   Suggested Outline for Answer: "Cybersales"

Question topic: Remedies
   Damage Analysis for Roocs Inc.

3. CONSTITUTIONAL LAW

Question topics: 10th Amendment, commerce clause, standing, 11th Amendment
   Sample Answer

4. CONTRACTS

Question topic: Formation
   Evaluation Sheet: "*Kim v. Coe*"

Question topic: Remedies
   Evaluation Sheet: "Amy and the Convertible"

Question topics: Parol evidence and interpretation
   Evaluation Sheet: "The Hearsay"

Question topic: Requirements contracts
   Sample Answer: "The Delicious Donut"
      Evaluation Sheet: "The Delicious Donut"

Question topic: Parol evidence
   Sample Answer: "Shuzzies, Inc."
      Evaluation Sheet: "Shuzzies, Inc."

Question topic: Conditions
   Evaluation Sheet: "Celebrity Sandals"

Question topic: Commercial impracticability
   Evaluation Sheet: "Farmer Green's Tomatoes"

Question topic: Frustration of purpose

Evaluation Sheet: "George and the Scooter"

Question topic: Formation under UCC 2-207
Evaluation Sheet: "The Shoelaces"

Question topics: Fraud and unconscionability
Evaluation Sheet: "Katie and the Dancing Lessons"

5.   CRIMINAL LAW

Question topic: Felony murder
Evaluation Sheet: "Murder of the Federal Express Man?"

6.   EVIDENCE

Question topics: Hearsay, relevancy, character evidence
Sample Answer

7.   PROPERTY

Question topic: Rule of capture
Evaluation Sheet: "Chester the Parrot"

Question topic: Adverse possession
Evaluation Sheet: "The Matter of Al Verse"

8.   TORTS

Note: If you are a first year student, "Ben and Jessica" is the first question you should try to answer. If your Torts class covers intentional torts, you will have covered the substantive law within the first two weeks of classes and you're ready to begin practicing what you've learned. I've included a step-by-step thought analysis guide. Read it to help direct and organize your thinking before writing an answer. Then you can compare what you have written to the sample answer and Evaluation Sheet.

Question topics: Assault and battery
Evaluation Sheet: "Ben and Jessica"
Sample Answer: "Ben and Jessica"

Question topic: Intentional torts
Evaluation Sheet: "Farmer Dell's Cornfield"

Question topic: Intentional torts
Evaluation Sheet: "Cindy and the Scarf"

Question topic: Intentional torts
Sample Answer: "Hurricane Tara"

Question topic: Strict products liability
Evaluation Sheet: "Elaine's Bout with Botox"

■ BUSINESS ORGANIZATIONS

QUESTION TOPIC: AGENCY

While Sam was home with a cold, he developed a recipe for a caffeine-free latte that soothed his sore throat and opened his nasal passages. The next day, Sam brought a cup of latte to his friend Ben because he had a cold too. Immediately upon drinking the special brew, Ben, exclaimed, "Sam, you've cured me. I can breathe again!" Then Ben said, "You could make a fortune with this latte. It is far better than anything I've ever tasted." Sam responded, "You know, Ben, I was going to call my attorney. I am thinking about patenting the recipe and maybe going into business. But I am too sick to go out. Why don't you go and meet with him for me so we don't waste any time. Let me know what he says."

Ben agreed and met with Sam's attorney, Mr. Greene. Ben informed Mr. Greene that his friend and developer of the latte, Sam, was unavailable for this meeting. The attorney advised that they move immediately to patent the latte because recipe theft was common. Jerry hesitated a moment and finally said, "I suppose Sam would want to protect his recipe. Go ahead and do what you have to do." The attorney drafted the papers for Ben's signature. Mr. Greene said that the fee was $5000 for the work he had done and he would require another $5000 to set up the business. Ben said " Sam will send you a check."

Sam could not believe that Ben signed papers and Sam now owes $10,000. "Well, just forget it. I only told you to meet with him. I didn't tell you to sign anything."

Mr. Greene filed the papers and sent a bill to Sam for $10,000. When Sam refused to pay, Mr. Greene brought suit against him. Has Sam incurred this liability and if so, on what basis?

SAMPLE ANSWER: "THE LATTE"

Whether Sam has incurred liability for the contract with Mr. Greene depends on whether an agency relationship can be found between the parties. An agent is one who consents to act in a fiduciary relation on behalf of another, the principal, and is subject to the principal's control. An agent can act with either actual or apparent authority. Actual authority is the authority to act in a given way on a principal's behalf if the principal's words or conduct would lead a reasonable person in the agent's position to believe that the principal had authorized him to act. There are two types of actual authority: implied authority, which comes in conformity either with law or the general business customs of a particular trade, and express authority, which is the power that the principal has conferred directly upon the agent. Apparent authority, on the other hand, is an agent's authority to act in a given way on a principal's behalf in relation to a third party if the words or conduct of the principal would lead a reasonable person in the third party's position to believe that the principal had authorized the agent to so act.

With respect to Ben and Sam's relationship, Ben can be seen as Sam's agent for the purpose of meeting with Mr. Greene, Sam's attorney. Sam gave express authority to Ben when he told him to "go and meet with him for me so I don't waste any time. Let me know what he says." This can be construed as the source of Ben's authority to meet with Mr. Greene. It also defined the scope of Ben's authority because Sam told Ben to meet with the attorney and report back to him the substance of their conversation. Sam did not indicate Ben was to do anything more than meet and listen and tell Sam what happened during the meeting. While Ben could argue that Sam intended Ben do more than just meet with Mr. Greene because Sam instructed Ben to meet with him so that he would not "waste any time," this is too vague to provide genuine instruction and leaves Sam's intent open to speculation. However, Ben could argue that he was acting in Sam's best interests, in his fiduciary capacity as his agent, because Greene told him that recipe theft was common and that speed was essential to protect the recipe. In this case, Ben acted to protect Sam's interests which would be commensurate with exercising his fiduciary obligations and would be acting within the scope of an agent's authority. Sam would be bound.

With respect to Ben and Mr. Greene' relationship, it is possible to claim that Ben acted with apparent authority because Ben told Mr. Greene he was meeting with him at Sam's request. Further, Ben told him that Sam had developed the latte. This could cause Mr. Greene to reasonably believe that Ben was authorized to act for Sam. However, when Mr. Greene told Ben that there was a need to act quickly, Ben first "hesitated a moment" and then replied with equivocation when he said that "I suppose Sam would want to protect his recipe." To a trained professional like Mr. Greene, this expression of doubt should have signaled a problem and caused him to more deeply question the relationship. It does not seem reasonable that Mr. Greene did not question Ben further before proceeding to engage in such costly and time-consuming work. He had a duty to inquire. Consequently, Sam may escape liability on this basis.

On the other hand, Ben may not escape such liability. He may be liable for the contract to Mr. Greene under a warranty of authority because he held himself out as a party to the agreement with the authority to do so. If Sam as the principal is not bound, then Ben as agent breached the warranty of authority and is liable to the third party, Mr. Greene, for expectation as well as reliance damages, in this case, the bill for legal services.

■ BUSINESS ORGANIZATIONS

QUESTION TOPIC: PARTNERSHIP

When Ann learned that her great aunt Jenny had left her $50,000, she decided to use the money to open a muffin shop. She asked her friend Jerry if he would be interested in going into the venture with her. He said, "I don't have any money to invest with you but I would be willing to work in the store and use my show business connections to bring in customers." Ann agreed and they opened "Muffin Morning." They leased a store where they both signed as co-tenants, purchased kitchen supplies, and entered into a contract with a supplier of muffin mix.

The business prospered. Ann and Jerry worked long hours in the stop. Ann spent most of her time behind the counter and dealing with the suppliers, while Jerry baked the muffins and entertained the customers with his comedy routine. One afternoon while Ann had gone to the market to purchase fresh blueberries, Jerry was alone in the shop when he realized that it would be a great idea to sell novelty chef wear in the shop along with the muffins. Jerry had never purchased for the shop before nor had the vendor, "Baker's Wear," ever sold to the shop. Still, Baker's Wear took Jerry's order for dozens of specialty aprons, chef hats, and bakers' pants. The order came to $1000 and was non-returnable. Jerry told the vendor to bill it to Muffin Morning. The vendor agreed and promised to ship the next day.

Soon Muffin Morning was attracting more business than it could handle. Jerry and Ann discussed expanding the business. They needed more space and even if they didn't move to a larger store, they needed to hire someone to help make the muffins. Jerry was eager to take out a business loan and build a new store, but Ann thought that was moving too fast. However, she agreed to hire an employee and they offered the job to Carl. Now with an employee to pay, the business needed to improve its cash flow. Without Ann's knowledge, Jerry went to the bank and negotiated a small line of credit to cover operating expenses.

Shortly thereafter, a man came into the shop and asked Jerry if Muffin Morning would be interested in acquiring another muffin store. The man explained that it had just come on the market and was available at a terrific price. Jerry realized that it would require more capital than Muffin Morning had available. Still, Jerry told the man that he was very interested and would get back to him the next day. Jerry realized that this was an excellent business opportunity and decided to borrow the money from his parents. Jerry called the man and accepted the offer to buy the store.

The following week when Ann arrived at the shop she found the shipment from Baker's Wear. She yelled at Jerry, "This shop is not in the clothing business. I insist you return everything immediately." Jerry refused. He told Ann that unless she was willing to go along with some of his ideas to expand the shop, he was going to leave. Ann told him to go.

Ann and Carl continued to run Muffin Morning. One morning as Ann was serving a customer, he congratulated her on the opening of her second shop. She was shocked. She immediately went to see what all the fuss was about. She found Jerry behind the counter. He had opened up another muffin shop but three blocks from Muffin Morning. Finally, Jerry told Ann about the offer he had received and accepted for himself. Ann was too surprised to say a word. Instead, she turned and walked out of the shop.

Ann has regained her composure and now seeks legal advice. She wants to sever all contact with Jerry and wants to know how to proceed legally. She is also concerned about the obligation Jerry incurred for Muffin Morning with the bank, the invoice due Baker's Wear, and whether she has any interests in the new muffin shop.

SAMPLE ANSWER: "MUFFIN MORNING"

The issue is whether Ann has established a relationship with Jerry that is recognized by law. In this case, the question is whether they were either partners or shared an employer/employee relationship. Under the Uniform Partnership Act, a partnership is defined as an association of two or more persons to carry on as co-owners a business for profit. A partnership may be based upon evidence of an agreement between parties, either express or implied, to place their money, effects, labor, and skill in business with the understanding that profits will be shared. There need not be a written agreement; evidence of a partnership can be inferred from the parties' conduct. When there is no written agreement, however, the courts will look to the provisions of the Uniform Partnership Act.

Here, Ann did not promise a salary to Jerry nor did she set regular work hours, responsibilities, or identify a job title, traditional hallmarks of an employment relationship. Thus it is unlikely Ann considered Jerry an employee. Instead, she invested the money she inherited and Jerry promised to labor in the store and use his connections to bring in customers. A party need not contribute money to the partnership; labor or other skills can qualify as well. Jerry's contribution would be his labor and connections. Further, it would appear that they intended to join their efforts on behalf of the business because they jointly signed a lease, purchased kitchen supplies and entered into a contract with a supplier. While no single factor is dispositive of a partnership, taken together they would indicate an intent to work together in a business. Therefore, it is likely that Ann and Jerry can be viewed as partners.

The next question is whether Jerry had authority to order from Baker's Wear. Under UPA 9, every partner is an agent of the partnership for the purpose of its business and the act of every partner for apparently carrying on in the usual way the business of the partnership of which he is a member binds the partnership. Here, Jerry purchased specialty aprons, chef hats, and bakers' pants for Muffin Morning. He placed the order for the store because he thought it was a good idea to sell such items along with the muffins. If Jerry was a partner, he had authority to make contracts in furtherance of the partnership's business. While Ann might argue that the ordinary business of the shop was to sell muffins so that the purchase of clothing items was not in the usual course of business, it is not uncommon or unusual for food shops sell more than just food. The clothing items that Jerry ordered were all related to baking and cooking. Although Jerry had never purchased for the shop before nor had the vendor, "Baker's Wear," ever sold to the shop, this would not be sufficient to invalidate an otherwise valid exercise of Jerry's authority. The vendor had no reason to believe that Jerry lacked authority to act on behalf of Muffin Morning. It is likely Jerry had authority to make this purchase and Muffin Morning must pay the invoice.

A similar argument can be made with respect to Jerry's authority to negotiate a line of credit with the bank to cover operating expenses for the business. The issue is whether negotiating a line of credit is usual or ordinary to the partnership. Under UPA 18(e), all partners have equal rights in the management of the partnership business. As a partner, Jerry could exercise his authority to act on behalf of the business. Here the line of credit was to cover operating expenses. Jerry had not negotiated a loan to expand the business but rather to make sure that the business had enough cash to cover its expenses. Therefore, this would most likely be considered an act within the usual business of the partnership and the partnership would be bound.

The next issue is whether Jerry was required to tell Ann about the offer to buy another muffin shop. Under UPA 21, a partner is accountable to every other partner as a fiduciary. Consequently, a partner owes his co-partners the duty of the finest loyalty while the enterprise exists. Because partners operate in a trust relationship, one partner cannot usurp a partnership opportunity for himself. Here, Jerry owed it to Ann to tell her about the offer. Even though he knew that the partnership did not have enough capital to make the purchase and that Ann had shown hesitation to take out a bank loan, his duty was nonetheless to share the information with her. The partnership had the right to accept or reject the opportunity. Once rejected, Jerry could then decide whether to accept the offer for himself. This opportunity rightfully belonged to the partnership and Ann would have a choice of remedies: damages or disgorgement. A party who breaches the fiduciary duty of loyalty must disgorge all profits gained from the disloyal act. Jerry must disgorge the benefits from the new store.

Alternatively, since the new store was the same kind as Muffin Morning, the new shop might be considered partnership property. Jerry's dealings when he discussed the matter with the man who offered the opportunity to him would have constituted a transaction connected with the conduct of the partnership so it rightfully belonged to the partnership. In this case, it becomes one of the assets of the partnership.

Note: By now you should have a good sense of how to proceed from one issue to another and weave together rule and fact. There are still several issues to discuss but from here I'll leave you on your own to craft the words and provide instead a summary of the issues you need to resolve.

ANN'S OPTIONS:

(1) *Ann can dissociate from the partnership*

(a) Since it was an at-will partnership, each partner has the power and the right to dissociate. Dissociation is the separation of a partner from the partnership. This in turn will trigger dissolution.

(b) Need to discuss whether a dissociation occurred when Ann and Jerry disagreed over his ideas and she told him to go or when Jerry usurped a partnership opportunity for himself. Were one or the other or both acts wrongful?

(2) *Dissolution issues*

(a) Distinguish between the power and the right to dissolve the partnership and the consequences, i.e., whether the dissolution was "rightful" or "wrongful." In some jurisdictions, a breach of a fiduciary duty can cause a wrongful dissolution.

(b) Determine whether the dissolution was rightful or wrongful. This determination dictates the subsequent analysis of the winding up and settling of accounts.

(c) Dissolution does not end the partnership; it is the beginning of the end.

(d) Winding up of partnership affairs: the liquidation of the partnership accounts. Identify the settling of accounts with third parties and among the partners.

(e) Termination: this occurs when the winding up of the partnership affairs is complete.

■ CIVIL PROCEDURE

QUESTION TOPIC: PERSONAL JURISDICTION

Reprinted with permission of Professor Myra Berman

A New York City jazz nightclub, calling itself Club Cornet, has registered a trademark with the federal government. Under this trademark, they operate Club Cornet in New York City, as well as other Club Cornets situated in cities around the world.

Joe Prince, who lives in Columbia, Arkansas, also owns a jazz club he happens to call Club Cornet. Columbia is a college town and Prince, thinking to attract college students to his club, creates a Web page and posts it on the internet.

The site contains information about coming events and the places, all in Columbia, Arkansas, where tickets can be obtained. The only interactive feature of the site is that people who log in are invited to cast votes as to what future acts they would like to see at the club. Casting a vote does not identify who the voters are or where they are located. No tickets can be ordered nor can additional information be sought through the site. The web is, of course, available internationally and Prince's page can be read in, among many other places, New York City, on any individual's personal computer and on the computer owned by New York City's Club Cornet.

The New York club owners see the website and sue Prince in federal court in the Southern District of New York. The Arkansas club moves to dismiss under FRCP 12(b)(2) for lack of jurisdiction over the person. The plaintiff responds, claiming personal jurisdiction based on the availability of the website to computers in New York and on the connection established by the voting feature.

You are the judge. What is your ruling? Why?

EVALUATION SHEET: "CLUB CORNET"

ISSUE:

Whether the NY court may exercise personal jurisdiction over a non-domiciliary defendant who has posted a website on the internet that allegedly violates a NY club's trademark.

RULE:

____ Jurisdiction as a constitutional issue, based on the 14th Amendment's due process protections

____ Recognition of *International Shoe* as controlling when:

    ____ Defendant is a non-resident

    ____ Defendant is not present in the forum

    ____ Defendant has not consented to the court's jurisdiction

____ "Minimum Contacts" test [Sufficiency of Contacts]

    ____ Nature and quality of contact

        ____ Whether the defendant purposefully availed himself of the benefits of the forum state

        ____ Whether the defendant's conduct and connection with the forum state are such that he should reasonably anticipate being haled into court there

        ____ Whether the defendant carries on a continuous and systematic part of its general business within the forum state

____ Differentiate between general and specific jurisdiction

        ____ General = continuous, systematic activities are of such a nature as to make the state's assertion of jurisdiction reasonable; activities may be unrelated to cause of action

        ____ Specific = sporadic, non-continuous, even single act contacts may be sufficient but only if the cause of action "arises out of" that activity or act

____ Not offensive to traditional notions of fair play and substantial justice

APPLICATION:

____ Prince is a non-domiciliary because he lives in Columbia, Arkansas

____ Neither Prince nor his club are present in NY [fairness in haling him into NY court]

____ Prince did not consent to the NY court's jurisdiction over him

____ Prince created a website, using the same name as a NY club, and posted his website on the world-side internet

_____ Prince created a website, using the same name as a NY club, and posted his website on the world-side internet

[Purposeful availment analysis]

_____ Prince created the site to advertise and promote his club

_____ Arkansas locations for the purchase of tickets are noted on the site

_____ New Yorkers could access and view the site [sufficiency of contacts analysis]

_____ Unless a New Yorker accessed the site, he wouldn't have contact with it [no pop-ups or e-mail contacts]

_____ No attempt to establish direct communications with New Yorkers

_____ The website was not interactive for the purpose of transacting business, not even in Arkansas [sufficiency of contacts]

_____ No sales could be made

_____ No tickets could be ordered

_____ The website was interactive in that it created a mechanism for voting on "favorite acts" that Prince ought to book at his club [purposeful availment]

_____ The voters were anonymous so no subsequent solicitation could follow

_____ The acts were clearly designated for an Arkansas Club

_____ Other possible direct or indirect contacts with NY [sufficiency of contacts]

_____ No NY office

_____ No NY telephone number

_____ No NY-based sales agents

_____ No sales to New Yorkers

_____ No solicitation or advertisement directed at New Yorkers

CONCLUSION:

_____ Since Prince did not avail himself of the benefits and protections of NY law nor are the quality and nature of his contacts sufficient under Shoe for the court to fairly and justly hale him into court, the motion to dismiss under Rule 12(b)(2) should be granted.

■ CIVIL PROCEDURE

QUESTION TOPIC: PERSONAL JURISDICTION

Reprinted with permission of Judge George Pratt

Cybersales Ltd. is a Georgia corporation with its principal place of business in Augusta, Georgia. It has no store, factory, or warehouse. It works out of an office building in Augusta and sells merchandise over the internet through its website "Suckers.com." It has arrangements with different manufacturers to ship ordered goods to designated addresses. A customer who wants to order an item need only reach the website on his computer, call up the display of items for sale, click on the item to be ordered, and enter his address and major credit card number. Cybersales directs the electronic order to the appropriate manufacturer who ships the item directly to the customer.

Cybersales has been phenomenally successful. Using manufacturers located in the United States, Mexico, Taiwan, South Korea, and China, it has in the past two years processed over $100 million in sales to customers in the United States alone, with purchasers in each state accounting for at least $500,000 in sales.

Lydia L. Bean, a citizen of Montana, bought a small propane-gas cooking stove from Cybersales and when she first used it on a camping trip near her home it exploded due to a faulty value and caused her serious injuries. Relying on a Montana long-arm statute that permits service of process on a nonresident defendant who commits a tort outside the state that causes injury in the state, Bean has Cybersales served at its office with a summons and complaint in a federal court action. Cybersales has moved to dismiss for lack of personal jurisdiction.

Question: You are the judge. Decide the motion, explaining your reasons.

SUGGESTED OUTLINE FOR ANSWER: "CYBERSALES"

Reprinted with permission of Professor Myra Berman

ISSUE:

Whether Montana district court has personal jurisdiction over Cybersales, a Georgia corporation, when one of its products caused an injury within Montana.

RULE: should include the following:

1. Under *International Shoe* and its progeny, personal jurisdiction ("PJ") is established when an absent defendant:

   - has "minimum contacts"
   - exercising jurisdiction is consistent with "fair play and substantial justice"
   - defendant could have anticipated being haled into a Montana court
   - meets "purposeful availment" analysis
   - meets foreseeability test – stream of commerce analysis

2. Statement differentiating between general and specific jurisdiction.

   - Answer to this question: does the cause of action arise out of or relate to contacts with the forum state?

     __ Yes – if contacts are sufficient, specific jurisdiction is established

     __ No – if contacts are not of the quality and nature to be deemed sufficient, no jurisdiction OR

     __ No – if contacts did not arise from the cause of action but rather are systematic and continuous within the state, then general jurisdiction is established

3. State must have a long-arm statute

   - PJ based on links with the forum state

     __ If defendant commits a tort within the state = PJ

     __ If defendant commits a tort outside the state that causes injuries inside the state, then to establish PJ, defendant must

       - Regularly do in-state business
       - Must receive substantial revenue from that business

APPLICATION: must analyze Cybersales' contacts with Montana

- Filled an order of a Montana resident based on ads on its website, available to everyone in the world for the specific purpose of selling its merchandise.
- Cybersales received payment through a credit card used by the Montana resident.
- Cybersales caused a defective stock to be shipped to Montana where it caused harm.
- Cybersales does substantial annual business throughout the U.S. – over $100 million – and at least $500,000 in Montana.

Connect each of the facts with the rules cited above. Cybersales' contacts should be deemed to warrant the district court's exercise of specific jurisdiction. The claim arose out of one of Cybersales' contacts with Montana. Its contacts, all of which are in the nature of selling goods to Montana residents are extensive. Cybersales should reasonably anticipate being haled into Montana to answer for harm caused by defective merchandise it sent there.

CONCLUSION: Motion to dismiss denied.

■ CIVIL PROCEDURE

QUESTION TOPIC: REMEDIES

Reprinted with permission of Judge George Pratt

For more than 30 years, Roocs, Inc. has manufactured beer in northern New York State, using water from Babbling Brook on Mount Marcy in New York's Adirondack Mountains. The legendary purity of Babbling Brook has been a central theme of Roocs' advertising for at least 10 years. About a year ago, Rawhide Tanning Co. opened a factory at a site about two miles upstream from Roocs, and about ½ mile distant from Babbling Brook. Six months ago, Roocs' tasters noticed an unusual obnoxious taste in the beer being produced. Chemical analysis revealed some highly toxic by-products of a tanning process to be in the water.

Roocs immediately shut down the brewery and had to destroy 10 vats of manufactured beer, as well as four truckloads of product that was ready for shipment. To resume production, Roocs had to dismantle and steam-clean all of its brewing machinery, pipes, and tanks. After the cleaning, in order to continue producing, it needed an alternative water supply, which it obtained by purchasing bottled water from the Sedate Spring Co. After intense investigation, Roocs discovered that Rawhide, in direct and flagrant violation of the Federal Clean Water Act, had surreptitiously installed a discharge pipe leading from its tanning factory, across land it did not own, and into Babbling Brook. The discharge had so polluted the Brook that its waters would not return to their original purity for at least two years.

Your firm has sued Rawhide on behalf of Roocs, seeking an injunction to stop the discharge, plus compensatory and punitive damages. On your motion for a preliminary injunction, Rawhide, caught with its hand in the cookie jar, consented to the injunction and conceded its liability, leaving damages as the only issue for trial. You are assigned the job of preparing for trial.

Discuss:

(A)   Each type and item of damage that Roocs might obtain

(B)   Briefly explaining each selection and

(C)   Describing what, if any, additional information you would need in order to establish each type or item

DAMAGE ANALYSIS FOR ROOCS, INC.

Reprinted with permission of Professor Myra Berman

(A) Compensatory Damages [fact-driven]

Four truckloads of beer. Loaded on trucks for shipment. Therefore, sales were already arranged. Damages would be the lost sales prices, which incorporates cost of production and profit.

Ten vats of beer. If sales agreements are already made for the beer, use lost sales prices. If not, determine the cost of producing the ten vats and add in a lost profit factor.

Recover all expenses for disposing of the tainted beer.

Recover material and labor costs for dismantling and cleaning the equipment [whether plaintiff does it himself or contracts to another. If contracted, then recover the contract cost.]

Lost profit for the period of the shut down: has to be estimated based on historical records of the volume produced and sold in comparable periods in the past.

Cost of the investigation to discover the source of the pollution.

Cost of the recall: but only if it was necessary to recall beer that had already been sold and delivered.

Lawsuits: if any lawsuits by consumers from sickness, costs of defense of suits and any damages paid out.

Cost of alternative water: purchase price plus any additional expenses in handling that may have resulted.

Loss of good will: this is aimed at lost future profits after production resumes, and includes any reduction in sales resulting from the tainted beer being actually distributed plus the inability to claim the mountain pure water any more. Also included here would be the lost investment in their advertising program touting the virtues of the water, plus the cost of a new advertising program for the bottled-water beer. Primarily, this would have to come through expert testimony.

(B) Punitive Damages

Purpose: to punish defendant, to deter defendant, to deter others by making an example of defendant.

Standard: whether defendant's conduct was wanton, intentional, reckless, malicious. Here it was unquestionably intentional because defendant surreptitiously installed the discharge pipe over someone else's property. Defendant also trespassed in the process and violated state and federal environmental laws.

Amount: essentially a blank check to be determined based on how angry we can get the jury at the defendant for its bad conduct. Court review will place limits on recovery following the BMW factors: degree of reprehensibility (here, very bad conduct); ratio to compensatory damages (yet to be determined by the jury); comparison to possible civil or criminal penalties for the conduct (these need to be investigated, but probably exist). Also need to look at defendant's wealth – the wealthier the defendant, the higher amount it will take to punish that defendant.

(C) Statutory Damages

Available only when authorized by specific statute. We would have to research to see if there are any statutory damages available under state and/or federal environmental statutes, beginning with the Federal Clean Water Act, the one the defendant violated directly.

■ CONSTITUTIONAL LAW

QUESTION TOPICS: 10TH AMENDMENT, COMMERCE CLAUSE, STANDING, 11TH AMENDMENT

Reprinted with permission of Vice Dean Gary Shaw

Note: *The following question was a mid-term examination worth 30 points. Students were given one (1) hour and 15 minutes in which to take the exam.*

In the year 2005, the United States faced a dilemma. As Asia and South America recovered from their economic slumps, demand for oil soared. At the same time OPEC seemed to recover its footing and effectively imposed new limitations on oil production. With increased demand and limited supply, the price of oil soared to $70 per barrel. The increase in energy supplies caused the United States economy to slump. This triggered a collapse of the stock market. Suddenly the United States was looking at a potential economic disaster at least on a par with the Great Depression of the 1930's.

As the economy plunged, crime rose swiftly. Indeed, most commentators and politicians described the situation as an "epidemic of crime." This was not just larceny or burglary. Rather, the unexpected plunge of the stock market seemed to trigger a tremendous amount of violent crime. Looking for a way to stem the tide of violent crime, Congress decided that creating a national data bank of fingerprints would make it easier to solve crimes. The problem was how to create such a data bank.

Congress quickly reached a consensus that the best way to create such a data bank was to require states to fingerprint all applicants for driver's licenses. Additionally, to ensure that fingerprints would be obtained quickly, Congress required each state to have its drivers renew licenses within the next calendar year. Accordingly, Congress passed the following statute:

> *After lengthy hearings, the members of Congress have determined that the increase on crime is having such a substantial negative effect on commerce in the United States that emergency measures are needed. We have also determined that the most effective way in which to combat this crime and help revive the economy is to create a national database of fingerprints. Accordingly, the following bill shall go into law beginning on January 1, 2006:*

> *Crime Prevention Bill 4066*

> *Each state shall require the drivers registered within the state to re-register for a new driver's license by January 1, 2007. As part of the registration process, the state shall take the fingerprints of the person registering for the new driver's license. The state shall then forward the fingerprints to the appropriate federal law enforcement authorities. States need not enact any legislation to implement this bill; they need only instruct the appropriate executives and administrators to carry out this directive.*

> *In any state that does not implement procedures to effectuate this law, any citizen may bring suit against the Governor in his or her official capacity in federal court to compel compliance with this statute. Such citizen shall be entitled to damages of $10,000 and an injunction shall be entered requiring the state to comply with the statute. Only one award of damages shall be made against any state official, regardless of how many suits shall be filed.*

Each state may also choose to create its own database with the fingerprints. In the event the state shall choose to do so, it may designate which state authority shall keep the database.

Crime Prevention Bill 4066 was passed in each house of Congress unanimously and was eagerly signed by the President. It went into effect on January 1, 2006.

Although the bill was passed unanimously, various states reacted differently. The Governor of Vermont refused to implement the bill. Dick Louden, a citizen in Vermont, was aware of the bill. Incensed that the governor of Vermont was not willing to do her share to combat crime, Louden brought suit in federal district court in Vermont against the Governor, Fran Lehi.

You are counsel for Lehi. What are the strongest arguments you can make on her behalf? Discuss all possible issues you would raise.

ANSWER TO CONSTITUTIONAL LAW EXAM

Reprinted with permission of Vice Dean Gary Shaw[1]

Lehi can make several arguments. First, she can argue that the statute is unconstitutional under the 10th Amendment of the United States Constitution. The 10th Amendment provides that all powers not delegated to the United States by the Constitution nor prohibited to the states by the Constitution are reserved to the states. In *Printz v. United States*, Congress commanded state law enforcement agents to conduct background checks of handgun purchasers. The Supreme Court held that the 10th Amendment precludes Congress from commanding states' officers to administer or enforce a federal regulatory program. Similarly, in Louden's suit against Lehi, Congress has enacted a regulatory program in which state officers are required to take fingerprints of the registering drivers. This is not any different from Congress requiring state law enforcement officers to conduct background checks. Since in Lehi's case Congress is commanding state officers to administer its federal program of creating a fingerprint data bank, the statute violates the 10th Amendment and is unconstitutional.

Lehi can also argue that the statute is unconstitutional because Congress has exceeded its power under the interstate commerce clause. The commerce clause provides that Congress has the power to regulate commerce between the states. In *United States v. Lopez* the Supreme Court stated that this power encompasses three categories: the use of channels of interstate commerce; regulation and protection of the instrumentalities of interstate commerce; and regulation of activities having a substantial effect on interstate commerce. Congress stated that it passed the statute in this case because crime was having a negative effect on interstate commerce. Therefore, the statute in this case deals with the third category–regulation of activities having a substantial effect on interstate commerce. However, Lehi can argue that Congress has exceeded its power in this respect.

In *United States v. Morrison*, the Supreme Court found the Violence Against Women Act to be beyond Congress' power to regulate interstate commerce. In *Morrison*, Congress passed the statute under the theory that violence against women had a deleterious effect on interstate commerce. The Court held that this was beyond Congress' power, finding that there was inadequate proof that violence against women had a substantial effect on interstate commerce. The Court reasoned that individual instances of crime do not have a substantial effect on interstate commerce. Further, the effects of individual instances of crime could not be aggregated so as to say that crimes against women taken as a whole would have a substantial effect on interstate commerce. The reason aggregation was inappropriate was that crime is not an activity that is economic in nature. Therefore, it is the individual instances that must be considered and an aggregation theory is impermissible. Second, the Court found that crime is local in nature and traditionally belongs to the state to deal with. Finally, there was no jurisdictional hook to save the statute. A jurisdictional hook exists when a Congressional statute is limited to those instances in which it is clear that jurisdiction exists. There was no hook that limited the Violence Against Women Act to only those situations in which Congress had power to act. It applied to every crime. As a result of these three factors, Congress had exceeded its power to regulate pursuant to the interstate commerce clause.

---

1 *There are three points to emphasize in this answer. First, this is a model answer. I would not expect a student to write this articulately under the time pressure of an exam. However, I do expect students to recognize the issues and address them. Second, and much more important, the students must answer the question asked. The question asks what Lehi's strongest arguments are. Therefore, they will get no credit for giving Louden's arguments and explaining why Lehi will lose. Third, in some instances issues must be addressed in a certain order because resolution of one issue affects the resolution of another issue. In this answer, however, the order is not important. If a student wishes to address the standing issue first, for example, that is entirely permissible and the student can receive full credit.*

Similar to *Morrison*, in the Lehi case Congress exceeded its power to regulate under the commerce clause. First, any individual crime does not have a substantial effect on interstate commerce. Just as in *Morrison*, crime is not an activity that is economic in nature and therefore its effects cannot be aggregated. Second, crime is local in nature and traditionally belongs to the state to deal with. Finally, there is no jurisdictional hook to limit the applicability of the statute. Therefore, the statute exceeds Congress' power to regulate interstate commerce and is unconstitutional.

Lehi can also argue that Louden does not have standing to bring the suit in federal court. Article III of the Constitution requires persons wishing to bring a suit in federal court to have standing. In order to have standing a person must have a sufficiently concrete interest in the suit to be allowed to bring the action. This means that the person must have suffered an injury in fact, the defendant must have caused the injury and there must be a substantial likelihood that the injury will be redressed by a favorable decision in the lawsuit. In *Lujan v. Defenders of Wildlife* the Supreme Court clarified that the injury suffered must be an individualized injury – a generalized grievance is insufficient to grant standing. In *Lujan*, the plaintiffs were challenging the constitutionality of an action by the Secretary of the Interior. The Court stated that they had not been individually injured by that action. Rather, the injury they complained of was one suffered by all citizens and such grievances were better redressed through the political system rather than the courts.

Similarly, Louden has suffered no individualized injury. He is simply unhappy with the decision the governor made. This is a generalized grievance of the sort in *Lujan*. Therefore, he does not have standing to bring the suit in federal court. Although the statute appears to grant Louden standing to bring an action, this part of the statute must fall. In *Lujan*, the plaintiffs had contended that Congress had granted citizens standing to bring suit in federal court to challenge such actions of the Secretary. The Court held that Congress cannot grant standing to a person who would otherwise not have standing under Article III. Since Louden does not otherwise have standing under Article III, Congress cannot grant citizens in his circumstances standing. Therefore, under *Lujan* he should not be allowed to bring the suit.

Finally, Lehi can argue that Louden's suit is barred by the 11th amendment of the Constitution. The 11th Amendment provides that citizens of one state may not sue another state in federal court. In *Hans v. Louisiana*, the Court held that the 11th Amendment also bars suits by citizens against their own states in federal court. In determining whether a suit has been brought against the state or a state official in her official capacity, one of the factors the Court looks at is whether the damages will be paid from the state treasury. If so, then the suit is deemed to have been brought against the state and is barred by the 11th amendment. In Lehi's case the statute is ambiguous, only stating that it authorizes payment of damages of $10,000. However, the statute does not say that the damages shall be paid by the Governor personally. It would seem then that this payment would come from the state treasury and this is barred by the 11th Amendment.

■ CONTRACTS

QUESTION TOPIC: FORMATION

Rob Coe, owner of a athletic-wear company, is a well-known sports enthusiast and world traveler. After returning from a prolonged exploration of the Australian outback, he realized that Americans were getting "soft." He decided to design a new line of sportswear to help Americans recapture their spirit and he would introduce them at the Coe Competitions, a series of endurance-type athletic events. Mr. Coe told Kim, his copywriter, that she should start writing the copy for the new athletic clothes. Then he added, "You know, Kim, there is nothing like exercise to keep a girl in shape. I bet if you started to work out now, you could be ready for the Competitions. In fact, I will pay you a bonus of $1000 if you get in shape for the Coe Competitions."

Kim thought to herself he must be kidding. He knew she considered a walk around Bloomingdale's rigorous exercise. Still, she had put on a few pounds because of all the muffins she had been eating, and this was just the incentive she needed. She did not say a word to Mr. Coe or any of her co-workers but went out and bought a pair of sneakers and several exercise outfits. Every morning she went for a two-mile walk with her friend Carly. Every night she exercised to some old Jane Fonda tapes. As part of her new health regime, she drank only high energy, low-fat shakes for lunch and eliminated all muffins from her diet. After six weeks, Kim lost 15 pounds and several inches. She was in the best shape she had been in since high school and ready to compete in the Coe Competitions.

Kim went to see Mr. Coe to collect her bonus. Instead of giving her $1000, Mr. Coe laughed and said: "The only competition you are in shape for the sale rack at the closest department store. Besides, I was only kidding." Kim is furious and wants to bring suit to collect the $1000. Can she recover?

EVALUATION SHEET: "KIM V. COE"

GENERAL ISSUE

Whether Kim can recover the $1000 depends on whether Coe made Kim an offer capable of acceptance

____ First sub-issue is whether an offer was made.

____ **RULE:** An offer is a proposal by one party to the other, manifesting a willingness to enter into a bargain and made in such a way (by words or conduct) that the other person is justified in believing that his assent (acceptance) to that bargain is invited and, if given, will create a binding contract between the parties. An offer creates the power in the offeree to make a contract between the parties by an appropriate acceptance. Consider the following in determining whether an offer has been made: (1) Has there been a manifestation of present contractual intent ? (2) Are the terms certain and definite ? (3) Has the offer been communicated to the offeree ? The offer must be communicated to the offeree; in no other way will it create a power of acceptance in him.

____ **APPLICATION:** Coe made an offer to Kim when he said, "I will pay you a bonus of $1000 if you get in shape for the Coe Competitions." The words spoken were definite and certain because they indicated an amount for the bonus ($1000), set a defined goal ("get in shape") and time for the performance (for the Competitions). It was communicated directly to Kim. A reasonable person in Kim's position could believe that her assent was invited and would conclude a deal. On the other hand, it is possible that "get in shape" is too indefinite a term in which case it would not be an offer. Still, the stronger argument is that an offer was made to Kim.

The next question is whether the offer called for acceptance by return promise or return performance.

____ **RULE:** The acceptance must be in the same manner requested or authorized by the offeror because the offeror is the master of his offer. If not specified in the offer, an offer is interpreted as inviting the offeree to accept either by promising to perform what the offer requests or by rendering the performance, as the offeree chooses. However, some offers may only be accepted by performance – the doing of the requested act – and not a return promise. Generally in this case notice to the offeror of acceptance is not required. The acceptance occurs through performance.

____ **APPLICATION:** Here, Coe was asking for Kim to get in shape. He wasn't seeking her promise to get in shape but to be in shape for the Competition. His purpose can be inferred from his interest in keeping Americans from getting "soft" and his sponsorship of competitions to encourage such activity. He wanted her to be ready to compete in the athletic competitions. Coe was not seeking her promise to get in shape but rather the act of getting in shape. Coe might claim that his offer was made in jest because he said, "I was only kidding" but the objective theory controls and the test is what a reasonable person in the position of the offeree would think were meant by the words or conduct of the offeror. Kim had no reason to believe Coe was kidding since he was fully committed to getting people back in shape. He was sports enthusiast himself and wanted to keep Americans from getting "soft." He designed a whole line of sportswear and was sponsoring athletic competitions for this purpose. Kim would have no reason to believe Coe was joking in making her the offer to get in shape.

The next question is whether Kim had begun performance.

____   **RULE:** if the offer calls for acceptance by return performance, once the offeree begins performance, the offer becomes irrevocable. The offeror's duty to render his return performance is conditional on the offeree's completing performance as specified in the offer but once performance has begun, he is no longer free to revoke but must allow the offeree to complete performance within the time specified or within a reasonable time. Irrevocability takes effect only when actual performance is commenced, not when preparations for performance are begun.

____   **APPLICATION:** Coe's power to revoke the offer became irrevocable when Kim began her performance by getting in shape for the Competition. She performed because she purchased sneakers and outfits to work out in and walked two miles every day and exercised every night. Further, she changed her diet and drank only high energy drinks for six weeks and lost 15 pounds. On the other hand, Coe will claim this simply signified preparations for performance and does not qualify as the actual performance of his promise. Still, even if buying clothes and sneakers could be seen as mere preparations, the actual acts of walking, exercising, eating properly, and losing weight would meet the criteria of "getting in shape." The offer did not require Kim to win the Competitions, but only to get in shape to compete. Further, it didn't specify what kind of shape. Only enough to compete. Kim said she was "in the best shape she had been in since high school and ready for the Coe Competitions." Hence, she got in shape and accepted Coe's offer by this performance.

____   *Reliance* argument: assuming the court fails to find a valid offer and acceptance, Kim can claim that Coe's promise induced her reliance (she went out to buy the clothes and exercised and dieted), it was foreseeable to him that she would rely (he offered a monetary incentive of $1000), she relied to her detriment (she spent money on the clothes and time exercising and foregoing her favorite muffins for six weeks), and the court should enforce the promise to avoid injustice. Coe will claim that she benefitted by losing the weight and getting in shape so he really did her a favor and there was no injustice. Still, she relied on his promise and would not have done it otherwise. His promise induced her reliance and therefore he's liable.

■ CONTRACTS

QUESTION TOPIC: REMEDIES

Reprinted with permission of Touro 3L Ed Grasmann

Amy arrives with her new white convertible at her summer cottage and realizes she needs someone to wash her car. Upon seeing her neighbor, Ben, she calls to him, "Hey, Ben, I need someone to wash my car for the next ten weeks. I will pay you $600 if you will wash and wax it every Friday for the summer." Ben replies, "Sure. I usually make $40 mowing someone's law on Fridays but I will cancel that. I will be glad to take care of your car and I could use the extra money but I need some stuff and I can't get it during the week." Amy says, "No problem. I will pick it up for you. Just tell me what you need." Ben answers, "Here's $50 and please get a bucket, brushes, some wax and AmorAll and I will see you on Friday." Amy responds, "Okay, see you Friday."

Amy realizes a few days later that she can get the job done for less money and she enters into a deal with Dan to do the same work for only $200. On Thursday, Amy tells Ben that the deal is off. Ben asks for his $50 back but Amy tells him that she doesn't have it and has to give it to him next week. The following day, Ben sees Dan along with his friends Carl and Dan washing Amy's convertible with the supplies he paid for. On Monday, Ben files an action in small claims court.

EVALUATION SHEET: "AMY AND THE CONVERTIBLE"

1. Threshold question: Was there a contract?

    ____   Need to identify the overriding question of whether enforceable promises were made. Here there was an exchange of promise to wash and wax a car for ten weeks and a promise to pay $600.

2. If so, what kind of contract?

    ____   Is it a contract for the sale of goods or services? Need to identify the nature of the parties' agreement to determine the rule of law to apply: whether the UCC or common law. Since the nature of the agreement is one for personal services (washing the car) and not a transaction in goods, the common law is applicable.

3. What are Ben's damages?

    ____   General rule: Every breach of contract entitles the aggrieved party to sue for damages. The general theory of damages in contract actions is that the injured party should be placed in the same position as if the contract had been properly performed, at least so far as money can do this. Compensatory damages are designed to give the plaintiff the benefit of his bargain.

Expectation damages

    ____   **RULE:** This interest represents the "benefit of the bargain" and would include all that Ben expected to earn over the course of the contract. It is what the injured party had expected to receive under the contract "but for" the breach, less expenses saved by not having to perform.

    ____   **APPLICATION:** Here, Ben would have earned $600 over the life of the contract, the amount she promised to pay him. He said he needed to spend $50 for supplies, so $550 was pure profit. The benefit of his bargain would entitle him to recover the $600 less the $50 he saved in not having to purchase supplies to do the job.

Reliance damages

    ____   **RULE:** This interest is protected where one party relies to its detriment on a promise and damages will be awarded to prevent injustice from the detrimental reliance. This is the amount of out-of-pocket expenditures made by the injured party in performing (any expenditure by P and for other detriment following proximately and foreseeably from D's failure to carry out his promise; i.e., to put P back in the position he occupied before the agreement)

    ____   **APPLICATION:** Here, Ben already had a regular source of income of $40 per week for mowing lawns for the 10 week period he had to cancel to wash Amy's car. As a result, he gave up $400 in reliance on Amy's promise that he would be washing her car. His reliance recovery would be $400.

Restitution damages

    ____   **RULE:** This is measured by the value to the breaching party of the injured party's performance (an amount corresponding to any benefit conferred by P upon D in the performance of the contract).

    ____   **APPLICATION:** Here, Amy is enriched by the $50 Ben gave her to buy brushes and wax which she did and used to clean her car. She is enriched to this extent and should be made to disgorge this benefit to Ben. If not, she would be unjustly enriched by this amount.

■ CONTRACTS

QUESTION TOPICS: PAROL EVIDENCE AND INTERPRETATION

One March morning, Ted and George decided to buy a sailboat so they'd have something to do all summer. The next Sunday, after wandering around a marina, they found a 30' sailboat named "Hearsay." Ted and George loved it. Sam, the owner of the marina, said he would sell Hearsay for $25,000. George whispered to Ted, "let's offer half of that." Insulted, Sam told George he should consider a rowboat because Hearsay was a steal at $25,000. It included an equipped kitchen, an outboard motor, bathroom facilities, and sleeping accommodations for six, complete with boat bedding and cushions. Not about to lose the boat because of George, Ted apologized and offered Sam $20,000 if Sam would include the cute little storage box on the dock and some sailing lessons. Sam said he could consider the storage box but that he wasn't about to give sailing lessons. Ted responded, "In that case, we won't be able to buy the boat because we're clueless about sailing." Sam didn't want to lose the sale so he said, "let me think about it. I guess I could teach you some of the basics but lessons really have nothing to do with the boat."

Sam took Ted and George on a tour of the boat, pointing out the kitchen and bathroom facilities, and the sleeping compartments. Ted asked whether the dishes and cooking utensils came with the boat and Sam said that they did. The parties went back and forth all afternoon about the price of the boat. They never discussed marina costs.

Finally, Sam said he had to think about it and to call him next week. During the week, Ted and George told their friend Kim about the boat. Kim asked Ted where the boat would be docked and how much that would cost. Ted said he assumed it would stay at the marina and that the docking fees must be included in the price of the boat.

Ted called Sam the following Sunday and asked if they had a deal. Sam said he wouldn't sell Hearsay for less than $22,500. Ted gave in and said, "You've got a deal." When Ted and George arrived at the marina, Sam was waiting for them with a contract which he had drafted. It read in pertinent part,

"Sam agrees to sell and Ted agrees to buy the 30' sailboat named Hearsay, for the price of $22,500. Hearsay comes with the following equipment and the following equipment only: an equipped kitchen, outboard motor, bathroom facilities, and sleeping accommodations for six."

Ted asked about the sailing lessons. Sam said not to worry, he'd give Ted and George some lessons as soon as it was warm enough. The parties signed the contract.

One May day, Ted, George, and Kim went to the marina to get the boat ready to sail. When they arrived, Ted had a hard time finding the boat because the little storage box was missing. Once on board, Kim cried out, "Ted, where are all the nautical cushions and bedding you said would be here?" Ted looked from starboard to stern but couldn't find a single cushion or pillow. Nor were there any dishes in the kitchen. Thinking there must be some mistake, Ted called Sam and asked him about all the missing items. Sam said there was no mistake. Then Ted asked about setting up his first sailing lesson and Sam just laughed and said, "Take a course with the local high school. And before you leave, here's your invoice for May's docking charges." Ted was shocked when he looked at the bill for $500.

Ted was too upset to utter a word at the time but he's since gained his composure and has consulted you to tell him his rights. What would you tell him?

EVALUATION SHEET: "THE HEARSAY"

I. Parol evidence issue

____ **ISSUE:** whether evidence of the parties' oral discussions about the sailing lessons, and other items are barred by the parol evidence rule.

____ **RULE:** UCC 2-202 applies because this is a sale of goods: a boat is a "good" pursuant to 2-105, where goods are all things movable at the time of identification to the contract.

____ **RULE:** where an agreement has been reduced to writing which the parties intend as the final and complete expression of their agreement, evidence of any earlier oral or written expressions is not admissible to vary the terms of the writing. If the parties had such an intention, the agreement is said to be "integrated," and the parol evidence rule bars evidence of prior negotiations for at least some purposes. If the parties had no such intent, the agreement is said to be "unintegrated," and the parol evidence rule does not apply.

____ *UCC:* allows terms to be explained or supplemented by course of dealing or usage of trade or course of performance but cannot be contradicted.

In applying the PER, ask two questions:

____1. *Is the agreement integrated or unintegrated?* The first issue is whether the parties intended the writing to be a final embodiment of their agreement. If so, there is at least a partial integration and the writing may not be contradicted.

____2. *If it is integrated, is it totally or partially integrated?* If the writing is a final expression of the parties agreement and complete with respect to all of its terms, it's a total integration and can't be contradicted by any type of evidence nor supplemented by consistent (non-contradictory) additional terms. A partial integration is final as to the terms it contains but not complete as to all the terms so it may be supplemented by consistent additional terms, but cannot be contradicted.

APPLICATION:

____ Whether it was integrated or unintegrated: it was integrated because it was reduced to a writing, signed by both parties, and stated that the Hearsay comes with the "following equipment only" which suggests the parties intended it to be a final expression of the terms the writing contained.

____ The next question is whether it was totally or partially integrated: appears to be only a partial integration because it contains some but not all the items the parties discussed. It identifies the boat by name and size and price and some equipment but the sailing lessons, bedding, and cushions were not mentioned, in addition to the usual items associated with a sale – for example, payment terms and transport.

With a finding of partial integration, each of the following must be analyzed:

____ *The bedding:* argue not barred by PER b/c supplements, not contradicts, the sleeping accommodations.

____ *Kitchen utensils:* argue not barred by PER b/c supplements, not contradicts, the equipped kitchen

____ *Storage box:* barred by PER b/c contradicts the language "following equipment only" and storage box is boat equipment

___ *Marina costs:* barred b/c no basis for admission; parties never even discussed

___ *The sailing lessons:* not barred by PER b/c does not contradict the terms b/c they speak to size, price and equipment only. Sailing lessons would be additional. Still, could argue either way whether they were "natural" to have been left out b/c they had nothing to do with the sale of the boat or they were so important to the deal (Ted wouldn't buy otherwise) that they naturally would be included. Would not be a condition precedent b/c the condition would have to be one which must occur before the agreement was to take effect. Here the parties performed the agreement by buying and selling the boat.

II. INTERPRETATION ISSUE

___ **ISSUE:** is the contract language "equipped kitchen" and "sleeping accommodations" subject to interpretation?

___ **RULE:** Interpretation is the process by which a court ascertains the meaning that it will give to the language used by the parties in determining the legal effect of the contract. The question is whether the written language is reasonably susceptible to more than one meaning. If so, extrinsic evidence is admissible to explain the meaning even if it would otherwise be barred by the parol evidence rule.

APPLICATION:

___ Sleeping accommodations: Ted will claim that he reasonably believedsleeping accommodations meant the boat bedding and cushions he saw on the boat and not just the physical compartments;

___ Equipped kitchen: Ted will claim that an "equipped kitchen" meant one that included all the utensils necessary to use the kitchen.

___ Usage of trade: each party could introduce evidence of the practices of the boat trade with respect to sales of personal boats to support the reasonable expectations of the party with respect to the transaction in question, i.e., what is customarily meant in the business by an "equipped kitchen" and "sleeping accommodations."

■ CONTRACTS

QUESTION TOPIC: REQUIREMENTS CONTRACTS

Hoping to cash in on the coffee craze, Kim and her friend Ted decided to open a business called the Delicious Donut to provide coffee and donuts to the morning breakfast crowd. They rented a store and entered into a contract with a supplier of donut mix. Muffin Man agreed to deliver to Delicious Donut all its donut mix requirements for a two-year period. No specific amount was stated in the contract. Muffin Man had similar contracts with coffee shops in the neighborhood.

After six months, the business was doing so well that Ted and Kim decided to expand operations when the store next to theirs suddenly became available. The rent was very low and they could afford the expansion in part because of the really good price they were paying for the donut mix. Business boomed and the demand for donut mix doubled after only two months and then remained relatively steady. Muffin Man met Delicious Donut's increased demand for four months but found it was having some difficulty meeting the increased requirements. Muffin Man called Delicious Donut and said, "I'm not sure I'm going to be able to keep supplying you with donut mix. I have other customers and I didn't agree to this."

Kim and Ted went into an immediate panic. Without donut mix, they might lose the business. And without donut mix at the price they had contracted for with Muffin Man, they would not make a profit because of the expenses involved in their enlarged operations. They demanded that Muffin Man perform and claimed that since the contract did not specify an amount, Muffin Man was obligated to meet its requirements, whatever they might be for the complete term of the parties' contract. What are Delicious Donut's rights, if any? What are Muffin Man's rights, if any? What would you advise?

EVALUATION SHEET: "THE DELICIOUS DONUT"

ISSUES:

____ Whether Delicious Donut ("DD") can enforce the requirements contract with Muffin Man ("MM") when DD doubled its requirements within months of entering into the agreement.

Sub-issues of good faith and unreasonably disproportionate demand

RULES:

____ UCC sale of goods; merchants (a merchant is one who deals in goods of the kind); 2-306 requirements contract (the quantity term is measured by the requirements of the buyer).

____ Good faith component

Definition of good faith. Good faith in the case of a merchant means honesty in fact and the observance of reasonable commercial standards of fair dealing in the trade. Good faith in context of requirements contract.

____ "Unreasonably disproportionate" component of 2-306.

Definition of unreasonably disproportionate as interpreted in requirements/output contracts.

APPLICATION:

____ Whether this was a contract for the sale of goods under the UCC.

This is a sale of goods because donut mix is a "good" under the UCC definition of a good as all things which are movable at the time of identification to the contract for sale. MM was a merchant because seller of donut mix; DD is a restaurant owner.

____ Whether this was a requirements contract.

This is a requirements contracts because the quantity term is defined by DD's requirements for donut mix.

Whether the increased demand was made in good faith:

____ In good faith

____ because Kim and Ted were new to the business and did not know for sure that demand would increase.

____ Even if they thought demand would increase because they enlarged the business, they would not know it would double.

____ In bad faith

____ because they counted on the good price they were paying for donut mix when they decided to increase operations.

____ They had to assume demand would increase because they enlarged the store.

____ They wanted to make more money and would be doing so while MM was bound to supply more at the same price. This would mean that MM was taking advantage of its contract with DD.

Whether the increased demand was unreasonably disproportionate:

____   Unreasonably disproportionate

        __ based on the parties' prior requirements which had been consistent for six months prior to increase.

        __ Further, doubling the demand might be seen as disproportionate to the comparable quantity DD supplied to the other coffee shops in the neighborhood.

____   Not unreasonably disproportionate

        __ because DD had supplied the increased quantity for four months so it could supply the amount, even if it might be losing money on the deal.

        __ It might be too soon to determine whether the demand had increased so substantially in comparison to prior requirements because DD had been supplying MM for only six months prior to the increase. This might be too soon to define DD's normal requirements. Further, the demand has leveled off and might even decrease.

SAMPLE ANSWER: "THE DELICIOUS DONUT"

My advice to Delicious Donut ("DD") begins with determining whether DD can enforce the requirements contract with Muffin Man ("MM") when DD doubled its requirements within months of entering into the agreement. Because this agreement involves a transaction in goods, donut mix, and goods are defined as all things which are movable at the time of identification to the contract, this contract is a sales contract and therefore subject to the provisions of the Uniform Commercial Code.

Under the UCC, an agreement sufficient to constitute a contract for sale may be found even though one or more terms are left open. The UCC will provide the missing term which is referred to as a "gap filler." Here, the facts indicate that DD entered into an agreement with MM for the purchase of "all its donut mix requirements" for a period of two years. The term specifying the quantity of donut mix was not defined. The question is whether parties may create contractual obligations for the sale of goods without committing to purchase a specific quantity. While quantity is usually the only term a court will not provide when it is absent from a sales agreement, it is not a problem in a requirements contract. Under UCC 2-306, a requirements contract is one in which the quantity term is measured by the requirements of the buyer. In this kind of contract, the parties create contractual obligations without committing to purchase a specific quantity. Here, the quantity term of the parties' agreement was measured by the buyer's requirements because MM agreed to deliver all of DD's donut mix requirements.

The UCC requires that a party's requirements occur in good faith. Good faith in the case of a merchant means honesty in fact and the observance of reasonable commercial standards of fair dealing in the trade. A merchant is one who deals in goods of the kind. Here, both parties are merchants: MM is a merchant because he is a supplier of donut mix and DD is a retail establishment. With respect to this particular agreement, MM met the requirements of the agreement for over six months but then DD doubled its demand. While it would seem that DD indeed had such requirements since it had increased demand for its donuts, the doubling of its demand might be seen as not occurring in good faith or as an unreasonably disproportionate quantity.

DD intentionally increased its demand for donuts by expanding its business. The question is whether this was a normal expansion undertaken in good faith or an attempt to take advantage of market opportunities at the expense of a fixed price. DD decided to expand operations by taking over another store in part because they were paying a good price for the donut mix. They knew that MM was bound to continue to sell at the contract price. Even if they did not know for sure that their demand for donut mix would increase, they had to assume it would because they were expanding the business. Even more likely, DD was counting on the increased demand so that business would be even more profitable. Consequently, if there were an increase in business, DD had to know its requirements for donut mix would also increase. This might be considered an act of bad faith in that it seeks to take advantage of the other party. It is possible that DD did not realize it might be taking advantage of its agreement with MM by doubling demand because it was a new business and it could not be sure of its requirements. Even if DD thought demand would increase because it enlarged the business, it would not know it would double. Still, it seems that DD knew it was taking advantage of the contract when it considered the price of donut mix as a factor in deciding to enlarge operations.

Even where one party acts with complete good faith, the UCC limits the other party's risk in accordance with the reasonable expectations of the parties. Conceivably, MM did not bargain for DD to double its requirements. While MM knew DD was a new business and so there were no comparable prior requirements, MM had similar contracts with other coffee shops in the neighborhood so it could approximate DD's demand with a reasonably foreseeable figure. Doubling the demand might be seen as disproportionate to the comparable quantity DD supplied to these other coffee shops. The doubling of requirements might also be seen as unreasonably disproportionate based on the parties' prior requirements. DD's requirements had been consistent for six months before the demand doubled. It was only after this increased demand had continued into the fourth month that MM called to say that it would no longer perform. In this case, MM might not be required to meet the increased quantity because it was unreasonably disproportionate to the prior demand.

On the other hand, it might be too soon to determine whether the demand had increased so substantially as to be considered an unreasonably disproportionate quantity. MM had been supplying DD for only six months before the increase in demand. This might be too short a time to define the DD's normal requirements and in this case an increase, even one that was doubled, would not be seen as unreasonably disproportionate. Further, since the facts indicate that demand has leveled off, MM might be required to meet DD's requirements for the term of the agreement.

■ CONTRACTS

QUESTION TOPIC: PAROL EVIDENCE

Carly and Simon decided to combine their resources and formed Shuzzies, Inc., a shoe manufacturing company. Carly would design the shoes and Simon would be responsible for business operations. Each party contributed $50,000 to start the business.

Carly planned a line of extravagant evening footwear that would appeal to celebrities. She knew they would be expensive to produce but her goal was to become shoemaker to the stars. Simon, on the other hand, was practical and planned a product line that would appeal to teenagers.

On January 25, 2003, Carly and Simon signed a written agreement that provided in relevant part:

> *"Upon written request by either party, Shuzzies shall, within sixty days of receipt of such request, re-purchase the interest of the requesting party at the original investment cost of $50,000."*

By March 2005, Carly was tired of spending all her time designing for teenagers and decided it was time to pursue her dream. She made a written request on Shuzzies for it to buy-back her interest pursuant to the agreement. Simon then reminded Carly that before the agreement was signed, the parties had orally agreed that the buy-back provision would only apply if the business was making a profit on the date of the request. As of March 2005, Shuzzies had not yet made a profit. For this reason, Simon told Carly that the business would not buy back her interest.

Carly duly commenced an action against Shuzzies for breach of contract, seeking to recover her $50,000. At trial, Carly's attorney objected when Simon sought to testify about the oral agreement limiting the buy-back provision. The court overruled the objection and permitted the testimony. Was the court's ruling allowing Simon's testimony concerning the oral agreement correct?

SAMPLE ANSWER: "SHUZZIES, INC."

The general question is whether evidence of the parties' previous oral discussion regarding the buy-back is barred by the parol evidence rule. The parol evidence rule determines the provability of a prior or contemporaneous oral agreement when the parties have agreed to a written agreement. Here, parol evidence may bar introduction of the parties' oral agreement regarding the buy-back terms because they had a writing with an express provision regarding a buy-back.

To determine whether Simon can introduce such evidence, we need to know whether the agreement is integrated or unintegrated. Where an agreement has been reduced to writing which the parties intend as the final and complete expression of their agreement, evidence of any earlier oral or written expressions is not admissible to vary the terms of the writing. If the parties had such an intention, the agreement is said to be "integrated," and the parol evidence rule bars evidence of prior negotiations for at least some purposes. If the parties had no such intent, the agreement is said to be "unintegrated," and the parol evidence rule does not apply.

To determine whether the agreement is integrated, we need to ask whether Carly and Simon intended the writing to be a final expression of their agreement with respect to the terms it contains even if it was not intended as a complete expression of all the terms. If the writing appears thorough and specific enough to be taken as a final agreement on the terms it contains, then the agreement is considered integrated with respect to those terms. Here, it seems that the agreement is integrated because it expresses their intent regarding buying out of the business. It provides the method by which it would occur, "upon written request," who could exercise the right, "either party," and when the money would be disbursed, "within sixty days."

Assuming the agreement is integrated, the next question is whether it is totally or only partially integrated. If the writing is a final expression of the parties agreement and complete with respect to all of its terms, it's a total integration and cannot be contradicted by any type of evidence nor supplemented by consistent (non-contradictory) additional terms. A partial integration is final as to the terms it contains but not complete as to all the terms so it may be supplemented by consistent additional terms, but cannot be contradicted. It is possible that this was a total integration because it includes all the necessary requirements for exercising the buy-back option, leading one to believe that it contains the complete expression of the parties' intent. Therefore, evidence of the parties' prior oral agreement would be barred.

Even if the agreement is a total integration, it is questionable whether the oral agreement was the type of collateral agreement that under the circumstances would naturally have been omitted from the writing. If so, then the parol evidence rule would not bar its admission as long as it does not contradict the main agreement. Here, it might not be natural to include mention of a company's financial profitability in a provision which simply outlines the procedure for re-purchasing the original interest. Conversely, if the parties intended that the only way the buy-back provision could be exercised would be if the company were in the financial condition to afford it, then they would certainly have included it in the writing and if it were not there, the court should not imply it.

Assuming, however, that this is a partial integration, the next question is whether this is an additional or contradictory term. Even if the writing is only partially integrated, extrinsic evidence of terms contradictory to one of the integrated terms is not admissible. Here, none of the terms regarding the buy-back deal with the issue of profitability. Instead, they specify written notice, a period of sixty days for Shuzzies to act on the request, and the specific amount of

$50,000. Therefore, a term regarding profitability could be seen as additional. However, since the profitability term expressly limits or modifies the buy-back provision, it could be seen as contradictory and thus inadmissible.

The court's ruling was incorrect because evidence of the oral agreement was barred by the parol evidence rule.

EVALUATION SHEET: "SHUZZIES, INC."

ISSUE:

___ Whether evidence of the parties' prior oral discussion about the buy-back is barred by the parol evidence rule

RULE:

___ The PER determines the provability of a prior or contemporaneous oral agreement when the parties have agreed to a written agreement. Where an agreement has been reduced to writing which the parties intend as the final and complete expression of their agreement, evidence of any earlier oral or written expressions is not admissible to vary the terms of the writing. If the parties had such an intention, the agreement is said to be "integrated," and the parol evidence rule bars evidence of prior negotiations for at least some purposes. If the parties had no such intent, the agreement is said to be "unintegrated," and the parol evidence rule does not apply.

APPLICATION:

___ The agreement is integrated because it expresses their intent regarding buying out of the business. It provides the method by which it would occur, "upon written request," who could exercise the right, "either party," and when the money would be disbursed, "within sixty days." It's also likely this was a total integration because it includes all the necessary requirements for exercising the buy-back option, leading one to believe that it contains the complete expression of the parties' intent. In this case, it might not be natural to include mention of a company's financial profitability in a provision which simply outlines the procedure for re-purchasing the original interest.

___ Alternatively, if the parties intended that the only way the buy-back provision could be exercised would be if the company were in the financial condition to afford it, then they would certainly have included it in the writing and if it's not there, the court should not imply it. Even if the writing is only partially integrated, extrinsic evidence of terms contradictory to one of the integrated terms is not admissible. Here, none of the terms regarding the buy-back deal with the issue of profitability. Instead, they specify notice, a period of sixty days for Shuzzies to act on the request, and the specific amount of $50,000. A term regarding profitability could be seen as additional. However, since the profitability term expressly limits or modifies the buy-back provision, it could be seen as contradictory and thus inadmissible.

CONCLUSION:

___ The court's ruling was incorrect because evidence of the oral agreement was barred by the parol evidence rule.

■ CONTRACTS

QUESTION TOPIC: CONDITIONS

Not one to give up on her dream of becoming a designer to the Hollywood stars, Carly, a shoe designer, decided to take her shoes directly to celebrities. She knew that designers often got their start if they could get just one celebrity to wear their designs. Carly learned from a friend that Oscar-nominee Sarah Jessie needed a pair of silver shoes to match her dress. Carly designed a pair of high-heeled silver sandals decorated with precious jewels in colors to match Sarah Jessie's gown. She photographed the shoes and sent a picture with the following note to Sarah Jessie,

> I have designed these shoes worth $5000 at my own expense and would be honored to give them to you at no charge provided that you wear them to the Academy Awards and take every single opportunity to tell anyone who asks that I, Carly Carpeta, designed the shoes.

Sarah Jessie replied she'd be delighted to wear her shoes. Carly shipped the shoes and Sarah Jessie wore them to the Awards ceremony. Joan Rivers stopped to interview her on the red carpet. Joan noticed the bejeweled shoes and shouted in delight, "Whose shoes are you wearing? Wherever did you find them?" Sarah Jessie simply smiled and said, "a little angel sent them to me." Both before and after this interview, whenever anyone asked her that night who designed the shoes, Sarah Jessie told them it was Carly Carpeta of New York. She was lavish in her praise. The only one she didn't tell was Joan. Carly was watching on television and all she heard was what Sarah Jessie told or rather, didn't tell, Joan. Carly immediately sent a letter to Sarah Jessie demanding $5000 for the shoes. Sarah Jessie refused to pay anything. Carly retains you to represent her. What result?

EVALUATION SHEET: "CELEBRITY SANDALS"

ISSUE:

____ Whether Sarah Jessie failed to meet an express condition so as to keep the sandals at no charge.

RULES:

____ A condition is "an event, not certain to occur, which must occur, unless occurrence is excused, before performance under a contract becomes due." An express condition is one agreed to by the parties and can be determined by such language as "if," "on condition that," "provided that," "in the event that," and "subject to."

____ A promise, according to Rest 2d is a "manifestation of intention to act or refrain from acting in a specified way, so made as to justify a promisee in understanding that a commitment has been made."

____ If a party's performance of an act is treated as a condition to another's duty, a non-performance of that act completely discharges the latter from his obligation, even though the failure of the condition to occur has damaged him little or not at all.

____ A party who breaches a promise is only liable for whatever damage he causes by the breach. Thus, if a party's performance deviates only slightly from that specified in a contract, the result to him is less harsh if his performance is treated as a promise which he has breached (in which case he is liable for only nominal damages) than if it is treated as a condition to the other party's performance (in which case the other party's duty to perform is discharged completely).

APPLICATION:

____ Here, Carly stated expressly that Sarah Jessie could have the sandals at no charge "provided that" she told everyone who asked that she designed the shoes. The words were specific in requiring that Sarah Jessie had to "take every single opportunity to tell anyone who asks." This would include Joan Rivers. It's not enough to have told every other person who asked both before and after the interview with Rivers or that she was lavish in her praise if the express term required that she tell anyone who asked. To meet the condition, Sarah Jessie had to tell absolutely everyone who asked and she didn't.

____ On the other hand, it might be considered only a promise and not a condition and Sarah Jessie substantially performed by wearing the shoes to the Academy Awards and telling almost everyone who asked about her shoes. Carly wanted people to know that she was the designer and she substantially received this performance because Sarah Jessie told everyone but Joan Rivers that Carly designed the shoes. Further, Sarah Jessie was lavish in her praise to anyone who asked and therefore Carly received that which she bargained for – her shoes were worn to the Academy Awards and people learned that she was the designer.

CONCLUSION:

____ It is likely a court would find an express condition because of the specific language and therefore Carly would recover becasue Sarah Jessie failed to meet the conditions.

■ CONTRACTS

QUESTION TOPIC: COMMERCIAL IMPRACTICABILITY

Farmer Green contracted to sell 10,000 pounds of tomatoes to the Acme Grocery Store. Both parties knew that Farmer Green expected to grow the potatoes on his own farm, although the contract said nothing about the expected source of the tomatoes. A tornado swept through Green's farm and destroyed the entire tomato crop. Is this an excusing event under UCC 2-615? What if the loss of the crop was caused by rabbits?

EVALUATION SHEET: "FARMER GREEN'S TOMATOES"

ISSUE:

___ The first question is whether the tornado would be an excusing event to Farmer's Green promised performance to deliver tomatoes.

RULE/APPLICATION:

___ Here the transaction involves the sale of tomatoes, which are goods pursuant to the UCC and so the UCC Article 2 applies. Further, the parties are merchants because Green was a farmer in the practice of raising and selling crops and Acme was a grocer in the business and buying and selling produce.

RULE:

___ A party may be excused from performance when that performance as agreed has been made impracticable by the occurrence of a contingency the non-occurrence of which was a basic assumption on which the contract was made.

APPLICATION:

___ Here the agreed performance was the delivery of the tomatoes and the contingency was the tornado which destroyed the entire crop. Generally, changes in weather are foreseeable and farmers are not excused if they undertook to deliver a stated quantity. They would have to secure the tomatoes elsewhere. However, here both parties expected the tomatoes to come from Green's property so it was a basic assumption that the property would yield the tomatoes. When the tornado destroyed the entire yield on Green's land, this would be a contingency the non-occurrence of which was a material part of the agreement and sufficient to discharge Green's performance.

SECOND ISSUE/APPLICATION:

___ The next question is whether Green's duty would be discharged if the crop were destroyed by rabbits. It's not likely because Farmer Green is in the position to guard against rabbit infestation and should have taken appropriate steps to guard against it. He could have used such a simple device as a fence. Between Green and Acme, Green would bear the risk of the rabbits.

■ CONTRACTS

QUESTION TOPIC: FRUSTRATION OF PURPOSE

George entered into a contract with Oscar Meyer for $5000 to dress up like a hot dog and ride a motor scooter in Macy's Thanksgiving Day Parade on Thursday, November 20. Since he didn't own a scooter, he went to a store and signed a contract to buy one for $8000 from Brands, Inc. for delivery on or about November 19. George explained that while he had always wanted a scooter so he could go riding in Central Park in the spring, he needed the scooter by November 19 because he had a contract to ride in the Thanksgiving Day Parade on November 20. George waited all day on November 19 and at 5:00 p.m. Brands called to say that the delivery would be made on November 21. As a result, George could not ride in the parade and was paid nothing by Oscar Meyer, which hired a replacement. George refused delivery on the 21st, claiming that his performance as a hot dog had been frustrated. Brands sued and George counterclaimed. What result and why?

EVALUATION SHEET: "GEORGE AND THE SCOOTER"

ISSUE:

____ Whether George's principal purpose in purchasing the scooter was frustrated when it wasn't delivered in time for the parade.

RULE:

Where the bargained for performance is still possible, but the purpose or value of the contract has been totally destroyed by some supervening event, such frustration of purpose will discharge the contract. The purpose that is frustrated must have been a principal purpose in making the contract. The object must be so completely the basis of the contract that without it, the transaction would make little sense.

____ (1) Some supervening act or event.

____ (2) The supervening act or event was not reasonably foreseeable at the time the contract was entered into.

____ (3) The avowed purpose or object of the contract was known and recognized by both parties at the time they contracted.

____ (4) The supervening act or event totally or nearly totally destroys the purpose or object of the contract.

APPLICATION:

____ (1) What was the supervening act? The failure to deliver in time for the parade.

____ (2) Was it foreseeable? It was "foreseeable" because the agreement called for delivery on or around November 19 so it was foreseeable that delivery could come after this date.

____ (3) Was the purpose known by both parties at the time of contract? George told Brands he had a contract to ride in the Thanksgiving Day parade and he needed the scooter by the 19th to do that. On the other hand, George also said he had always wanted a scooter to ride in Central Park in the spring and he was ordering in November so there would seem to be no problem with a delivery delay of a day or two.

____ (4) Did the late delivery totally destroy/frustrate the purpose of the contract?
If the sole purpose was to ride in the parade, then that purpose was lost. However, George can still ride the scooter in Central Park. It is arguable whether the sole purpose of the scooter was to ride in the parade since George was to earn only $5000 for dressing up like a hot dog and the scooter cost $8000. Because it cost $3000 more than he was to earn from the parade contract, it is very possible that George's purpose in purchasing the scooter was for more than just riding in the parade. Therefore his principal purpose is not substantially frustrated.

■ CONTRACTS

QUESTION TOPIC: FORMATION UNDER UCC 2-207

Reprinted with permission of Professor Theodore Silver

On August 1, 2005, Bart, a shoelace distributor in New York, and Ernie, owner of convenience store in New York, formed a written contract requiring Bart to deliver to Ernie on August 14, 2005, 400,000 pairs of white standard nylon shoelaces for a total purchase price of $100,000 to be paid by Ernie to Bart.

On August 1, 2005, in order to secure the shoelaces promised to his customer Ernie, Bart signed and sent Sarah, a shoelace manufacturer in New York, this fax:

> "We wish to purchase 400,000 pair of your standard nylon shoelaces, at a total price of $80,000 for resale to our New York customer Ernie, to arrive at our warehouse on August 10. Shoelaces must be packed in wooden crates – otherwise we cannot and will not make the purchase."

Sarah received the fax on August 1. In response, Sarah signed and sent to Bart this fax:

"Your offer to purchase is absolutely accepted. *Shoelaces will be sent, however, in card board boxes, not wooden crates.*"

Bart telephoned Sarah to restate that Sarah should pack the shoelaces in wooden crates. Sarah told Bart that she could not do that and that the sale was therefore canceled. Bart insisted that Sarah perform but Sarah repeated that the sale was canceled and that she would not now perform under any circumstances.

Bart files a complaint in a New York court alleging that Sarah has breached their contract. Sarah moves to dismiss Bart's action on the grounds that the alleged facts do not describe the formation of a contract and therefore do not give rise to a cause of action. The court grants the motion.

Was the court correct in granting Sarah's motion to dismiss?

EVALUATION SHEET: "THE SHOELACES"

Reprinted with permission of Professor Myra Berman

ISSUE:

____ Whether a contract for the sale of shoelaces was formed when the acceptance contained a term different from the offer.

RULES:

____ Identification of contract for sale of goods under the UCC; definition of a "good as all things which are movable at the time of identification to the contract for sale."

____ "Merchant" means a person who deals in goods of the kind

____ Unlike the common law "mirror image rule," the UCC may find an acceptance even if the terms in the acceptance vary from those expressed in the offer.

____ 2-207 provides that an expression of acceptance operates as an acceptance even if it sets forth terms that are additional to or different from those of the offer, unless that acceptance makes itself conditional upon express acceptance of the additional or different terms.

____ If the dealings are not between merchants, contract is formed solely on offeror's terms. The additional or different terms are mere proposals to the contract.

____ If the dealings are between merchants, the additional or different terms become part of the contract UNLESS

   ___ the alterations are material, or

   ___ the offer expressly limits acceptance to the terms of the offer, or

   ___ the offeror has already given notice of objection to the alterations or does so within a reasonable time after notice of them is received.

APPLICATION:

____ This is a sale of goods because shoelaces are "goods" under the UCC.

____ The parties were merchants with respect to the goods because Bart was a shoelace distributer and Sarah was a shoelace manufacturer.

____ Because both parties are merchants, 2-207(2) will apply to determine whether the question of boxing vs. crating.

It is unclear whether the packaging term at issue, wooden crates vs. cardboard boxes, is material. It seems that it is not material because both are methods of packing the shoelaces for shipment and there are no facts to indicate that shoelaces require special packaging to protect them during shipment or for any other reason. Still, they did not become part of the contract for the following two reasons:

   ___ (1) Bart's offer indicated that it would not contract unless the shoelaces were packed in crates. Notice of objection to any other form of packaging was part of the offer.

   ___ (2) Further, Bart even contacted Sarah after she notified in her acceptance that the shoelaces would be packed in cardboard boxes to voice his objection.

CONCLUSION:

____ No, the court should not have granted Sarah's motion to dismiss.

■ CONTRACTS

QUESTION TOPIC: FRAUD AND UNCONSCIONABILITY

Reprinted with permission of Professor Myra Berman

Back in 1985, when disco was in its heyday, newly divorced sixty-year old Katie decided that she'd benefit from dancing lessons at the Night Fever dance studio. Poor Katie had never held a job, never gone beyond high school in terms of education, and never lived on her own. Her husband of thirty-five years, Tom, had just run off with a twenty-two year old woman. Katie had no other family; she was alone in the world. Learning how to do these dances, and then going out clubbing on a regular basis, would, she hoped, help her meet a new man, or, at the very least, give her a new interest in life. Although she had never been a very good dancer, she was hopeful that the lessons would help her improve.

And so, when Katie arrived at the Night Fever studio on January 2, 1985, she was immediately targeted by manager John as a prospective student. He took her off to a private room where he repeatedly remarked on her poise and beauty as well as on the contours of her body, which – he assured her – were perfect for disco dancing. He offered her a standardized contract, eight (8) lessons of one hour apiece, to be used within a 30 day period, for the low price of $50.00 cash, payable upon signing. When Katie said she'd like to think about it, John pulled her onto the dance floor of their private room, began dancing around her stationary body, and told her that the contract had to be signed now or he simply couldn't offer it to her at that price in the future; it was a take-it-or-leave-it deal, John said, as he leaned towards her while continuing to dance. She couldn't resist. She signed the agreement.

Over the next six months, Katie was induced to renew this contract and others like it numerous times and also to purchase even more lessons, all due to John's ongoing statements – which were false – regarding Katie's grace and developing skills on the dance floor as an "accomplished dancer," his constant barrage of flattery, and his flirtatious handling of her which, given her vulnerable position, she perceived as the promise of a future romantic relationship. At the end of 1985, Katie had spent her entire divorce settlement on the dancing lessons that John had sold her. She was penniless, without education, without a new man in her life – all without being an accomplished dancer.

Finally, several of Katie's old friends confronted her and helped her recognize that she'd been "had" by John and the Night Fever dance studio. Katie filed a complaint claiming that John and the studio had procured her money and induced her to repeatedly sign contracts through false representation that she had potential to become an accomplished dancer, and that she was improving in her skills. Katie further claimed that John and Night Fever were aware that she had no dancing aptitude whatsoever, that they withheld the truth from her for the sole purpose of deceiving and defrauding her.

Katie asks the court to void the contracts on the basis of (1) fraud or misrepresentation and (2) unconscionability. What result?

EVALUATION SHEET: "KATIE AND THE DANCING LESSONS"

Unconscionability issue:

ISSUE:

____   whether Katie can avoid the contract with Night Fever based was unconscionability.

RULE:

____   An unconscionable contract is one that is manifestly unfair or oppressive – a contract which no one in his right senses and not under a delusion would make. It must be unconscionable at the time of its making. In determining unconscionability, the court looks to see whether it is procedurally and substantively unconscionable.

> __   Procedural unconscionablity: characterized by an absence of meaningful choice. The court looks to the relationship between the parties to determine if there was unequal bargaining power, a lack of opportunity to study the contract and inquire about the terms, and whether the terms were non-negotiable.

> __   Substantive unconscionability: is found when the terms of the contract are so unfairly one-sided as to be oppressive. A one-sided agreement may be found where one party is deprived of all the benefits of the agreement or left without a remedy for the other party's breach or there is a large disparity between the prevailing market price and the contract price.

APPLICATION:

____   Whether the process of forming the agreement was unconscionable.

John told Katie to sign then and there; the terms were non-negotiable in a standardized contract drafted by Night Fever. Since she had to sign immediately or would lose the deal, she could not study the terms (even though she asked) and negotiate them. There was an imbalance in bargaining power b/c of the disparity in commercial sophistication between the parties. Although not a child, Katie is not a business woman and has never even held a job. John, on the other hand, is the seller of dance lessons and works for dance studio. Moreover, Katie is in a vulnerable state as a newly divorced woman with only a high school education and no experience in the business world. While we don't know any more about John other than his prowess on the dance floor, he seized the opportunity to make Katie sign by dancing around her and telling her that the offer had to accepted then or there to get that price. Further, he said her body was made to disco, relying on her physicality and his to create a deal.

____   On the other hand: Katie was a grown woman and a high school education and could have walked away from the deal. He was merely twirling around her, not holding her hostage. She was a willing dance partner.

____   Whether the terms of the agreement were unconscionable.

The terms were oppressive and one-sided b/c the contracts were repeatedly signed without benefit to Katie b/c she wasn't improving in her dancing. Even if there's no guarantee one will become a great dancer, she was still required to use 8 lessons within 30 days which is oppressive. It is oppressive because Katie must attend lessons 3 to 4 times per week or lose money. Typically, dance classes are taken once a week and here they were required to be taken 3 to 4 times a week to meet the contract. The oppression is not that you're danced to death but that you're forced to pay for so many lessons in a short time when the usual industry rate would be four lessons in a month, not a week.

CONCLUSION:

_____ The contract was procedurally and substantively unconscionable at the time of formation and thus voidable by Katie.

Misrepresentation issue:

ISSUE:

_____ Whether Night Fever made fraudulent misrepresentations to induce Katie to enter into the dance contracts.

RULE:

_____ A misrepresentation is an assertion not in accord with the facts. The general rule is that the misrepresentation must be one of fact rather than opinion to be actionable but there are exceptions:

> __ where there is a fiduciary relationship between the parties
> __ where there has been some artifice or trick used by the representor
> __ where the parties do not in general deal at "arm's length"
> __ where the representee has superior knowledge (expert)

_____ Katie must show (1) a misrepresentation existed (2) it was material (3) it induced her to execute the contract (4) her reliance was justified.

_____ Even where there's no duty to disclose, if a party undertakes to make a disclosure, he must disclose the whole truth.

APPLICATION:

_____ To induce Katie to sign, John told her repeatedly she was becoming an accomplished dancer. John was an expert in the field so his stated opinions about her dancing abilities would be considered a misrepresentation.

_____ Katie's dance aptitude was the material basis on which she assented to the deal. She had no way of knowing an expert wasn't telling her the truth about her abilities, especially when he told her she had the poise and body contours made for dancing. She relied on his assertions in buying more and more dancing lessons.

_____ John's statements were made in bad faith with knowledge of their falsity since Katie was anything but a good dancer. His sole purpose was to sell dancing lessons.

_____ John's constant barrage of flattery and flirtatious overtures led Katie to believe in him.

CONCLUSION:

_____ Night Fever misrepresented Katie's dancing skills to induce her assent; the contract is voidable by her.

■ CRIMINAL LAW

QUESTION TOPICS: FELONY MURDER

It was late in January and George was having a terrible day. Nothing was going right and then Federal Express was late in making a delivery. George shouted at the delivery man when he finally arrived: "Where have you been all day. This was supposed to be an AM delivery and now it's after 3:00 PM and you show up with no apology and you just drop the box on the floor. Now my Mickey Mantle collector plate is smashed." George called Federal Express to complain about the late delivery, the surly delivery person, and the broken plate. Federal Express offered to pay the damages but George was not satisfied. Instead, he threatened, "I'll get that delivery man and teach him a lesson. We'll see if he likes to have his property destroyed. I'm going to rip something to shreds!"

The next day at 6:30 p.m., George went looking for the Fed Ex man. He put a scissors in his briefcase. He was walking the streets of the city when it started to rain heavily. He ducked into the very first open door he could find which happened to be a fitness center. George walked around for a while, checking out the exercise equipment and the locker rooms and then he noticed a closed door at the end of the hall. George opened the door and went up the stairs. It led to an apartment above the gym. It was still raining and George was hungry so he went into the kitchen and opened the refrigerator. He made himself a peanut butter sandwich, opened a can of soda, and sat down to read the newspaper. George cut out some coupons from the newspaper and placed them in his pocket. Finally, it stopped raining. Just as George was about to leave, the Fed Ex man came through the door. Panicked, George threw his briefcase at him without even looking and ran out the door. The briefcase hit him in the head and knocked him to the floor. George had not known that he had been in the Fed Ex man's apartment. The man died of his injuries. George has been charged with felony murder.

You have been hired to defend George in this common law jurisdiction. What is the likelihood of successfully reducing the charges to involuntary manslaughter?

Note: This hypothetical can be easily adapted for use in your class. Based on what the professor emphasizes in class, answer the question based on your state's statutory law, the Model Penal Code, or the common law rule.

EVALUATION SHEET:
"MURDER OF THE FEDERAL EXPRESS MAN?"

Reprinted with permission of Professor Myra Berman

ISSUE:

____ Whether, in a common law jurisdiction, a defendant's felony murder charge can be reduced to an involuntary manslaughter charge when defendant unintentionally caused the death of another during the commission of a crime.

RULE(S):

Felony Murder

____ Unintentional homicide that occurs during the commission or attempted commission of a dangerous felony.

____ If defendant is acquitted of the underlying felony, there can be no felony murder conviction.

____ No intent to kill need exist; however, intent needed as element for the "murder" is replaced with the required intent to commit the underlying [or predicate] felony.

____ Includes any death that occurs during the *res gestae* of the underlying crime or in immediate flight therefrom.

____ Defenses to felony murder are:

____ Defendant was unarmed AND

____ Defendant did not commit the homicide AND

____ Defendant had no reason to believe that his conduct was likely to result in death

Involuntary Manslaughter

____ Two types of involuntary manslaughter under the common law, with *mens rea* of either recklessness or negligence.

____ Defendant is aware that there is a substantial risk of death [but not a grave risk, as required for Depraved Heart Murder] yet still proceeds to act recklessly, causing another's death.

____ Negligent Homicide: defendant fails to perceive substantial risk of death, and this is a gross deviation from the conduct of a reasonably prudent person.

Burglary

____ Unlawfully entering [breaking and entering] or remaining in a dwelling [a structure used for sleeping purposes] at nighttime, with the intent to commit a crime therein.

____ Under the common law, burglary is considered a dangerous felony and is one of the underlying felonies that can sustain a felony murder charge.

Larceny

____ Wrongfully taking another's personal property [requiring only the slightest movement of the chattel] with the specific intent to permanently deprive the owner of that property or to deny the owner of possession for an unreasonable length of time or to use in a manner that deprives the owner of economic value.

____ Under the common law, larceny is not considered to be a sufficiently dangerous felony to sustain a felony murder charge.

APPLICATION: *To sustain a felony murder charge:*

____ Fed Ex man's death was unintentionally caused by George when George threw the briefcase at him [and the man died from those injuries].

____ George committed this act of throwing the briefcase as he was fleeing from the site of the underlying crime, thus his act was within the time frame parameters established for a felony murder charge.

____ George expressed the intent, the *mens rea* to knowingly, purposely harm another or another's property when he said he'd "get that delivery man and teach him a lesson" and "rip something to shreds" [e.g. the Fed Ex man and/or his belongings]; to that end, George armed himself with a scissors which he placed in his briefcase and went looking for the man. George therefore was armed with a potentially deadly weapon and intended to commit an act of violence upon the man or his belongings, once he found him. George's statement, "We'll see if he likes to have his property destroyed" combined with the fact that it was George's property that was damaged, is a strong indication that George's intent was to damage property. This could constitute the element of intent required for the dangerous felony of burglary or merely for the felony of larceny.

____ George would have had to commit a burglary for the felony murder charge to be sustained. While George's act in seeking shelter from the rain by entering the fitness center was clearly not criminal [indeed, it was open to the public], he did enter an apartment through a closed door at nighttime. It is questionable whether walking through a closed but unlocked door would be deemed "breaking," a requirement under the common law for burglary. Further, George was in a public place where entering a closed but unlocked door would not be considered unlawful.

____ To have committed burglary, George – upon unlawfully entering the dwelling – would have had to have the intent to commit a crime therein. The facts indicate George was merely looking around, checking out the fitness center while waiting for the rain to stop. George did not know he was in the Fed Ex man's apartment. Therefore, George lacked the requisite intent for burglary; his intent to damage/destroy the man's property has no causal connection with his entry into this dwelling.

____ George did commit a larceny. George knew he was in someone's apartment, yet he ate the owner's food and cut up his/her newspaper. He wrongfully and permanently deprived the owner of items of economic value. Larceny, however, is not a predicate crime for felony murder.

To reduce the charge to involuntary manslaughter:

____ When George saw the Fed Ex man enter the apartment, he panicked, throwing his briefcase without even looking at the man. Given these facts, George's *mens rea* with respect to the act of throwing the briefcase was neither knowing nor purposeful, not even reckless. Since George did not look or aim at the man, he did not perceive a substantial risk and then recklessly disregard it. At most, George acted negligently in that he failed to perceive the substantial risk of harm that could result from throwing a briefcase. This would constitute negligent homicide, which under the common law is involuntary manslaughter.

CONCLUSION:

____ George should not be charged with felony murder because:

    __ He did not have the requisite *mens rea* required for the underlying dangerous felony of burglary so there can be no transfer of intent to the homicide AND he did not even commit the *actus reus* of burglary, so there is no underlying dangerous felony.

____ Since George did not commit an underlying dangerous felony, but did engage in a negligent act that cause the death of another, George's charge should be reduced to involuntary manslaughter.

■ EVIDENCE

QUESTION TOPICS: HEARSAY, RELEVANCY, CHARACTER EVIDENCE

Reprinted with permission of Vice Dean Gary Shaw

Note: The following question was a mid-term examination worth 30 points. Students were given one (1) hour and 15 minutes in which to take the exam.

Dan Davis was walking down the streets of Huntington, New York on the evening of October 30, 2002, when he saw Peter Palmer walking towards him. Davis knew Palmer from their college days together at Stony Brook University from 1998-2001. They hadn't seen each other for just over a year and had renewed their acquaintance a few days earlier while at a bar. Unfortunately, the re-acquaintance had gone badly.

Davis had been sitting in a bar talking with a woman, Susan Worth, he had just met a the bar. They were having a nice conversation and Davis had decided to ask her for her phone number. Just as Davis had asked her for her phone number, Palmer had shown up. It turned out that Worth lived with Palmer and had been waiting for him at the bar. Palmer had shown up and was walking towards Worth just as Davis asked for her phone number. Palmer heard this and became very angry. He grabbed Davis by the shirt and threatened to beat his brains out if he ever saw Davis talk to Worth again. Davis, who was much smaller than Palmer, immediately ran out of the bar.

Now Davis saw Palmer walking towards him. Palmer was scowling and his hands were clenched into fists. Davis, afraid, crossed to the sidewalk on the other side of the street. Ten seconds later, Palmer crossed to the same side. As they neared each other, Davis, fearing Palmer, pulled out a gun and shot Palmer. He then ran away. Palmer collapsed to the ground. Bystanders who heard the shot called the police. Officer Chone was the first to arrive on the scene. He asked Palmer what happened and Palmer replied "Davis killed me." Ultimately, Palmer survived, although he had to have three operations and was out of work for a year. Palmer is a citizen of New Jersey and Davis is a citizen of New York. Palmer properly brought suit in federal court for the Eastern District of New York based on diversity jurisdiction. Palmer sued under a tort theory of assault and battery. In his pleadings, Davis denied liability, claiming he acted in self defense.

At trial, Palmer's attorney, Gail Beber, called Officer Chone as her first witness. After preliminary questioning, Beber asked what had happened on the night of October 30, 2002. Chone replied that he had answered a call for help and had found Palmer shot on the ground. He then testified that when he asked Palmer who shot him, Palmer responded, "Davis killed me." Davis' attorney, Darren Allen, immediately objected, claiming that this was hearsay. The judge overruled the objection, saying it was not hearsay. After some further testimony, Chone was allowed to step down.

Palmer was the next witness. After preliminary questioning, Palmer testified that he had known Davis in college. Palmer testified that he had been a member of a fraternity that Davis had tried to join. However, Davis had not been asked to join. At this point, Allen objected, claiming that this was not relevant. At a sidebar, Beber told the judge that if permitted to continue along this line of questioning, the relevance would become clear. The judge overruled the objection and Beber was allowed to continue questioning Palmer. Beber then asked Palmer how Davis had reacted to being denied admission to the fraternity. Palmer replied that there had been five members of the committee who had decided whom to admit to the fraternity. Palmer stated that over the next three years, he had seen Davis shoot the other four members of the committee. Allen immediately objected, claiming that this was inadmissible evidence. The judge overruled the objection. Palmer then testified to the medical expenses he had incurred and the amount of lost wages.

On cross examination, Allen asked Palmer, "Isn't it true that in 1996, you were convicted of aggravated assault?" Beber immediately objected, claiming that this was irrelevant and inadmissible. At a sidebar, Allen offered to show the conviction and the fact that Palmer received a fifteen month sentence. The judge overruled the objection.

After Palmer testified, the plaintiff rested his case. Allen then called Davis to testify as his first witness. Davis testified that on October 22, 2002, he had been talking to a woman in a bar when Palmer grabbed him by the shirt and threatened him. He testified that on October 30, 2002, he had seen Palmer walking towards him. He testified that he had been afraid and that he had acted in self defense. Upon questioning, he stated that Palmer had said at the bar, "I'll beat your brains out the next time I see you." Beber objected, claiming that this was inadmissible hearsay. The judge overruled the objection. After further testimony, Palmer was allowed to step down.

Were the judge's rulings correct or incorrect? Why?

ANSWER TO EVIDENCE EXAM

Reprinted with permission of Vice Dean Gary Shaw[2]

The first issue is whether the judge's ruling that Chones' testimony–that when Chones asked Palmer what had happened, Palmer replied, "Davis killed me."– is hearsay was correct. Hearsay is an out-of-court statement introduced to prove the truth of the matter asserted. (Federal Rule of Evidence (FRE) 801(c)). What Palmer said is an out-of-court statement. It is not being made for the first time before the trier of fact. The key issue is whether or not it is being introduced to prove the truth of the matter asserted. Clearly, Davis did not kill Palmer so the statement is not being introduced to prove its literal truth. However, there is an intended assertion implied from the actual assertion–that Davis shot Palmer. Chones testimony is being introduced in order to show that Davis shot Palmer. Therefore, the out-of-court statement is being introduced to prove the truth of the matter asserted (that Davis shot Palmer) and is hearsay and the judge's ruling was incorrect.

The second issue is whether the judge's permitting Beber to continue to question Palmer about being a member of the fraternity that turned down Davis was correct. The objection was that this testimony is irrelevant. Testimony is relevant when it makes a fact of consequence to the litigation more or less probable than it would be without the evidence. FRE 401. By itself the fact that Palmer was a member of a fraternity several years earlier does not make it more or less likely that Davis shot Palmer. However, pursuant to FRE 104(b) the judge may allow the testimony to be introduced subject to being connected up to other evidence to establish its relevance. If the testimony is not ultimately connected up then it must be stricken. However, in this case it was connected up by showing that it went to Davis' common plan or scheme. Therefore, the judge's ruling was correct.

The third issue is whether the judge's ruling that Palmer's testimony that Davis shot five other members of the fraternity was admissible was correct. Under 404(b), this evidence is not admissible for the purpose of showing propensity; i.e., to establish a character trait of violence in order to show that Davis had acted in conformity with that character trait. Thus, it may not be introduced to establish that because Davis shot the other four fraternity members, he shot Palmer. However, it is not being introduced for that purpose. Rather it is being introduced to show a common plan or scheme–that Davis was gaining revenge on everyone who had refused him admission into the fraternity. Because it is not being introduced to establish conduct in conformity with a character trait, it is admissible under FRE 404(b). Therefore, the judge's ruling was correct.

The fourth issue is whether the judge's ruling that the Palmer's conviction for aggravated assault was admissible was correct. This evidence is being introduced for impeachment purposes–to attack Palmer's credibility. Therefore the relevant rule is FRE 609 (a)(1), which states that for the purpose of attacking a witness' credibility, evidence that a witness other than the accused committed a crime shall be admissible, subject to FRE 403, if the crime was punishable by greater than one year in jail. In this case the witness was Palmer, who is not the accused (the defendant in a criminal trial). The crime was punishable by more than one year in jail. Therefore, if the evidence is not kept out under FRE 403, it is admissible. FRE 403 states in pertinent part that relevant evidence may be excluded if its probative value is substantially outweighed by the danger of unfair prejudice. Here the probative value of the evidence deals with its relevance on the issue of credibility. Numerous courts have held that assault and

(continued next page)

issues and address them.

battery are generally not very probative of a witness' credibility. On the other side of the equation, there is a danger that Palmer will be unfairly prejudiced by the jury hearing this evidence. The unfair prejudice will take the form of the jury deciding that because Palmer committed an aggravated assault, he is a bad person who does not deserve to recover any money even if he was wronged. The question is whether the unfair prejudice substantially outweighs the probative value. Although the probative value with respect to Palmer's credibility is weak, it is hard to say that the danger of unfair prejudice substantially outweighs the credibility of the evidence. The judge is probably correct in allowing the evidence in.

The fifth objection is whether the judge's decision to admit Davis' testimony that Palmer had said, "I'll beat your brains out the next time I see you" was correct. The objection was that the statement was inadmissible hearsay. This was an out-of-court statement in that Palmer did not say it for the first time before the trier of fact. However, it was not introduced to prove the truth of the matter asserted, that Palmer really would beat Davis' brains out. Rather it is being introduced to show that Davis was truly afraid of Palmer and was acting in self defense. The statement need not be true to be relevant. It need only be shown that Davis heard it and believed it. An alternative theory is that even if this were introduced to prove the truth of the matter asserted, this is an admission by party opponent and is therefore not hearsay under FRE 801(d)(2)(A). This is a statement made by the opposing party (Palmer) in his individual capacity being offered against that party. Therefore, under either theory this is not hearsay and the judge's ruling was correct.

■ PROPERTY

QUESTION TOPIC: RULE OF CAPTURE

Reprinted with permission of Professor Rena Seplowitz

Chester is a parrot. He is fourteen inches tall, with a green coat, yellow head and an orange streak on his wings. Red splashes cover his left shoulder. Chester is a show parrot, used by the defendant ASPCA in various educational exhibitions presented to groups of children.

On June 28, during an exhibition in Kings Point, New York, Chester flew the coop and found refuge in the tallest tree he could find. For seven hours the defendant sought to retrieve Chester. Ladders proved to be too short. Offers of food were steadfastly ignored. With the approach of darkness, search efforts were discontinued. A return to the area on the next morning revealed that Chester was gone.

On July 5, the plaintiff, who resides in Belle Harbor, Queens County, New York, had occasion to see a green-hued parrot with a yellow head and red splashes seated in his backyard. His offer of food was eagerly accepted by the bird. This was repeated on three occasions each day for a period of two weeks. This display of human kindness was rewarded by the parrot's finally entering the plaintiff's home, where he was placed in a cage.

The next day, the plaintiff phoned the defendant ASPCA and requested advice as to the care of the parrot he had found. Thereupon the defendant sent two representatives to the plaintiff's home. Upon examination, they claimed that it was the missing parrot, Chester, and removed it from the plaintiff's home.

Upon refusal of the defendant ASPCA to return the bird, the plaintiff now brings this action in replevin.

The issues presented to the Court are twofold: One, is the parrot in question truly Chester, the missing bird? Two, if it is in fact Chester, who is entitled to ownership?

The plaintiff presented witnesses who testified that a parrot similar to the one in question was seen in the neighborhood prior to July 5. He further contended that a parrot could not fly the distance between Kings Point and Belle Harbor in so short a period of time, and therefore the bird in question was not in fact Chester.

The representatives of the defendant ASPCA were categorical in their testimony that the parrot was indeed Chester, that he was unique because of his size, color, and habits. They claimed that Chester said "hello" and could dangle his legs. During the entire trial the Court had the parrot under close scrutiny, but at no time did it exhibit any of these characteristics. The Court called upon the parrot to indicate by name or other mannerisms an affinity to either of the claimed owners. Alas, the parrot stood mute.

EVALUATION SHEET: "CHESTER THE PARROT"

ISSUE 1:

____ *Is it Chester?*

RULE:

____ Identification: the more unique qualities about it, the more able you are to show that the bird is in fact Chester.

ANALYSIS:

____ The parrot had rare markings, an orange streak on his wings and red splashes over the shoulder, which make it more identifiable.

____ It is unusual to find parrots flying around Queens, New York since they are not native to the area and even so, this particular bird had unique markings. It's very likely Chester.

ISSUE 2:

____ *Assuming it is Chester, who has ownership rights?*

First, this depends on whether Chester was a wild or domesticated animal.

RULE:

____ The hunter has a burden to determine whether it is a wild animal and subject to capture or one which is tame and domesticated and subject to prior ownership.

> *Ferae naturae*: a wild animal which will always seek its freedom. It is in the nature of the animal, his species, to be wild.

> *Animus revertendi*: a trained or tame animal. Like Bambi.

The questions to be asked:

____ 1. Did the captor know in fact that the animal was previously owned/domesticated?

____ 2. Should the captor have known by the circumstances that the animal was owned or domesticated? Were there sufficient indicia to suggest that the animal was or was not *ferae naturae*?

APPLICATION:

____ Here, plaintiff should have known that the parrot was domesticated and someone else had prior possession and therefore could not be captured for himself. He was on notice because:

> ____ Parrots are not native to Queens; Plaintiff should have known that the parrot either escaped or some person brought it to the area.

> ____ Parrots in general are tame and live in homes, zoos, pet stores. They do not fly about free in Queens. The parrot walked into the house and appeared to be comfortable around people since he eagerly accepted the food from Plaintiff. If it were a wild animal, it would probably have flown away. Instead, the bird accepted three meals a day for two weeks.

____ *Did Plaintiff "capture" Chester?*

Even if Chester were wild and subject to ownership through capture, Plaintiff would have to capture him, which he did not.

____ Rule of capture: A wild animal *(ferae naturae)* becomes the property of the first person to put it under his/her control; capture is required, merely chasing the animal is not enough. Whoever takes possession has ownership *(Pierson v. Post)* The public policy is that society wants animals caught. The policy encourages people to go out and hunt. On the other hand, domesticated animals are valuable to society and this effort to tame wild animals should be rewarded.

APPLICATION:

____ Plaintiff did not hunt Chester, but found him in his backyard and no chase was involved. Plaintiff's offer of food was readily accepted and although Plaintiff continued to offer Chester food three times a day for two weeks, Plaintiff did not have to do anything more but offer the food and Chester came into Plaintiff's home. Plaintiff did not trap Chester, unless it could be said he trapped him with kindness. Arguably, plaintiff put Chester under his control and "captured" him when he put him in a cage but here too Chester walked into the house willingly where he was "placed" in the cage.

■ PROPERTY

QUESTION TOPIC: ADVERSE POSSESSION

Reprinted with permission of Professor Seplowitz

Greenacre is a plot of ten (10) acres of land with a house on the northeast corner and a small cottage on the southwest corner. The cottage has a fence around it enclosing exactly one (1) acre. Blueacre is a plot of 15 acres on the east side of Greenacre adjacent to it. In 1965, Mr. Greene was the owner of Greenacre in fee simple and lived in the cottage, and Mr. Blue was the owner of Blueacre in fee simple. Mr. Blue did not occupy his land. In 1974, Dudley Dowrong conveyed Greenacre and Blueacre to Al Verse by an invalid deed. Mr. Verse moved into the house on Greenacre. In 1985, Mr. Verse left the property for one year to care for his sick mother, returning in 1986. In 1995, Mr. Greene died suddenly leaving Junior as his only heir. Junior, while inspecting the property, discovered Al in the house and Al showed him the deed. Junior warned Mr. Blue about Al's invalid deed to Greenacre and Blueacre so he could protect whatever interest he had in his property. Assume the statute of limitations in the jurisdiction is 20 years.

Please answer the following questions as they apply when Junior inherited Greenacre.

1.   After the smoke has cleared from the various lawsuits, who will own what?

2.   Assume that in 1984, Al had his cousin Alice "house sit" for him while he cared for his mother. He then returned in 1985. What result?

3.   Same facts as in 2, but Al has built a patio attached to his house on the extreme northeast corner of Greenacre, extending completely into Blueacre.

Suggestion: before beginning your analysis, draw a figure identifying the properties and locations of Blueacre, Greenacre, the house and its patio, and the cottage.

EVALUATION SHEET: "THE MATTER OF AL VERSE"

Analysis reprinted with permission of Touro Law 3L Randi Schwartz

GENERAL ISSUE: Whether Al Verse acquired the property through adverse possession.

1. Who owns what?

____ **RULE:** To establish title by adverse possession, the possessor must show an actual entry giving exclusive possession that is open and notorious, adverse or hostile and continuous for the statutory period. The elements are:

  __ a. Actual possession

  __ b. Open and notorious

  __ c. Exclusive

  __ d. Adverse/hostile to the true owner: possession must be without the owner's consent.

  __ e. Continuous for the statutory period

Adversity issue: was Al's possession hostile to the true owner by virtue of a defective deed?

____ Here, Al's claim is founded on an defective deed so his possession is hostile to the true owner under color of title. When a party relies on a defective deed, that party acquires title to all of the land described in the deed based on constructive possession unless the true owner is in possession of part of it. Since Blue was not in possession of Blueacre and Green lived in the small cottage on the southwest corner of Greenacre, Al can claim title to all the land described in the defective deed except the cottage occupied by Green.

Continuity issue: Was Al's possession continuous and uninterrupted for the statutory period?

____ **RULE:** To establish the continuity requirement, it must be shown that the adverse possessor used the property in the same manner as a real owner would.

____ **APPLICATION:** Here, it is not likely that a true owner would leave the land unoccupied for a year, no matter what the circumstances, even to care for a sick mother. Depending on whether this interpretation is reasonable, the Statute of Limitations is either tolled for that period of time or it begins to run again when the party returns to the property. If it is tolled for that year, Al would have acquired title (1974 -1985 = 11 years + 1986 - 1995 = 9 years; 9 = 11 = 20, the statutory period. On the other hand, if the time is not tolled and begins to run again, then Junior would own Greenacre and if Blue went to court or put a barrier up, he could successfully eject Al.

2. Cousin Alice: what is the effect of "house sitting"?

____ **RULE:** there is a distinction between leaving the land voluntarily and involuntarily. When an adverse possessor leaves the land involuntarily (i.e. physical threat) the statute of limitations may be tolled, and the subsequent possession may be tacked on to the previous possession. But, if the adverse possessor left voluntarily, then there would be a break in continuity, and the statute of limitations would begin again when the adverse possessor returned.

____ **APPLICATION:** However here, even though Al left voluntarily, he had Alice look after the property, and since Alice was able to act as his agent/caretaker, there was no break in continuity, and thus, no tacking issue.

3. Whether the encroachment made by the patio satisfies the open and notorious requirement so that Al can claim Blueacre.

_____ **RULE:** the adverse possessor must occupy the property in an open, notorious, and visible manner, thus putting the true owner on notice. The acts must look like the typical acts of the property owner. However, no presumption of knowledge arises from a minor encroachment.

_____ **APPLICATION:** The act of building a patio is typical conduct of a true property owner. It shows an intent to cultivate and use the property. Here, Al built a patio for his house on Greenacre which encroached onto the Blueacre property. However, simply building a patio which abuts the house might be insufficient to satisfy the open and notorious element. A patio is relatively small in size when compared to a house, is flat and level to the land, and might not even be visible to someone passing by the property.

■ TORTS

QUESTION TOPIC: ASSAULT AND BATTERY

At 2:00 am in the morning, Ben began singing under Jessica's balcony. Jessica lived on the 5th floor of an apartment building. Jessica was not in the mood after a long day at work. She began shouting at Ben to keep quiet but he refused to stop singing. Jessica then yelled that she would kill Ben if he didn't stop, but Ben just continued to serenade her. In an effort to scare Ben away and get some beauty sleep, Jessica began throwing her fuzzy, high-heeled bedroom slippers out the window, first one and then the other. Ben was unafraid. One of the slippers hit Ben on the head. Ben, who had thin skin, died instantly.

What is the result in a suit brought by Ben's estate against Jessica?

EVALUATION SHEET: "BEN AND JESSICA"

ISSUE:

____ Whether Jessica committed a battery when she threw the slippers out the window and hit Ben.

RULE:

____ A battery is the intentional infliction of a harmful or offensive bodily contact upon another.

The conduct

There must be a contact, either direct or indirect. An indirect contact is one that results from a force set in motion by the defendant.

The intent

It is not necessary that defendant desires to physically harm the plaintiff; defendant has the necessary intent for battery it if is the case either that:

_____ D desires to cause a harmful or offensive bodily contact

_____ Or D acts with purpose or knowledge to a "substantial certainty" that a contact would result

_____ Or there is transferred intent from another intentional tort

APPLICATION:

____ Here we have a contact between Jessica and Ben because Jessica threw a slipper out the window which hit Ben. The contact was harmful since Ben is dead. Note the irrelevancy of Ben's "thin skin."

____ The question is what Jessica intended when she threw the slipper. The facts indicate she did not intend harm but only to "scare Ben away and get some beauty sleep." Still, it's not necessary that she intend to cause a harmful contact; it could be that she intended to cause an offensive bodily contact. Here too it's not likely she intended an offensive contact since she threw fuzzy bedroom slippers – which could be seen as romantic and sexy since Ben was serenading her and slippers are bedroom attire.

____ Still, it's possible that if she knew with substantial certainty that throwing her slippers out the window would result in hitting Ben, she could be liable for battery. Here, it's difficult to find knowledge to a substantial certainty because she threw fuzzy slippers and not a hard object (it wasn't a boot or even a shoe) out of a 5th floor window. Not only are slippers soft, but the distance had to be quite far – 5 floors above ground – for Jessica to believe a contact of any kind would be possible. Still, the slippers were high-heeled and she did throw both of them. However, it's still not likely that she knew with substantial certainty she would effect a contact because there's no indication in the facts that she took aim before she threw and because of the great distance between her room and the ground.

____ However, we could use transferred intent to establish liability for the battery if she had the intent to commit an assault.

ISSUE:

____ Whether Jessica committed an assault when she threw the slippers.

RULE:

____ An assault occurs when one intends to cause apprehension of an imminent harmful or offensive contact and the other is put in apprehension of such contact.

APPLICATION:

____ Here, Jessica intended an assault because she intended to "scare" him away by putting him in apprehension of a contact. She shouted at him that she was going to kill him and then she threw her slippers out the window. Words alone wouldn't be sufficient but here they are accompanied with a physical act. She intended for him to feel apprehension because she threw slippers – thus the intent for an assault is satisfied. Therefore, the intent to commit the assault is transferred to establish liability in battery. Jessica is liable for battery.

____ Ben must feel apprehension of an imminent contact for there to be an assault. This means he would have to be aware that the slippers were coming at him. The facts do not indicate whether Ben saw the slippers, either one of them, coming at him, so we do not know whether he felt apprehension. In this case there would be no assault.

The first question is whether Jessica committed a battery when she threw her slippers out the window to scare Ben. A battery is the intentional infliction of a harmful or offensive bodily contact upon another. The contact can be either direct or indirect where an indirect contact is one that results from a force set in motion by the defendant. Here we have a contact because Jessica threw a slipper out the window which hit Ben. Also, it was harmful because a slipper hit Ben on the head and he suffered such severe trauma that he is dead.

The real question is what Jessica intended when she threw the slippers. The facts indicate Jessica did not intend harm but only to "scare Ben away and get some beauty sleep." But she need not intend harm to have the requisite intent to commit a battery. It could be that she intended to cause an offensive bodily contact. Here, it'ës possible she did not intend an offensive contact since she threw fuzzy bedroom slippers – which could be seen as romantic and sexy because Ben was serenading her and slippers are bedroom attire. Nevertheless, she was not interested in being romantic because she wanted him to stop singing so throwing the slippers was not likely intended as a romantic gesture.

The next question is whether she knew with substantial certainty that a contact would result from throwing the slippers out of the window. (*Garratt v. Dailey*) If she knew with substantial certainty that throwing her slippers out the window would hit Ben, she could be liable for battery. Here, it may be difficult to find knowledge to a substantial certainty because she threw fuzzy slippers and not a hard object (it was not a boot or even a shoe) out of a 5th floor window. Not only are slippers soft, but the distance had to be quite far – 5 floors above ground – for Jessica to even believe a contact of any kind would be possible. Still, the slippers were high-heeled and she did throw both of them. However, it is questionable whether she knew with substantial certainty she would effect a contact because there's no indication in the facts that she took aim and the great distance between her room and the ground.

However, if Jessica had the intent to commit an assault, then she could be liable in battery as well because the intent to commit the assault is transferred to establish liability in battery. An assault occurs when one intends to cause apprehension of an imminent harmful or offensive contact and the other is put in apprehension of such contact.

Here, Jessica intended an assault because she intended to "scare" him away by putting him in apprehension of a contact. She shouted at him that she was going to kill him and then she threw her slippers out the window. Words alone wouldn't be sufficient but here they are accompanied with a physical act. She intended for him to feel apprehension because she threw slippers – thus the intent for an assault is satisfied. Therefore, the intent to commit the assault is transferred to establish liability in battery.

However, Ben must feel apprehension of an imminent contact for there to be an assault. This means he would have to be aware that the slippers were coming at him. The facts do not indicate whether Ben saw the slippers, either one of them, coming at him, so we do not know whether he felt apprehension. In this case, there would be no assault.

■ TORTS

QUESTION TOPIC: INTENTIONAL TORTS

Ben and Jerry were riding in Jerry's new convertible when Ben noticed some cornfields. Suddenly, he had to have fresh corn on the cob for dinner. He told Jerry to stop so he could pick some corn. Jerry said, "Look at that scarecrow. The owner of that field doesn't want the crows to get his corn and I bet he doesn't want you to get any either." Ben insisted that no one could possibly miss a few ears of corn. Jerry reluctantly parked the car on the side of the road. Ben got out of the car and entered the cornfield.

Jerry was sitting in the car when a gust of wind blew his cap off his head and into the cornfield. Jerry ran into the cornfield to retrieve his cap only to find that it had decapitated the scarecrow. Apparently, his cap had triggered a spring-gun. Thinking that it was not a good idea to hang around, Jerry turned to leave when he realized he was lost. The stalks were so tall he couldn't see where he was. Fortunately, he had a machete with him and he started hacking a path through the cornfield, knocking down the corn stalks in his way. He soon found Ben, contentedly picking up stalks of corn which had fallen to the ground. Jerry said it was time to go and the two started back to the car. Suddenly a voice rang out from behind, "Stop or I will shoot!" Ben and Jerry stopped and turned to find a farmer pointing a shotgun at them. The farmer said, "This is my property. What are you doing with my corn?" When neither Ben nor Jerry responded, the farmer shot his gun into the air. Ben dropped the corn and ran with Jerry close behind him.

Farmer Dell has sought your advice as to whether he has grounds for an action against Ben or Jerry or both. Discuss fully.

EVALUATION SHEET: "FARMER DELL'S CORNFIELD"

FARMER DELL V. BEN

Trespass to land

____ **RULE/TRESPASS:** (1) intent to enter onto, or cause an entry onto, the land; and that (2) unauthorized entry onto the land of another occurred.

____ **APPLICATION:** Ben committed trespass when he walked onto Dell's cornfield to pick corn. It's unauthorized b/c Ben did not seek to find Dell to ask. Further, the presence of the scarecrow, which Ben saw, indicated that Dell did not want visitors. He entered Dell's land because he wanted to get corn for his dinner. However, Ben could argue that even though he may have trespassed, Farmer Dell was not privileged to defend his property with a shotgun.

Trespass and conversion to chattel

____ **ISSUE:** whether Ben's picking up the corn up moved beyond trespass to conversion.

____ **RULE:** Trespass to chattel is temporarily depriving or interfering with another's possessory right to their property short of conversion. The intent is just to touch it, interfere, intermingle with the chattel. D is liable for any damage to the chattel. A conversion requires an intentional interference with the property that is so substantial as to destroy the goods or fundamentally alter them.

____ **APPLICATION/TRESPASS:** Ben might have committed a trespass because he picked up Dell's corn which had fallen to the ground. Ben interfered with Dell's property just by touching the corn. Because he did not sever the corn from the stalks, it's possible that all he was holding were defective stalks, of little or no value to Dell. Then there was no harm done to the property because it's not likely Dell could sell defective stalks. If he could sell them at all, it would likely have been at a reduced value and hence Ben could be liable only for the limited value. Still, Ben had the requisite intent to deprive Farmer Dell of his corn because Ben told Jerry he wanted to have fresh corn from Dell's cornfield for dinner. Further, he asked Jerry to stop the car so he could get out and pick the corn.

____ **APPLICATION/CONVERSION:** Ben's objective was to take Dell's corn and have it for dinner. So even if the stalks had fallen to the fallen to the ground, he picked them up, moved them from their original spot and planned to leave with them, thereby permanently depriving the owner of his property. It's possible that Ben did not *substantially interfere* with the stalks at all because he *did not sever* the corn from the stalks. He *merely picked* up what had fallen to the ground by itself. Still, Ben intended to take Dell's corn and eat it for dinner which would be a fundamental *alteration* of Dell's property – it would become Ben's dinner! But this had not happened yet, and all Ben did was pick up loose corn stalks. Further, when Dell shot off his gun, Ben dropped the corn, thereby *relinquishing control* over it altogether. Dell got his corn back and the most he could seek from Ben would be any reduction in the corn's value because of Ben's touching it.

Privilege to defend

____ **RULE:** A property owner is permitted to use reasonable force in defense of his property – both personal and real – on essentially the same basis as he would have to defend himself. First there is a duty to use words. The landowner must make a verbal demand that the intruder stop before using force unless it reasonably appears that violence or other harm will occur immediately so that the request to stop will be useless. Still, the landowner can never use more force than reasonably appears necessary and he does not have a general right to use deadly force even when the intrusion can only be prevented this way.

____ **APPLICATION/GUN:** Here, Farmer Dell shouted out a warning to "Stop or I will shoot" which would satisfy the requirement that a verbal request to stop be given. However, Dell accompanied these words with a shotgun pointed directly at Ben and Jerry, which in itself signifies the potential use of deadly force. Further, Dell then shot the gun when Ben and Jerry remained silent, making it the actual use of deadly force. Even though Dell shot the gun into the air and not directly at Ben and Jerry, this might nevertheless be seen as an improper use of deadly force to protect chattel – some stalks of corn – and would not be privileged. Even if Dell argued that he was a landowner protecting his land, shooting a gun would likely be seen as using more force than reasonably necessary to protect the property against the likes of Ben and Jerry. This assumes, however, that Jerry is not still holding the machete, which might give some basis for Dell to believe he was in imminent danger of death or bodily harm because a machete is a dangerous weapon. But the facts don't indicate whether Jerry was holding the machete at this time or whether Dell had even seen it. We do know that when Dell shouted the warning, Ben and Jerry both stopped in their tracks. Simply because they did not respond to his question did not permit Dell to shoot a gun when there did not seem any basis to believe that Ben and Jerry posed an immediate threat of harm to Dell.

____ **APPLICATION/SCARECROW:** It's also questionable whether Dell is privileged to defend his land against intruders with the spring-gun loaded scarecrow. A property owner is privileged to use mechanical devices only if he would be privileged to use a similar degree of force if he were present and acting himself. As we've just discussed, Dell was not privileged to use a shotgun to protect his property and therefore the use of the spring gun would similarly not be permitted as being an unreasonable use of deadly force.

BEN V. DELL FOR ASSAULT

____ **ISSUE:** Whether Farmer Dell's act of pointing a shotgun at Ben can be considered an assault.

____ **RULE:** An assault is the intentional causing of an apprehension of harmful or offensive contact. Apprehension can mean fear but it doesn't have to – but there must be an expectation or awareness of a contact.

____ **APPLICATION:** Dell intended to cause apprehension of a harmful or offensive contact because he shouted, "stop or I will shoot." One doesn't threaten to shoot another with a gun unless the intent to is cause apprehension. Arguably Ben and Jerry could not feel apprehension because their backs were turned to Dell and therefore couldn't see whether the gun was pointed at them, but they were threatened with being shot which could reasonably cause apprehension. Still, words alone are insufficient to constitute an assault. There must be some overt act, a physical act or gesture, before an assault can be claimed. Here, when Ben and Jerry turned around, they saw a shotgun pointed at them. This would seem to constitute the overt act necessary to constitute assault.

FARMER DELL V. JERRY

Trespass to land

____ **ISSUE:** whether Jerry committed a trespass to land when he entered Farmer Dell's cornfield to retrieve his hat.

____ **RULE:** same as written for Ben – no need to rewrite

____ **APPLICATION:** whether the intent element was satisfied if Jerry only went onto the property to get his hat when it blew off his head. Liability for trespass to land occurred the moment Jerry stepped onto Farmer Dell's land because he fully intended to do so. The intent requirement is simply that the party intentionally, with purpose or knowledge, enter the land of another. It doesn't matter that he just wanted to get his hat back.

Trespass and conversion to chattel

____ **ISSUE:** whether Jerry committed trespass or conversion to chattel when he took his machete and hacked a path through Dell's cornfield

____ **RULE:** same as written for Ben – no need to rewrite

____ **APPLICATION:** Jerry's act of chopping his way through the cornfield would amount to a conversion of the corn because he substantially interfered with Dell's property by effectively destroying the corn with his machete. He intended to get them out of his way so he could pass, thus fundamentally altering their appearance and value.

____ *Necessity defense:* It's possible that Jerry was privileged to cut a path through the cornfield based on necessity. He was lost in the cornfield and, desperate to find a way out, he cut a path through the stalks. In this case, he would be permitted to interfere with another's property but required to pay for damages to the corn.

JERRY V. DELL FOR ASSAULT

Same as above analysis for Ben but Jerry would have his own claim against Dell based on the same set of facts.

■ TORTS

QUESTION TOPIC: INTENTIONAL TORTS

Ben and Dan were sitting and talking about nothing when Dan asked Ben for some advice. Dan met a woman online and they had been e-mailing each other for a couple of weeks. They met for the first time last week and Dan thinks he is in love. But there is something odd about Cindy because she insists on wearing a scarf around her neck – all the time. She even wore one when they went swimming. Ben agreed that this was odd behavior and suggested that maybe she was hiding something.

Dan decided he had to know what was under the scarf. He offered to make dinner for their next date. He prepared an 18 pound turkey for the two of them, hoping that the turkey dinner would put Cindy to sleep and he could sneak a peek at her neck. After eating half of the turkey, Cindy fell asleep on the couch. Dan carried her into the bedroom and placed her on the bed. He drew the blinds and closed the door. He went over to Cindy and started to untie her scarf. It was in a knot and secured with a gold pin. Dan was all thumbs — he had trouble untying the knot and then he stuck Cindy with the pin. Before he could get the scarf off and while he still had his hands around her neck, Cindy awoke, looked around the darkened room and started to scream, "Where am I and what are you doing to me?" Dan stammered, "You fell asleep on the couch and I moved you in here to make you more comfortable. I thought you were choking on a turkey bone, so I was untying your scarf." Cindy replied, "Let me out of here." Dan stood aside as she ran out the door.

Now Cindy is threatening a lawsuit. She claims she can no longer eat turkey for fear of falling asleep and when she does sleep, she has nightmares about having her neck exposed. Dan wants to know if Cindy has any viable causes of action against him.

EVALUATION SHEET: "CINDY AND THE SCARF"

Assault

____ **RULE:** An assault is the intentional causing of an apprehension of harmful or offensive contact. Apprehension can mean fear but it doesn't have to – but there must be an expectation or awareness of a contact.

____ **ISSUES/APPLICATION:** there are a couple of possible assaults but only one likely: when Cindy awoke with Dan's hands around her neck untying the scarf. The other possibility fails b/c Cindy was asleep and lacked awareness, i.e., when he tried to untie her scarf (would be assault b/c she would find this an offensive contact b/c she didn't want anyone to see behind her scarf and Dan coming at her to untie the scarf would create apprehension, but she was asleep).

Battery

____ **RULE:** A battery is the intentional, harmful or offensive touching/contact with another. There must be a contact/touching, either direct or indirect. An indirect contact is one that results from a force set in motion by the defendant. The act must be intentional or substantially certain, but the consequences need not be. Separate the defendant's act from the consequences of that act. It is not necessary that defendant desires to physically harm the plaintiff; defendant has the necessary intent for battery it if is the case either that: (1) D intended to cause a harmful or offensive bodily contact or (2) D intended to cause an imminent apprehension on P's part of a harmful or offensive bodily contract.

____ The intent element is satisfied not only when the actor intends harmful or wrongful behavior, but if he acts with purpose or knowledge to a *"substantial certainty."* This means that the actor need not have understood his act to be "wrongful" to have formed the requisite intent: he need only to know with substantial certainty that a contact would result from his act.

____ **ISSUES/APPLICATION:** here there are several possible batteries: does it constitute battery when Dan fed Cindy turkey hoping she would fall asleep so he could untie her scarf? This one relies on Dan's knowledge/purpose in inviting her for a turkey dinner. The other more obvious batteries are: (1) when Dan carried Cindy into the bedroom (a woman may find it offensive to be picked up and carried, especially after eating a half a turkey and feeling fat!); (2) when Dan untied the scarf; (3) when Dan stuck Cindy with the pin; (4) when he had his hands around her neck.

False Imprisonment

____ **RULE:** There is intent with purpose or knowledge to confine another. P must (1) be confined against his will (2) be aware of such confinement (if actual harm occurs b/c of confinement, then may recover even if unaware of confinement) (3) have no reasonably safe means of escape (4) confinement may be by force, threat of force, or false assertion of legal authority. Words alone may be enough (can be confined for fear of losing your personal property) (5) Spatial confinement: physically prevented from leaving a certain space. Doesn't have to be a closed space.

____ **ISSUES/APPLICATION:** Must examine the elements in light of each of the facts – there might be intent to confine because Dan brought her into a room when asleep, something she might not have allowed while awake (against her will), the confinement was spatial since she was in a room with closed and darkened windows and a closed door. However,

Cindy was not aware of the confinement until she woke up. Only then would there be awareness. That moment might be enough for FI. But another form of confinement would be when Dan had his hands around her neck. She screamed and asked where she was and what he was doing to her, indicating she didn't know what was going on. While Dan let her go as soon as she asked to leave, it's possible for that brief interval she was confined when she awoke with his hands around her neck.

Intentional Infliction of Emotional Distress

____ **RULE:** the intentional or reckless infliction by extreme and outrageous conduct of severe emotional or mental distress, even in the absence of physical harm. Intent : (1) D desires to cause P emotional distress; or (2) D knows with substantial certainty that P will suffer emotional distress; or (3) D recklessly disregards the high probability that emotional distress will occur. D's conduct must have caused P's distress. D's conduct must be beyond all possible bounds of decency.

____ **ISSUE/APPLICATION:** whether Cindy has a claim in ED when she can no longer eat turkey for fear of falling asleep and suffers nightmares of having her neck exposed when she sleeps. An argument can be made to satisfy all the elements except Dan's conduct being extreme and outrageous. Since when is feeding someone a turkey dinner beyond all bounds of decency? Might argue that it's an extreme way to get a look at a neck, but cooking dinner for a girlfriend fails to qualify as outrageous behavior.

Dan's defense: consent

____ **RULE/APPLICATION:** a person may consent to an interference with his person or property and if established, operates as a complete defense. Consent must be informed, voluntary, and by one with capacity to consent. Here Cindy consented to dinner with Dan because she voluntarily came to his apartment. She wasn't forced to eat, let alone consume half the turkey. However, she didn't voluntarily and knowingly consent to being picked up, moved to another room, or touched because she was sleeping.

■ TORTS

QUESTION TOPIC: INTENTIONAL TORTS

Reprinted with permission of Associate Dean Nicola Lee

Scarlett O'Hara has lived in New Orleans, Louisiana, for the past 50 years. For a number of those years, she has had an on-again, off-again relationship with her neighbor, Rhett Butler. Last week, as news spread of a hurricane developing in the Caribbean, Rhett decided to take a long-deferred trip to Las Vegas to sample the gambling at Harrah's. He urged Scarlett to leave town too, but she declined.

As predicted, the aptly named Hurricane Tara made landfall in New Orleans, wreaking havoc. While the water in Lake Charles started to rise, Scarlett was mildly concerned for her safety, but when a couple of levees near her home were breached, she realized it was time to leave. By the time she had put together the possessions she thought she could carry, the water was up to the top of the steps leading into her house.

Scarlett, knowing that Rhett was out of town and certainly not in need of his boat, decided to take Rhett's canoe, which he kept on the porch of his house. She waded across the waist-high water in the street and dragged the boat back to her house, where she loaded in her few possessions and set out for dry land.

After paddling for some time, she encountered another neighbor, Ashley Wilkes, who was standing on a deck on the top floor of his house, from which he had an unobstructed view across the city. He called to Scarlett that the water level around their respective homes seemed to stabilized, and he suggested that she join him in his home, which he assured her had ample provisions for two for at least a month.

Welcoming his offer, Scarlett steered towards the steps in front of Ashley's house and, reaching them, climbed out of the boat, which at this point had sprung a leak from a small gash in its side. Scarlett managed to drag the canoe up onto the porch beside her, then she fell to the floor and began to weep.

Identify and analyze the intentional tort claims suggested by these facts.

> **Comment:** *Dean Lee provided the sample answer for her problem. When you review it, please note that the rule of law is in bold and the analysis portion is italicized. This is done to draw it to your attention. Essentially, each issue is analyzed in IRAC form. Also, you might also consider using the sub-headings in your answer – here and on your exams – to make for a more organized essay answer.*

SAMPLE ANSWER: "HURRICANE TARA"

BUTLER V. O'HARA FOR TRESPASS TO LAND

The issue is whether Butler can assert a claim of trespass to land against O'Hara. *To succeed, Butler must show that O'Hara had (1) intent to enter onto, or cause an entry onto, the land; and that (2) unauthorized entry onto the land of another occurred. O'Hara demonstrated the requisite intent when she manifested the thought to enter Butler's property and, of her own volition, initiated action by going onto the land, including the porch to his house. The intent here is merely to enter, so it is reasonably easy to satisfy. Since Butler was not at home and the facts do not mention any other form of communication between the parties, O'Hara could not have obtained Butler's permission, making her entry onto his land seemingly unauthorized. However, whether or not the entry was unauthorized, entry is determinable based, in part, on the prior dealings between the parties. O'Hara may claim that her entry was consensual (implied consent because of an on-again, off-again relationship with Butler) and therefore, authorized.*

In her defense, O'Hara may invoke private necessity, which creates, in the case of emergency, the privilege to enter the land of another to prevent serious harm to self or property. Given dire flood warnings and rising water, O'Hara will likely be successful in asserting this defense (to enter Butler's land for the purpose of removing his canoe); however, if she caused any damage to the land, she will have to pay for it.

BUTLER V. O'HARA FOR CONVERSION

The next question is whether Butler has a claim in conversion. *To succeed, Butler must show that O'Hara had (1) intent to exercise dominion and control over a chattel, which means to affect it in a substantial way; and that (2) exercise of substantial dominion over the chattel of another/serious interference with the owner's right to control the chattel occurred. O'Hara demonstrated the requisite intent when she manifested the thought to take Butler's canoe and, of her own volition, initiated action by taking the canoe. By removing the boat from Butler's property, filling it with her possessions, climbing in, and paddling away, O'Hara was treating the canoe as her own. Interference with the owner's right to control is considered serious when the actor might justly be required to pay the owner the full value of the chattel. In this instance, since the canoe received a gash in its side, and a hole defeats the very purpose of a boat, this may be sufficient to show O'Hara's exercising substantial dominion over the chattel. It is a question of fact, but her initial action of taking and using the canoe for an indefinite length of time and in unknowable conditions, suggests serious interference with the owner's right to control. It is irrelevant that Butler was away and not in use of his canoe, since the law focuses on the owner's right to control which does not require physical proximity to effect. For example, he could have intended for someone else to use it.*

Whether or not the taking of the canoe was a conversion or a trespass to chattel depends on such factors as (a) the extent and duration of defendant's interference; (b) defendant's intent to assert a right inconsistent with plaintiff's right of control; (c) defendant's bad faith; and (d) the expense and inconvenience for plaintiff. The damages for conversion are the market value of the chattel; the damages for trespass to chattels are for the actual harm (diminution in value) or the dispossession (approximately the rental value). Given that O'Hara used the canoe for a relatively short time and Butler was not in need of it at that time, having left New Orleans, it is more likely to be treated as a trespass to chattels (see the following), subject to the defense of private necessity.

BUTLER V. O'HARA FOR TRESPASS TO CHATTELS

The next issue is whether Butler has a cause of action against O'Hara in trespass to chattels. To succeed, Butler must show that O'Hara had (1) intent to intermeddle with the chattel of another; and that (2) actual intermeddling occurred, causing either harm to, or dispossession of, the chattel. O'Hara demonstrated the requisite intent when she manifested the thought to take Butler's canoe and, of her own volition, initiated action by removing the canoe from Butler's porch. O'Hara's use of the boat was sufficient to show intermeddling, but the law requires that any dispossession be for a substantial period of time in order to be compensable. This would be difficult to establish because: first, Butler was out of town and unaware of the dispossession; and second, it was for only a short period of time. However, the intermeddling is also actionable if it results in harm. O'Hara is responsible for damage to the canoe, a gash in its side, which occurred when the chattel was in her possession.

Regardless of whether this is found to be conversion or trespass to chattels, *O'Hara may invoke the defense of private necessity, which creates, in the case of an emergency, the privilege to interfere with another's chattel, so as to prevent serious harm to herself or her property. Because of the existence of rising water, the use of a boat was necessary as the only means of escape, O'Hara will likely be successful in asserting this defense; however, she would be responsible for the cost of any damage to the canoe.*

■ TORTS

QUESTION TOPIC: STRICT PRODUCTS LIABILITY

Amy was getting her hair cut when her stylist, Joe, said to her, "You know, Amy, since your bangs have grown out, the wrinkles on your forehead are really noticeable. Have you considered a little Botox?" Amy said, "I've thought about it. Do you know where I should go?" He replied, "Deb, my dermatologist is terrific. She gives Botox parties for her private "patients" so it's affordable. Here's her cell number."

The next day, Amy called Deb and met with her. Amy asked about Botox treatments. Deb said, "I've been giving Botox treatments for about six months at my office but so many of my friends couldn't afford the treatments that I've been giving private parties." Deb is a licensed dermatologist who works part-time for the ABC medical group. She provides routine dermatologic care, including Botox treatments to the medical group's patients. Deb works for ABC four days a week and her hours are flexible, except she must work Saturdays and afternoons from 4:00 pm - 6:00 pm so that she's available for school-age patients. Deb said, "I started doing my own parties on the side because with all of the adolescents I've been treating at the office, it has cut way down on my Botox treatments. And that's where I earn most of my income because ABC pays me a percentage on the Botox patients but only an hourly salary for my time at the office."

Amy asked when the next party would be, how much it would cost, and whether she could come. Deb said, "it just so happens that my friend, Kate, is hosting a party Friday night at her home. I'll have enough Botox by then because I get my supply on Thursday from my friend Sue who works for the manufacturer, Botoxica. I use the needles from my office so everything is as if you were coming to see me at my office. Each session is $100 and it looks to me like you'll need at least five sessions." While Amy didn't like the way Deb looked at her when she said that, she said she'd come to the party.

On Friday night, Amy went to Kate's house. When she arrived, there were four other women in the living room, watching the manufacturer's video about the many benefits of Botox. The video identified possible side effects and included a special warning for women who were pregnant or might become pregnant. Deb introduced Amy to Kate and the other women. It turns out that the women were there for their third treatment. As far as Amy could tell, everyone looked fine. Amy turned to the woman seated next to her and asked whether she'd had any side effects. The woman said not at all, that the product was perfectly safe and that she should know because she worked for the manufacturer. Amy realized that this woman must be Deb's friend Sue.

Sue came to the party straight from her job as marketing director of Botoxica where she had access to Botox. Sue was friendly with the warehouse manager and every week he gave her the batch overruns. Botox was manufactured on a daily basis. Each day was a new batch and each batch was identified with a unique batch number. There was nothing wrong with the overruns. They were just not needed for customer orders and all overruns were automatically discarded. Sue brought five (5) vials of Botox from the same batch to the party, one for each of the women at the party.

Amy knew it was now or never so she volunteered to be the first patient of the evening. Deb took Amy into the bathroom and proceeded to prepare for the injections just as she would at the office. Deb opened a sealed packet that contained the needle. When she threw the wrapper in the garbage, Amy could read the warning on the label, "Warning: Shelf Life of Needle is Three Years. " Deb had taken the needles from ABC's supply room where they had been stored for the past 3½ years. The industry standard for hypodermic needles is a shelf life of 2½ years. Further, the industry standard for the material composition of hypodermic needles is a 50% aluminum alloy. Alpha needles were made of only a 45% aluminum alloy.

Deb filled the needle with Botox from the vial. About ten minutes and a few injections later, Amy walked out of the bathroom and joined the other women. When Amy looked in the mirror, there was just a bit of redness and puffiness at the injection sites. Deb said it would pass in a couple of hours.

Amy went home and went to bed. When her alarm went off in the morning, Amy found that she couldn't open her eyes. Apparently, her entire forehead had swollen to twice its normal size. Panicked, Amy called her friend Jon. Jon rushed over and nearly fainted when Amy answered the door. Jon said, "Amy, what happened to you? We've got to get you to the hospital." When Amy arrived at the emergency room, a doctor took one look at her and admitted her for surgery. During surgery, the doctor removed a needle point from Amy's forehead. It appears that it had separated from the needle and remained in her head.

The doctor told Amy that she'd recover, but she'd be left with deep wrinkles at the sites of the injections, deeper than what she had before the Botox. "Deeper wrinkles?" Amy cried, "I was supposed to get rid of the wrinkles altogether and now I have these grooves in my forehead. Someone is going to pay for this!"

As soon as possible, Amy went to speak to Deb. Deb took one look at Amy's forehead and knew something was wrong. Amy told her about the needle point getting lodged in her head. Amy asked if this had ever happened before and Deb said no. None of the other women who had Botox treatments that night had any problems.

Unbeknownst to Deb, her office had switched suppliers of hypodermic needles from the Alpha Company to the Beta Company. ABC switched manufacturers because while the Alpha needles were less expensive, the shelf life of the needles was only three years. After this time, the tips could separate from the base of the needle. Deb was still using the old needles and she had used Alpha needles for all the Botox treatments at Kate's party, including Amy's treatment.

Amy has sought your advice. She wants to know her rights. Discuss fully. *Do **not** discuss any negligence issues.*

EVALUATION SHEET: "AMY'S BOUT WITH BOTOX"

While the problem raises negligence issues, the following addresses only those arising in strict liability:

AMY V. ABC MEDICAL GROUP

____ **ISSUE:** Whether Amy can bring suit against ABC for her injuries depends on whether it is vicariously liable for Deb's conduct in giving Botox parties. This depends on whether Deb was an EE or independent contractor.

____ **RULE:** Factors to determine whether person is an EE: (1) works exclusively for employer; (2) paid wages by employer; (3) taxes and social security paid by employer; (4) under control of employer.

Factors to determine whether person is an independent contractor: (1) works for several employers; (2) provides own workers, hires and fires and pays them; (3) owns his own equipment; (4) regulates his own work hours; (5) manages own work flow; (6) there is a contract with the employer; (7) self-financed.

____ **APPLICATION:** Deb is an EE because ABC is where she earns most of her income, she works for them four days a week and while her hours are flexible, she is required to work Saturdays and afternoons, thus showing ER control. Although ABC pays her hourly like an EE, it also pays her a percentage on the Botox patients, which could make her seem like an independent contractor. This combined with her flexible work hours might indicate a degree of control to make her an independent contractor but it's probably insufficient and she's more likely an EE with typical part-time flexibility. Although she earns money through her Botox parties, they are not her primary source of money and they are given at private homes in small parties. She even used ABC's supplies of needles at her parties.

AMY V. ALPHA

____ **ISSUE:** Is the manufacturer Alpha liable for Amy's injury under a products liability theory?

____ **RULE:** one who manufactures or sells a product that is defective and thereby unreasonably dangerous is liable for any personal injuries incurred as a result of the defect. There are three types of strict products liability causes of action: manufacturing defect, design defect, and failure to warn. Analyze under the Rest §402A

   __ 1. Applies to anyone who sells a product - manufacturer/retailer

   __ 2. Product must have a defect which makes it unreasonably dangerous

   __ 3. The defect must exist when it leaves the manufacturer's control

   __ 4. Causation: the defect must be the proximate cause to a lesser-extent of the injury

____ **APPLICATION:** Generally, any foreseeable purchaser or user of a defective product has standing to sue the manufacturer or seller under a strict liability theory. Here, Alpha manufactured the needles and it was purchased and placed into the stream of commerce by ABC. Although Amy was not a purchaser of the needles, she was a reasonably foreseeable user because it was foreseeable that a medical practice such as ABC would purchase needles and use them on their patients. Amy was receiving the type of procedure, Botox injections, that would be a foreseeable and intended use for the needles.

Was there a manufacturing defect?

Amy must show that the defect existed when the needle left Alpha's control. Since the needles were individually wrapped in sealed packets and stored in ABC's supply room, no one touched the needle until it was used on Amy. This would indicate the defect existed while the needle was in the possession of both Alpha and ABC. Further, only the needle used on Amy had a problem with the tip separating from its base. None of the other needles used on the four women receiving Botox treatments that night separated from their base.

Was there a failure to warn?

Amy could claim that the warning on the needle wrapper that the "shelf life of needle is three years" was inadequate because it was merely on a label on the wrapper which was ripped and thrown away to get at the needle. Alpha should have known that the warning would be discarded with the wrapper. Further, the warning that the shelf life is three years is not a strong enough warning to let users know of the danger of broken needle tips. It is far too vague. On the other hand, the warning is intended for the doctor and not the patient so Alpha might claim that Amy is not the intended party to benefit from the warning.

Was there a design defect?

Amy can claim design defect because the needles Alpha manufactured had a shelf life of only three years when the industry standard for such needles was a shelf life of only 2 ½ years. At three years, the tips could separate from the base of the needle and this made the design defective and unreasonably dangerous. Even though Deb used a needle that was 3 ½ years old and exceeded the warning on the label of three years, it was still beyond the industry norm. Further, Alpha needles were made of a 45% aluminum alloy where the industry standard was a 50% alloy. This indicates that the needle has a structural weakness which would make the design unreasonably dangerous.

ABC V. ALPHA

ABC can proceed in its own claim against Alpha as a purchaser.

Analyze similar claims in manufacturing, design, and failure to warn claims by ABC against Alpha. There is no need to repeat the rule of law; weave the elements into the analysis of the facts.